MEMOIR
OF A NOBODY

MEMOIR OF A NOBODY

by Steve Bluestein

BearManor Media
2018

Memoir of a Nobody

© 2017 Steve Bluestein

All rights reserved.

For information, address:

BearManor Fiction
P. O. Box 71426
Albany, GA 31708

bearmanormedia.com

Typesetting and layout by John Teehan

Published in the USA by BearManor Media

ISBN — 978-1-62933-251-2

Table of Contents

Preface xi
The First Entry 1
Garage Sale 4
The Shredder 5
Temple Gig 6
Explaining Anxiety 8
An HMO Visit 9
The Problem 11
I.B.S. 13
Sports-Berg 16
Estelle Harris Comes To Dinner 18
The Mudslide 21
Geary's Sale 23
Home Depot 25
Food Shopping 27
The Oscar Party 29
Taking My Mother To Australia 31
My Fiftieth Brithday 35
Vern 38
Return From Hawaii 41

My Last Vegas Gig	44
The New York Trip – Part 1	47
Trip To Paris – Part 2	50
Trip To Paris – Part 3	53
My Car Gets Stolen	56
Maggie	59
The Brady Bunch Variety Hour	62
The Playboy Playmate Awards	65
Two Million and No Linen Closet	69
Howie Mandell	72
My Insane Life	74
Satellite TV	77
The Israeli Accident	80
The Niacin Affair	83
Unemployment	85
Memorial Day	88
Childhood Memory	91
Kathy Griffin	93
The Duck Story	96
Mary Travers	99
Todd	102
Vegas Dribs and Drabs	105
Streisand	108
Jan	111
Frankie Avalon	114
Albert Hammond	118

The Old Man In the Mountain	123
Jenny Jones	127
Crosby I	130
Crosby II	134
B'hai Story	137
The Last New York Story	142
Chicken In the Projects	146
Penny Marshall	149
Mike Douglas	152
Candid Camera	155
Mac Davis	160
Jim Bailey	163
David Copperfield	166
Charo	169
Judy Garland	171
Van Johnson	175
The Freezer	180
Gary	184
Miami	187
Melissa Manchester	191
Kenny Loggins/Frankie Valli	195
Nancy Walker	199
Lauren Bacall	203
Alan Thicke	207
Chapter One	210
Rita Moreno	214

Barry Manilow 218
Donna Summer 224
Linda 228
A Year At the Top 233
Fox News 237
Tina Turner 240
Maggie Vomit 244
Surprise Gardener 247
Amy Heckerling 251
Mills Brothers 254
Vegas First Time 256
Polio 260
Sha Na Na 263
Morristown, TN 267
Celebrity Sighting Fest 270
Actor's Studio 273
John Ritter 275
Alan Landsburg 278
Ella Fitzgerald 282
Celebrity Sightings 285
Twenty-Five Years 289
More Celebrity Sightings 292
Sharon Tate's House Party 294
All Night Talk 296
The Anxiety Attack 299
Only I Can Change Me 301

Singing Waiter	303
NYC Drugs	307
The Famous Manager	311
Getting Into Emerson	315
Even More Sightings	318
A Mary Willard Christmas	321
Rosie O'Donnell	325
A Thought	328
Eiplogue	331

Preface

WHEN I WALKED INTO the Comedy Store in 1972 I knew my life would change forever. I had no idea how much it would change or what direction it would take, I just knew my life was about to be different. I'd no longer be the assistant buyer at The May Company, I'd be "somebody"; I was right. Because of my career as a stand-up comedian, TV writer, and playwright, I've traveled the world and worked with some of the biggest names in show business. I have fond memories and some I'd like to forget. My personal life has always been a mesh of bad relationships, lost souls and natural disasters, yet I seem to have come to the surface like the flotsam of a shipwreck. I'm a survivor, as they say. This is my story.

Who would have thought words alone could change a life? My profession is making people laugh. I worked in comedy clubs. I did stand-up. I'm no author; authors are Arthur Miller, Tennessee Williams, and Truman Capote. Authors live in Connecticut. I live in Bel Air. I'm not an author, yet that's not what my readers tell me. My readers tell me my writing has changed their lives. I'm feeling like a real writer today but inside I never feel like a real anything. My book was just a lark, something to take up my time, to stretch my funny, to record my thoughts. I had no idea it would turn into my passion. I never thought my life would interest anyone. After all, I never became a star like some of my friends. I didn't find the cure for any disease. I'm not a political leader. Yet the readers tell me I matter. They write to tell me how much my words mean to them. My knee jerk reaction, "Get a life." Yet, I thank them for being so supportive. Writing the book hasn't been easy. As a comedian, I am so used to hearing the instantaneous reaction to my words, but I am now learning via email that my jokes amuse. I'm learning that my words have worth. I'm learning about me as you, the reader, learns about you. They call that a symbiotic relationship, the host benefiting from the parasite and vice versa. Don't ask me which I am.

Before you start on this journey with me, I need to explain something. The stories are not chronological. This whole book is a dyslexic's wet dream. Oh, and I've changed a few names to protect the guilty.

Just one final note, I wrote these words for you but it is I who has gained the benefit. I gained the self-confidence and shed a life of negative familial connections. It is I who started writing as an adult child and ended up an adult. I am the author, not the parasite; I am the host. Welcome to my world.

The First Entry

It's Friday at about 11:30 a.m. and I've started writing. My good friend, Carole Propp, talent producer, suggested that I should document my life for all to see because, "Who'd believe the crap that happens to you?!" I guess I would, Carole, I'm living it. Now I invite you, the readers, to live it along with me.

As we speak the "handy man" is in my garage trying to open the garage door, which fell on my car last night. Oh, it's not one of those sectional garage doors you buy from Sears, with the row of tacky windows at the top. Oh no, it's a solid wood, made by hand, weighs-a-ton door. Right now, it's sitting on top of my car, the one that I was rear ended in last week by an eighteen year-old Israeli without insurance.... That car. I try to look on the bright side; the damage done by the Israeli can be repaired at the same time as the damage done by the garage door. I hope the body shop is having a two-for-one special. Couldn't you just kill me now?

So, the garage door has fallen and inside the garage are my car *and* the contents of the antique shop. What antique shop, you ask? The shop I opened in the hopes that it would give me something to do when I was not on the road, the hobby to keep my anxiety down, the place for me to go on Saturdays...that antique shop. It's the one that, after I opened, got sold to a developer who gave me three months to get out. That one!

After filling the shop with thousands of fine antiques, I had to empty it into my car... before it got rear ended... then crushed by my garage door. I brought home all that crap—I mean fine antiques—made my nice clean garage look like a flea market, and put out the garage sale notices on Craigslist: "Come buy the antiques they're half off." However, those antiques are sitting in my garage, which has no other access but the garage

1

door and are being held hostage by a two-thousand-pound garage door built by some guy without a green card.

Let me explain my house to you. It's in Bel Air—the slums of Bel Air but still Bel Air—and it has been built into the side of a mountain. The same mountain that gave way last February and destroyed thirty years of memories when it filled my office with mud and water; that mountain (Feeling better about your life yet?). Okay, back to the house. You enter on the street level and travel up four flights of stairs as they carry you through the house. The foyer is on level one; my office is on level four. The garage is on level zero...street level.

I needed to tell you this so you'd appreciate the following. The handyman calls me on his cell phone from the garage (I told you it's a big house) and asks me to come down and hand him his toolbox. Why? There's no way out of the garage and after he squeezed in, the door closed just enough to trap him. He's trapped in there with the car and the antiques and my tools and my trashcans and all the stuff one keeps in a garage. I walk down the four flights of stairs, hand him the toolbox through a crack just big enough to pass a wrench through and head back into the house. I find my dog, the new one, the one that weighs eighty-five pounds and eats whatever he feels like, that one. I find him with a wet coffee filter in his mouth and behind him a mountain of coffee grounds spread all over the living room. His tail wags rapidly so proud, *look what I did*. I stop and begin the process of cleaning up the wet coffee grounds that have fallen into the cracks of my antique pine planked floor. This process takes thirty minutes. I head back to my office on the fourth floor, the phone rings. It's the handyman, "Can you come down and help me?" I make the trek back down the four flights of stairs to find him peeing in an antique spittoon he found in my garage. Seriously, just kill me now.

We get the door opened. He rinses out the spittoon, which I plan to bury in my back yard after he leaves. What he's left me with is a two-by-four holding up the remnants of the garage door and five thousand dollars' worth of antiques exposed to the street. It's sort of like a homeless person's wet dream.

It's 12:45 p.m. The Garage Door Doctor is coming at three o'clock. This is not some name I've made up. This is a company that does nothing but fix garage doors. There are all kinds of "doctors". I've seen the Door Doctor and the Rooter Doctor and the proverbial "Doctor" Doctor but this guy is the Garage Door Doctor. You'd expect him to show up in a white coat with rubber gloves. Instead you get a 350-pound Italian guy on parole for non-payment of spousal support. A guy you'd run from in a dark alley, and this guy is going to fix my garage door. I'll fill you in on what good news he gives me after my consultation. That's what they call it. He's not coming to look at the door; he's coming to give me a consultation. What, in reality, he's coming to do is to suck out whatever is left in my checking account. See, he's like a real doctor.

Later that day I get a call from the Garage Door Doctor's office, "The Doctor is on his way." I am thrilled because no one comes when they say they will. I hang up and the doorbell rings on level one, and I'm on level four. I make a mad dash for the front door expecting to see the doctor, instead I see two cherubic girls who look like they're from the dance group The Lockers, featuring Fred Berry. *Oh Shit, they saw the antiques in the driveway. I'm gonna get hit for a donation.*

I open the glass doors and greet them in the portico, "Can I help you?"

It was then it started..."Sir, we'd like to wish you a happy day." If they really wanted me to have a happy day they would have rung my neighbor's doorbell.

I make a decisive move, "Look, I'm not buying anything. I've bought before. I bought the peanut brittle for $18. I bought the pen set for $16. I got the magazine subscription to *Arizona Highways*. I'm not buyin' nothin." Long cold stare.

"How about a donation?"

"No!" I reply firmly. And then it happened...she went all ghetto on me.

"You be livin' in this big house with all them antiques in the driveway and your white ass is telling me you can't make no donation to poor starving kids who's just trying to make a little money so they can go to college!!!"

We stare each other down. "Yeah, basically that's it in a nutshell," I reply.

Beat… beat… "Okay. Have a nice day," and they both leave.

It's the end of the day and the doctor just left, "Can't do anything until next Tuesday," so my garage stays open until next Tuesday. Please, someone, anyone, come steal the crap in my garage and make it a perfect day!

Garage Sale

HOUSES ON BOTH SIDES OF ME are for sale. This means that little people from the valley run to see how the rich live in Bel Air. The place is crawling with lookie-loos. Since I can't leave the house until the garage door is fixed, I thought, *hey, why not try to dump the rest of the antique crap?* I opened a Garage Sale. Right away I sold $69 worth of stuff, actual value $150. Then, just as suddenly as it got busy, it dropped dead. Not a single person until one of the lookie-loos stumbled in.

I, trying to make conversation, say, "Are you looking at the house next door?"

"I wouldn't live around here, dude," he said, in his valley accent.

"What do you mean you wouldn't live here... dude?"

"I like the country."

"Which country?" is all I could get out.

He laughs, the moron doesn't know I'm insulting him. He holds up an item and asks the price. I double it just so he'll go away. He buys it. He'll buy anything at any price. He's not looking so bad now. I try to get him to buy more stuff. Whatever he asks, I double it. He buys it. The kid is an asshole. The Gods have sent me my reward for yesterday's torment. The asshole takes his purchases and leaves. Oh, happy day, happy, happy day!

I close the garage sale because despite the fact that I have made $500, it will cost me $600 in therapy. I can't fall into one of my depressions again. Now this may sound like a joke, but it's not. I battle depression. When I say battle it's more like an on-going struggle. Once, I was so depressed I watched *Schindler's List* just to cheer myself up. I can't let myself slip into one of those depressions…. I'm going to watch *Munich*. Nothing cheers me up like a Spielberg film. I've got an Academy DVD and my afternoon is free.

The Shredder

I HAD NO IDEA WHAT I SHOULD write about; then I looked down at my shredder and got inspired. Printed along the top of the shredder is a picture of a paperclip with the universal red slash through it. Next to it is a picture of a hand, with the same universal sign. And I'm wondering who goes into an office and thinks, "*Gee, I wonder if my hand will fit in the shredder?*" Our society has become so sue-crazy; manufacturers feel they have to protect themselves by putting all these stupid warnings on their merchandise. People will sue for anything. I'm fat, it's McDonald's fault. I'm anorexic, it's Lean Cuisine's fault. If they hadn't built that freeway, I wouldn't have been going to McDonald's, and today I wouldn't be anorexic. What we all need to do is take a deep breath and stop shoving our hands into our shredders. Kennedy—the good one—hit the nail on the head when he said, "Ask not what your country can do for you…" Today it's, "Ask not who can sue for you, but who you can sue."

I was sued by a man who said that beating me up and breaking my rib caused him to have a heart attack at a wedding a year later. He got $5 thousand. It pissed me off so much I sued him and got $65 thousand. He counter-sued my counter-suit and was thrown out of court. This process took a year out of my life and wasted a lot of people's time. However, I did buy a new home out of the deal. Basically, I'm a pimp and you shouldn't listen to a word I say. It's my fault there's that stupid air bag warning on the visor of your car. Basically, I'm just as bad as the next guy. Oh, do me a favor. Promise me you'll keep your hands out of your shredder. If you should happen to do so, please don't sue Target; I love their towels.

Temple Gig

I START EACH DAY GRATEFUL that yesterday is over and that today is a new adventure. It's 9:57 a.m.; I have a migraine and diarrhea. It's raining and I've had to take an allergy pill. My head is pounding and the arm just fell off my desk chair. Worse than all that, I just got booked for an April 1st gig in town, no travel, nice Money, in a temple. A temple filled with my mother in different dresses. I hate these gigs and here is why.

About ten years ago I was asked to work a Temple here in town. The booker called and offered me the gig and I turned it down. Why? I only like to work professional venues. This stems from an experience I had when I first started out. I worked a private party where the buffet was set up in front of the stage and I had to work behind the ice sculpture. I digress. I turn down the temple gig and the booker calls back with more money. I turn him down. He calls back with more money. I turn him down. He calls back with more money. This goes on for a week until the gig was five mortgage payments. How do you turn down five mortgage payments? I accept.

It's the night of the gig and I'm driving to the temple as the committee between my ears begins. *What are you doing this for, you're not going to be happy, they're not going to like you, the stage won't be right, the lights won't be right. Why did you accept, there's more to life than money.* By the time I get there I'm looking for a tower to start shooting from. It's 8:55 p.m. I pull myself together and go up to the front desk.

"Hello, I'm Steve Bluestein. I'll be entertaining here tonight."

The woman looks up at me and says, "Oh, I know you! You almost made it big!"

Slam-dunk.

She tells me there is a little problem. The caterer forgot to bring trays and the waiters have to carry the dishes out two at a time. The 9 p.m. show began at 11 p.m.; that meant that for two hours I had to hear in my head, *you almost made it big*. The show begins; I hate everyone in the room. I hate the valet; I hate the guy in the men's room who hands out towels. I hate people who hate people. I hate my neighbor with the camper in his driveway. I hate people I never even met. I am insane. I am getting ready to go on when I hear the M.C.

"Before we bring out Steve Bloomsteen, Mrs. Rosenberg would like to say a few words."

Cut to me on a table having electric shock therapy.

Mrs. Rosenberg takes the stage, "When my Harold died.... blah, blah, blah... the Cancer. ... blah, blah, blah .... My entire world was shattered... (Crying) blah, blah, blah." Forty-five minutes. She spoke for forty-five minutes. The only thing she did not do was bring out dead babies from the Holocaust.

"And now the comedy of Stevie Bloomberg."

It's 11:45 p.m. At this point I don't care about the show, I don't care about the crowd, Mrs. Rosenberg, saving the whales, or what my mother is going to say when she finds out I cashed in my Bar Mitzvah bonds. At this point I have jumped off the tower I was shooting from. I say the first thing that comes into my head. I look at Mrs. Rosenberg, who has a front row seat,

"Nice speech, hon. I think you lost them in the last thirty-five minutes."

The crowd screams with a scream of laughter I have never heard before in my life. From that minute on, the show went wild. No matter what I said, they screamed. They were with me every single joke. Mrs. Rosenberg was laughing harder than anyone. I finished to a standing ovation, got in my car and felt really great! That show taught me something: I *did* make it big.

Explaining Anxiety

I WOKE UP THIS MORNING and my mind was a complete blank. Perhaps it's that banging anxiety in my chest. I'm like a flushed toilet. Empty. I thought about the hilarious story of the day my house was hit by twenty-six tons of mud and debris. Oh God, what a romp through comedy land that was. Nothing seems right, nothing seems important enough or funny enough or… enough. It's the anxiety. I have suffered from it most of my life. I remember telling a nurse, "I think I'm having a heart attack." I was eight at the time.

Anxiety is anger turned inward, or is that depression? I always get the two confused. They are my constant companions. With me, it's nondescript anxiety. That means for no reason I wake up one morning wanting to rip my heart out, stomp it on the floor and dance the Meringue. It's a healthy way to start the day, no? Over the years and after sitting in God knows how many shrinks' offices, I've learned to ride it like a wave. It passes, it always does, and it doesn't kill me unless I let it. It's lots of deep breaths and moving forward one step at a time.

The HMO Visit

I HAVE A DOCTOR'S APPOINTMENT. Why? It appears my blood pressure is stroke level. It's genetic. Some people get blonde hair and washtub abs; I get high blood pressure and an allergy to shrimp. I belonged to an HMO: A Horrible Medical Organization. Once I fell and thought I broke my leg. I was rushed to their Emergency Room. On the wall was a sign, "Time heals all wounds". Who would want a doctor who thinks an HMO is what he went to medical school for? I think I'd rather live in the Mexican desert and wait for one of those planes. You know, the ones from Houston full of doctors who take big moles off Mexican children... with a camera crew. So dedicated.

3:40 p.m.
I'm back from my HMO. I'm on blood pressure medication and officially have become my grandfather. It's all downhill from here. I'm looking for a coupon for walkers.
Let me tell you what a visit to my HMO is like. I walk into the waiting room and they've got *Jerry Springer* on the TV. *Jerry Springer* in a doctor's office... that's like playing the Osama Bin Laden tapes at a Bar Mitzvah. The most intellectual magazine I could find was *American Rifle* with four of the pages stuck together. I take a seat between Lenny from *Of Mice and Men* and two women: one wet, just out of the shower, and one with her hand in a cast and in desperate need of a shower. They are gripped by the *Springer* show. I guess they never saw a transvestite hooker who was looking for his birth mother from a prison line up. Suddenly, shower girl takes out a brush and begins combing her flaxen locks onto my pants.

Mid comb she parts her hair, bends over and shows her scalp to the dirty girl. They looked like two baboons grooming.

The door opens and the nurse shouts out, "Roger R."

No one moves.

"Roger R."

Nothing.

"Roger Ripelli?"

Lenny gets up. I guess the "R" thing threw him.

I am called next, "Steve Blue-sssss---t-t-t-," I'm in the door. Now here's something I need to know: shouldn't the nurse look at you when she's taking your history? This girl is so detached I'm beginning to think I sexually assaulted one of her children. She takes my blood pressure and gives off a reassuring, "Whoa!!" The doctor comes in and I remember why I go to him. He knows my name, he knows my history, he's concerned, and he's a Jew! I got the only Jewish Doctor who didn't go into private practice, he joined an HMO. He wants to see me in a couple of months. I fill my prescription and I'm outta there.

On the way home, I stop at Trader Joe's. Is it just me, or do they intentionally build Trader Joe's with parking lots made for demolition derbies? It's a huge store with a teeny-tiny parking lot with six-inch spaces and seventy-year-old hippies. Love the food, hate the parking lot; hate the hippies, which I call the "Birkenstock-and-Bunion" set.

I love Trader Joe's. I started going there for the dried papaya and soy cheese—both of which they no longer carry. My present addiction is rice crackers and dried peas. If you look in my car, in the space between the console and the seat, you'll find $1,600 in rice cracker and dried pea crumbs. Leave me alone; at least the anxiety is gone.

The Problem

BAD SHIT DOESN'T HAPPEN to me every single day of my life. It's not like I take the trash out and I'm kidnapped and held hostage for the release of Adele's new CD. Some days nothing happens, and on those days, I am forced to face the boredom that is my life. Case in point, last night. Last night I went to a dinner party with some Hollywood types. The food was magnificent, the company was wonderful, and I had no problem finding the house. No drama. Okay, I did forget my only winter coat there and they are leaving for Palm Springs today and won't be back until Sunday, but in comparison with the rest of my life, this is a piece of cake.

The only problem I have today is the harness I bought for my dog, Tori Spelling. She has a small head just like the real Tori Spelling, and she pulls out of a conventional collar, just like the real Tori Spelling. So, I bought her one of those harness contraptions that goes around her tummy and over each leg. Here's the problem: when I took it off the cardboard it melted into a macramé of belts and buckles. I put the dog's head through one hole and her paw through another; she looked like the cover of an S&M magazine. I put her head through another hole and her paw through here. She looks like my grandmother in her corset—it's hanging here, it's tight there. I put her head through this hole and pull her leg through that one. It won't fit. So now I grab her foot and pull it. *Pop!* It's through, and she's wearing a push up bra. I start over, only now the dog growls at me. Evidently, she *wanted* a push up bra. I can't get the thing off her; she looks like Mae West. She runs into her doghouse; I follow. It smells like shit in there. Why? There's shit in there. I pull her out, telling her calmly that if she doesn't let me get this harness off, I'm going to have her put to sleep. I get it off and now I've got it lying on the ground, and next to it I've got a map of the dog and a map of the harness. I think I've got it this time. I pull and push, presto change-o, the straps are running horizontally. They should be vertical. I pull it off. Now the big dog comes. He picks up the harness and runs into the backyard with it. I'm thinking gun, I'm thinking bomb, I'm thinking hostages at Petco. He will not give it back. Not for a bone, not for a toy, not for my favorite Prada shoes he ate the night before. He wants the harness, and he's a big dog. If I get a pony cart I could make money in Beverly Hills pulling kids around birthday parties.

Two hours later I finally get the harness away from him and on her. That dog is going to die with that harness on her. It's never coming off… ever. It could be faded, stink and be on fire and I'm not removing it. It would just be simpler to get her a bigger head.

I.B.S.

Do you see the time? Do you?? I have been up since 4 a.m. with irritable bowels. That's what my doctor says it is, but he's with an HMO so I'm probably pregnant. To me, "irritable bowels" sounds like my bowels are too temperamental. I don't know if you know what irritable bowels are, but I now have a direct connection to any woman with monthly cramps. My hat is off to you ladies. I don't know how you do it. From now on, when you flip me off on the freeway around the twenty-fifth of the month (that's the international sign for PMS), I'll understand because we now have a bond. Cramps. This is the kind of pain you wish on your ex.

I got no sleep last night—maybe four hours—but the blood pressure pills have slowed down my system so badly I feel like Billie Holiday at a recording session. I am so slow on the uptake; it doesn't feel like me. How can you be agitated and sluggish at the same time? I hate it. How can I vacuum? It's my only form of relaxation. I do Zen vacuuming. Up one chair down the other, up one chair down the other, up one chair down the other. Ohm.

It's 6 a.m., my day has not even started yet, and it's started. I go in for my morning pee and the phone rings. I don't know about you, but I can't stop mid-pee and it feels like last night I drank Lake Superior. It would not stop. I have to get the phone before the sixth ring because then the answering machine picks up and it's on the fourth floor and has an annoying *beep* sound when a message has been left, which means that I will not be able to go back to sleep because all I'll hear is *beep... beep... beep...* to infinity. I am now pushing the last of the Great Lakes out of my bladder and run to the phone.

"Hello?" My heart sinks... it's one of my bipolar celebrity friends and they're having an episode.

"Remember two years ago when we had dinner at your house?"

"No."

"Oh yes you do. You told everyone I was mentally ill. Well how could you do that to me?" How does one respond to that in pee stained pajamas?

"You're having an episode. That never happened."

"I *know* it never happened but how could you tell people I was mentally ill?"

I stay on the phone with this person until I can take it no more, "I've got to go now."

Just as insanely as they called, they say, "Okay, have a good morning!"

Why me? How do I collect these people? I've got a ton of them. There's the crier, the obsessive-compulsive, the sex addict, the alcoholic, the drug addict, and the sociopath. They're my closet friends. I love them all so much because I can relate. I've had every one of their illnesses and if I can make it through, so can they. All they need is a friend that will listen. That's what I needed. I had one shrink tell me that with my childhood, I should be proud I am not in a state facility making wallets. To which I added, "yet". The bottom line is these friends are my family and I love them with their warts and farts because lord knows I farted and created warts with the best of them.

Now the morning doesn't end there. My bipolar friend calls back an hour later at 7:30 a.m.

"I'm sorry I called you so early, but I was just thinking…" *Your first mistake.*

Then, like an unraveling roll of toilet paper, I get a laundry list of accusations. I lay the phone down on the counter and let the person spew. I butter my toast until I hear the murmuring stop.

"Okay, thanks for calling. I'll see you tomorrow." Click.

Now most people would be angry but I know it's the illness talking and not my friend. I love this person. I want to see them well again; nothing would make me happier. I am of the conviction that we all should be there for one another. What this world needs is less self-obsession and more compassion… and a cure for irritable bowel syndrome.

Now I'm off to Bank of America to fight with a teller.

12:02 p.m.

The strangest thing just happened. I went to the bank, there was a space right out in front. I took it and entered the bank. There was no one in line and I walked up to the teller, handed him my deposit slip, he stamped it and handed me a receipt. "Thank you. Anything else?" is all he said. I said no and was out of the bank in five minutes. There's something very wrong here. Where was the lady who is always in front of me depositing $157 in nickels? Where was the ninety-eight-year-old man who couldn't figure out how to use the ATM? Where were the Iranians? There's always Iranians at the bank. Some people visit relatives, Iranians visit their money. Something is very, very wrong. Maybe I've found the parallel universe. The entrance is in the Bank of America in Beverly Hills. Or maybe, just maybe, this is what it's like living in Utah.

Sports-Berg

I WAS WATCHING THE OLYMPICS as Sasha Cohen skates between her falls and I'm thinking, *See, Cohen should not be in sports. Cohen should have a going-out-of-business dry goods store on Long Island.* Be serious, Jews were not meant to be sports figures, run heavy machinery, or fly airplanes. Once, I was flying Los Angeles to New York and heard the announcement, "I am Stewart Rosenberg and I will be your captain today." I turned to woman next to me and said. "We're all gonna die." Jews aren't pilots. Jews are in the back of the plane complaining, "I had a special meal."

In any case, I'm watching Sasha and suddenly there is a bright light floating in front of my eyes. It turns to a chevron that obscures most of the TV. Then my vision begins to narrow and I can't see anything peripherally. My head starts pounding. I think, *I'm having a stroke.* I run to the phone and call my HMO doctor who by now has given me his private number (he's afraid I'll bad-mouth him in my book). I describe my symptoms and tell him where my will is. He laughs—which is exactly what you want to hear from your doctor when you're having a stroke.

He says, "You're having a visual migraine."

"Are you sure? How do you know? Maybe you were absent that day."

He reassures me the symptoms are textbook and to take two Tylenol.

Okay, let's review, shall we? I have irritable bowels and now visual migraines. I can't just have a heart attack and die, I have to go out piece by piece. They'll bury my naval in a three-piece suit. He tells me what to expect and the migraine follows the exact course he predicted. I make it through the night and am here to write this morning. It scared the shit out of me, but not as much as my bipolar celebrity friend.

Estelle Harris Comes To Dinner

ESTELLE HARRIS, OF *SEINFELD* FAME, had read one of my plays and agreed to do a staged reading here in Los Angeles. She is a wonderful woman, a fine actress, and I immediately fell in love with her. I wanted to thank her for all her efforts on my behalf and so one night I invited her over for dinner. I should have taken a gun and shot her; it would have been a lot less painful for her. You see, I completely forgot: I can't cook. Can't boil water; I can make toast if I have the recipe.

It was holiday season and I thought I'd make the traditional Christmas meal... Russian brisket. I started at 8 a.m. I got out the crock pot and cut up the veggies; one, two, three, four, five, six, seven, eight, nine, ten fingers—veggies go in the pot. I added the meat. I added the seasoning. I plugged in the crock-pot. God is good. I left for the day knowing that dinner would be ready when I arrived and I'd have plenty of time to prepare for Estelle. She was coming over at 7 p.m.

At 3 o'clock when I returned and opened the door, there was no brisket smell in the air. I ran to the kitchen; the crock is ice cold. I forgot to turn it on. Estelle will be here in four hours and I go into panic mode. I empty the crock into a casserole dish and pop it in the oven. I set the electronic oven, which I have used two times, to have the meal done by 7 p.m. and go about the task of setting the table. It's around 5 o'clock now and we have brisket smell. God is good. I need to make the rice. I open the cupboard, grab for the rice, hit the oatmeal container and three pounds of oatmeal come pouring out. It's a Lucy sketch. I'm covered in oatmeal, the floor is covered in oatmeal, the counter is covered in oatmeal; Estelle arrives in two hours. I have never done this but I call for the dogs, "MAINTENANCE!!!" I scream and dogs come running. Within three minutes they have eaten all the raw oatmeal off the floor. All I have to clean is the counter and myself. That's done and the dogs go back to the bedroom. I start all over. I grab for the rice, the bag rips and four pounds of long grain brown rice take up their position where the oatmeal just was. There is rice everywhere. My kitchen looked like the bride and groom just left for their honeymoon. I remember I need this rice for the meal. No dogs, but they hear the noise of falling food and are in the kitchen like in ten seconds. Picture me fighting them off with a broom. One dog has the broom in his mouth while the other is sucking up raw rice at one pound a minute. I wrestle the dogs outside and survey what's left.... about one cup and seventeen hairs. I can do this if I F.H.B. (Family Hold Back) the meal. I know! I'll make steamed veggies and that will take up the slack. I get to the kitchen that I now have to clean *again*. I prep the steamed veggies, I make the rice minus the hair and I set the table. God is good.

It's now 7 p.m. and the doorbell rings. It's Estelle and her husband. They enter the house and want the tour. Jews always want the tour, "This is the master bath, this is the guest room, this is where the dogs sleep." It gives the guests something to talk about on the way home, "What a shit hole they live in." So, I give the tour and we sit in the living room and talk and talk and talk for way over an hour. Finally I say, "Are you hungry?" and head for the kitchen where I learn I have set the oven incorrectly. This marvel of electronic wizardry did not shut off at 7 p.m. God is NOT good. From a six-pound brisket, I'm left with about one pound of shriveled, blackened, shoe leather. Estelle walks in and looks over my shoulder.

"We'll make do. We have rice and veggies."

I insist we can salvage the meat and put it on a platter. On that huge platter, the brisket looked like a refugee raft floating in from Cuba. I get the meat to the table and Estelle says, "I smell burning plastic." I had forgotten to put water in the steamer and the steamer has melted—more like fused itself to the burner. I pull out some untouched veggies and throw them in the microwave. They come out like petrified wood. The entire meal is now a science project.

Back at the table Estelle's husband is attempting to cut the brisket. "No, No. Allow me." I make the first cut; the knife slips and a piece of meat shoots across the table into Estelle's husband's lap. I get all the food on the plates and watch as Estelle pushes it around like its radioactive, which at this point I'm not sure it isn't.

"The rice is good," she says pulling a hair from her teeth. We make small talk.

"So, wanna go out and get something to eat after this?" Their faces smile; their eyes tell a different story. They just want to flee for their lives.

As if things weren't bad enough the dogs have opened the bedroom door and joined us. They take their position in the corner of the dining room, hovering like vultures. Within three minutes Estelle covers her nose with a napkin. "What the hell is *that*? Did your cow die?" Apparently, oatmeal and the dog's digestive system don't mix. They are farting up a storm, long, deep, farts that linger in the air and will not dissipate. I turn on the A/C. Estelle is freezing. I shut it off. It's smells like the pound. Estelle and her husband are truly good, wonderful people and make the best of a horrific situation. Suddenly there's a huge crash from the kitchen. What now? A porcelain turkey platter has fallen off the shelf and shattered into a million pieces.

"What was that?" Estelle shouts from the other room.

"The dishes are committing suicide," is all I could get out.

I won't even tell you about the dessert, but suffice it to say it entailed sprinkling paprika on vanilla pudding instead of cinnamon. To this day, whenever I'm with Estelle, no matter who we are with, no matter where we are, she'll turn to the person next to me and say, "Did you ever eat dinner at his house? No? God is Good."

The Mudslide

I HAD BEEN SITTING at my desk when I got up to pace. The rain had been making me very nervous. My neighbors were building an Ark. I walked down the hall, about six feet from my desk when I heard a loud explosion, like someone had dumped a load of gravel on the roof. I turned and I was standing in the garden. The whole back of the house was gone; however, I did have a waterfall in the bathroom.

I run to the phones to dial 911. The phones are dead. I try my cell but I know if I call 911 on my cell I'll get highway patrol, so I dial the Bel Air fire house on Sunset.

"Bel Air Fire."

"You have got to come to my house. I just had a mudslide; the whole back of my house is gone!"

Long pause. "How did you get this number?"

I then have to beg them to come to my house. When they arrive, all cool and collected, I am in full panic mode, "Can you guys do something to divert the water?"

"No."

"NO?"

"It's dangerous back there."

"Don't you guys run into burning buildings?"

"Yes, but not mud."

"Should I set the house on fire? Would that help?"

About this time the guy with the big white hat comes up to me, "Sir, when you have an emergency you should really dial 911."

"My phones were dead."

"But sir, you should dial 911."

"But I couldn't reach you on my cell so I dialed you directly."

"Sir, that's why we have 911."

I hit the roof, "I have a river flowing through my house! There is mud up to my ass. You guys won't help, and now I get a lecture on how to dial 911. Get out of my house!" I throw the fire department out! Literally, I threw them out of the house.

My neighbors began collecting at the front door. They start a bucket brigade. I call my best friend, my brother, plastic surgeon Michael Churukian. It's his day off; he's here in twenty minutes and gives me Botox. He runs to the back yard and jumps waist high into the mud. I have a plastic surgeon, a guitar designer, two attorneys, a jeweler, and a medical staffer digging out the back of my house, while the fire department went to Starbucks for a Latte. Oh, they did shut off the gas, the electricity, and phones before they yellow-tagged my house. It shouldn't be a total loss for them. I'm homeless; their day is complete. This is my greatest fear: no home and two dogs. I can see myself pushing a shopping cart through Beverly Hills. I spend the night on a friend's sofa and begin six months of pure hell dealing with the city pencil pushers, or as I call them: Morons Anonymous. Rash on my hands? I'm lucky I didn't get shingles on my prostate.

Six months later the house is all back together thanks to State Farm and Guatemala. However, when it rains it all comes back and I shit my pants. Oh God, you're so strict!

Geary's Sale

GEARY'S OF BEVERLY HILLS is a very "fah-fah" kind of store. They have forks for $400. It's very bourgeois, very expensive, very out of my shopping experience. Once a year they have a sale. It's a big event, and every year I buy shit I won't use and can't give as gifts because it's "too good" for them. Unless you've been to this sale you cannot even imagine what it's like. Picture Ruta Lee mud wrestling a mid-eastern woman for a candelabrum. It's the most insane group of people you have ever seen. Last year I put my hand down on the counter and a Russian woman bought it. When I told her it was mine, she demanded I give it to her because "I haf von jest like."

Let me try to set the stage for you. The store is piss elegant. It's filled with Steuben, Waterford Crystal, Lalique, sterling silver tea sets from England, linens from Ireland, and Jews from New York. You can't shit in that store for under $200. But when they have the sale, the center of the store is removed and replaced by one huge table filled with markdowns. Picture a bargain basement at Windsor Castle.

The first two days of the sale are invitation only. Yours truly is invited and I think it's going to be rich Beverly Hills types shopping with their maids. Instead, there was an Ellis Island reunion. No one spoke English and everyone looked like a suicide bomber. And the smell. How can I describe it…Chanel No. 5 and scrotum. I'm pushing my way through the crowd; I feel like a salmon trying to spawn. I see a bowl and I reach out for it. At the same time a hand with 126 bracelets and nine clean fingernails grabs the same bowl. Our eyes meet and she knows my last name ends in –stein. She ain't giving up.

"I saw it first," I bleat.

She spits in the bowl, "OK, maybe you saw it first."

I've kicked and scratched my way through a sea of Louis Vuitton Burkas. I've come up with one item: a picture frame. I take it to the counter where the line extends back to 1847. I'm at the end of the line. People are churning butter behind me. After about an hour I get to the register and hand the girl—who is crying—my credit card, and the register begins to print out my receipt. *Tick... tick... tick.* It's the dot matrix printer that Edison used in his experiments to invent the light bulb. I have never seen a printer print so slowly. It took so long, half way through I needed to shave. It finally finishes and I sign the check, but where's my package? Gone. Evaporated. They search the counter; it's crossed over into the fifth dimension. Now I need a refund. *Tick... tick... tick.* "Here's your package!" The sales clerk shouts. I want to shove knitting needles in my eyes and we start the process all over again. I hold the package this time.

I get to my car, my pants are ripped, I'm bleeding, and I need drugs. Any drugs. I'll take Pamprin at this point. But I got a $500 bowl for $250. Tomorrow there will be no morning gym. I will be at Geary's with kneepads, hardhat, and a gun. I wouldn't miss that sale for the world.

Home Depot

I JUST WALKED IN THE DOOR from Home Depot. Somebody get me a Valium. God does not want us shopping for doorknobs in a warehouse bigger than Houston. Oh my God! I've never seen a place filled with employees who don't want to help. Who runs the place, Al Qaeda?

I needed a fence post so I go to lumber where there are skeletons of customers who have died waiting for service. I see an orange vest and a mullet... it's either an employee or a friend of Ellen DeGeneres.

"Can you help me?" I shout. They avoid eye contact like if they see me they'll turn to a pillar of salt. I go up the next aisle and standing in front of me is the biggest Home Depot employee I have ever seen, maybe he's 450 pounds. He looks like someone Maury Povich should be interviewing.

"Can you help me?"

"Sure!" he says with sweat dripping off his nose, "What do you want?"

"Fence posts."

And he says, "They're right over there by McDonald's."

Ok now I think he's on crack but low and behold... there is a McDonald's inside Home Depot. I grabbed a roll of masking tape and taped my mouth shut, otherwise something like, "Is that *your* McDonald's or can anyone use it?" will come spewing out like some comedy suicide bomber.

He waddles me over to the fence posts. It's twenty-five feet; he has to sit sixteen times. I'm refreshing CPR in my mind as I watch him squeeze down the fifty-foot aisle.

"Do you want me to carry this to the register for you?"

"No," I wanted to say, "Just lay down on a flatbed truck and let me push you to Weight Watchers."

Then I remember other sales people I have seen there. Once, a dwarf in the ladder department helped me. I kept thinking, *does anyone else see the humor here?* There was a guy in a wheel chair in hardware and a blind man in lighting. Who does the hiring at Home Depot, Tim Burton?

I get the fence post to my car; it's too big to fit into the car. By now 3,500 illegal aliens have gathered to watch me try to get the fucker into my back seat. "Gringo... ju need help?" I roll the windows down and stick the post out the side of the car. I look like I'm about to joust with an Infiniti. I get the post home and reflect on my shopping experience. Costco, Home Depot, Office Depot, it made me wonder how many of these depot stores there are. I did a Google Search.... here's the funniest one I found. Enjoy. http://www.edepot.com/buddha.html Can anyone install a fence?

Food Shopping

I CAN'T COOK, and if you don't believe me, ask my beloved Estelle Harris. But what I didn't tell you was what happened the day before Estelle came to dinner when I went to Ralph's to buy the food. What I hate more than cooking is shopping for food. I hate the parking lot. I hate the aisles. I hate the women on their cell phones, "Do we have oregano?" How insecure can you be that you have to call home for reassurance on spices? I hate the whole shopping experience. I wish I could just take a pill, and that would be dinner. However, if you *have* to food shop I have discovered that if you shop at 6 a.m. you have the store to yourself and you can get in and out in ten minutes.

This particular morning Ralph's is completely empty. It's like there is a ricin scare and nobody told me. It's ten thousand square feet of Pop Tarts and anti-itch cream and it's all mine. Just me and this 189-year-old woman with a walker. I do my shopping in five minutes and this includes coupons. I head for the check out at the exact time the 189-year-old lady gets to the check out. She has a gallon of milk and Preparation H. Being a gentleman I say, "After you," and she shuffles ahead of me. Now what I am about to tell you is the God's honest truth; on my father's grave.

The checker totals the two items, "That'll be $9.07," and Grandma Moses gets this look on her face like she's the poster child for Alzheimer's.

"Ah... ah... did I get a lettuce?"

Checker says "No."

"Oh, I need a lettuce," and she takes her walker and begins the mile-long trek back to produce.

Checker says into the microphone, "Over ring!"

"Can't I just scoot in and buy my stuff?" I ask.

She shakes her head no. The manager shows up with "the key," they sign the paperwork, they reset the register, recount the money, throw a rattlesnake at the moon, and face Mecca. I bought my house with less red tape. Meanwhile back at produce Mrs. Senile is thumping lettuce heads. I scream at her across the store.

"It's a lettuce not a heart and lung machine!"

She heads back to the check-out stand, lettuce in hand. The checker totals the three items. It's now 6:29 a.m.

"That'll be $10.18".

The woman reaches into her purse and pulls out a $100 bill.

Checker over loud-speaker, "Manager.... Change!" Now it's 6:45 a.m. and the manager comes with the change for a hundred. The checker counts out the dollars and the woman hands her back a twenty.

"I need two rolls of quarters".

"Manager.... Change!".

He arrives, "Sorry we're out of quarters." It's 6:55 a.m.

The woman begins a long dissertation, "You see I do my laundry at that nice place on Westwood Blvd. and the last time I was there the change machine was broken. I told them it was broken but the kid who services the machines doesn't listen to me. I'm not the only one who complains. Mrs. Lathem also told him and I think..."

KA- BOOM!!!! The top of my head blows off.

"For crap sakes will you buy your food and let me get out of here? It's Ralph's not the Federal Reserve. Do you go to the Bank of America and ask them for Depends??"

And this sweet little old lady, with grey hair and a walker looks at me and in complete innocence says, "Oh blow it out your ass."

And that is why I don't like to cook.

The Oscar Party

I'M INVITED TO THE SAME PARTY every year. It's a black and white Oscar Party, where everyone has to wear black and white. Hence the name, Black and White Oscar Party. Duh. It's really quite a great event. You arrive at the house and there is a limo parked in the driveway. Behind the limo there is a scenic backdrop of a movie theater and photographers are hired to photograph you as you "step out of the limo." It's a lot of fun, especially if you're from Ohio and don't get out a lot. But I'm telling you, I love this party and the people who throw it, so like Estelle Harris, I make do.

I have been looking forward to this party for weeks. I even bought a new sport coat at J. Crew for the occasion. The party is called for 5 p.m. I'm meeting friends at my house and we're all going together. Around 4 p.m. I step into the shower and immediately cut my foot on a razor left in there by Juanita, my homicidal housekeeper. It looked like a scene from Psycho. I shut off the water; I bandage the foot. I go back in. No hot water. I wait for the water to build up. I take the shower. I have done one "S" of the "3 S's" of manly grooming (shit, shower, and shave) and am heading for the second "S" when the phone rings. It's my friends; they're going to be late. Why? They're at the Geary's sale. The Geary's sale again.

I "S & S", no problem. I'm getting dressed when I notice the jerk at J. Crew has left the security tag on the hem of my new jacket. It's not one of those little ones you cut off…it's the big one that needs the machine to remove. However, I am delusional and think I can get it off. My first attempt is with a hammer. I lay the jacket on the kitchen counter and give it a whack. It bounces; dent one on the counter top. Not being of sane mind, I do it a second time… dent two on the counter top. Matching dents, just

29

what I always wanted. Now I try to remove the tag with a screwdriver. Slam Bam; a six-inch hole in the brand new, never worn jacket. Steam is pouring out of both ears. It's a Roger Rabbit moment. I call J. Crew.

"And what would you like me to do, sir?" she gurgles.

I'd like you to shove this jacket up your ass and remove the security tag is what I'd like to say, what I actually say is, "Will you please exchange it?" I am such a wuss. Bottom line. Tomorrow, forty-five-minute drive to return the jacket some teenage airhead sold to me with a security tag as a bonus.

The question arises, "How did I get out of the store with the security tag on?"

The answer, "Just lucky I guess."

My friends arrive an hour late, which is perfect because with the security breach at my house I'm still in my bathrobe. I pick out the closest thing I have to black and white... red and green and am prepared to hear three hundred times, "Didn't they tell you it was a black and white party?" We get to the party late and the food is being packed up. I run into the kitchen and grab the serving tray, as the maid is about to dump it in the disposal. We're eating drippings and crumbs and look like homeless people by the freeway.

The Oscars were interesting (yawn) and so entertaining (yaaaawn). I don't know how anyone could… zzzzzzzzzzzzzzzzzzzzzzzzzzzzzzzz.

We leave with the perfect parting gift provided by our hosts, a full-sized chocolate Oscar. These people thought of everything. I wish they had worked at J. Crew. We say our good-byes and as I enter my car, I slam my head into the car door. I wanted to see stars and I just did.

Taking My Mother To Australia

THE FOLLOWING STORY IS TRUE and infamous amongst my friends. Whenever a group of us get together and there is a new member of the group, eventually someone will say, "Hey Steve, tell so-and-so about when you took your mother to Australia." And then I am forced to relive one of the biggest nightmares of my life!

First, you have to know my mother. When *you* think of Mom you think of that sweet lady who is baking cookies in the kitchen. When *I* think of Mom I think of a staff sergeant with all the tenderness of an acid burn. I didn't really have a mother; I had a Vice President in charge of maternal affairs. She was a wonderful person; she was a horrific mother. She was the kind of woman who should have never had children and has zero mothering skills. We had a love-hate relationship that seesaws because both of us never get our needs met. We lived in a constant state of battle. She had one finger that she used just to push my buttons and apparently, I did the same to her. But she was my mom and I learned to deal with her... if you call two nervous breakdowns and a failed marriage dealing with her. So that's my mother.

Back Story

In 1985, I starred in a show in Sydney, Australia and fell in love with the country, the lifestyle, and the people; especially one Judy Robertson and her entire family. Judy was the most insanely wonderful person I ever met (she passed a few years ago and I still grieve the loss). I worshipped the ground she walked on; she was wise and funny and talented and adored me unconditionally (does anyone know how to spell Freud?). It was important to me to make several trips to Australia to see my adopted family, The Robertsons. About 1990 (I'm foggy on the dates) my stepfather died and my mother was beside herself. I was making my weekly calls to my mom, trying to be supportive, trying to tell her it would be okay. Time heals all wounds...blah, blah, blah. However, it's like trying to be supportive to quicksand. She sucks you in and pulls you under.

I was making idle conversation when I said, "Guess what! I just earned enough miles on American Airlines for two first class tickets to Sydney." I was about to say, "I'm going to sell one ticket and use the money for a vacation in Australia."

Before I could get that sentence out my mother jumped in with, "I'd love to go."

HUH?

"No one has ever done anything nice for me in my life...and I would love to go to Australia." I hear the sound of a prison door slamming. My knees began to shake. She goes on like a martyr, "I won't mention it again. I'll just wait for someone to make me happy."

I think, *if I don't mention it again, she'll forget*. For the next four months, she mentioned it every time we spoke.

"Did you make the reservations?"

"When do we leave?"

"Do they keep kosher in Australia? Should I bring meat?"

I called Judy to tell her I might be bringing my mother. Her immediate reaction, "Love, are you out of your mind? You can't go to dinner with your mother, and you're thinking of taking her half way round the world." Judy was right, as she always was; there was no way I could take my mother on a vacation. Flash cut. My mother and I sitting in the first-class lounge of Qantas Airlines. We're on a sofa next to an elderly woman and my mother is chatting up a storm, "My husband just died. It was a long illness. Longer for him than for me." Out come the tissues. In mid-sentence, she stops and notices the food table in the corner, "Look there's a buffet," and goes back to boring this stranger about the details of her husband's death. "We didn't have an open casket... he wasn't that good looking alive I'm certainly not going to show him dead." I cringe. Someone asks me a question, I look away for one tenth of a second and when I look back, my mother is gone. I scanned the room and found her. The blood drained from my face. There was my mother at the buffet table with her purse wide open cramming whatever she could get her hands on. Oranges, bananas, apples, napkins, silverware, toothpicks... you name it, she was shoveling it. I ran to her.

"What are you doing??"

"We'll need food on the long flight."

"We're going first class. This is Qantas not a Lewis and Clark expedition."

"SHUT UP. I want this fruit."

We are five minutes into the trip and they need a crowbar to get my hands from around her neck. I grab my suitcase and I leave for the gate. I want nothing to do with her. I'm walking down the long corridors at LAX which are divided by moving walkways. Behind me I hear the *click, click, click* of my mother's high heels. *Click, click, click,* then silence as she gets on the moving walkway. *Click, click, click,* silence as she gets on the walkway. *Click, click, click,* then "Oomph!" I don't turn around, but an orange rolls past me. I turn and she's spread eagle on the floor surrounded by oranges and grapes and pineapples, napkins and forks. I walk back, "You ok?" She nods and I step over the body as she sits there gathering her groceries.

Cut to me on the plane sitting in first class. My mother soon follows behind... she's eating a banana. Now I don't know if you've ever been in first class on a 747 but it's huge and at the bulkhead of each seat is a large storage bin. My mother opens it and dumps in her cache of stolen food. About this time the flight attendant approaches with a leather amenities kit. My mother takes hers and tosses it into the bin. The flight attendant leaves and my mother hits the call button. Another flight attendant approaches.

My mother says, "I didn't get an amenities kit."

To which I say, "What!"

My mother's eyes open to the size of dinner plates. I know this look. This is the "Shut your mouth or you're out of the will" look.

Cut to baggage claim. Our suitcases come up and my mother says with glee, "Look, they ripped my luggage!" Now you have to know what this luggage is. What's lower than K-Mart, Salvation Army? That's what this luggage looked like.

I beg her, "Don't start. Please. We just arrived in a foreign land. Don't declare war." She's off to the claims office. I sit there for an hour and finally go to find her. I open the door of the claims office and as God is my judge I hear my mother saying, "No, what do YOU think it's worth?" She gets an entire set of new luggage from Qantas because, "I'm not traveling with an unmatched set," this coming from a woman who re-washes zip-lock bags.

The trip was a never-ending story of battles and losses. Wherever she went, she stole. She took the towels from the hotel, the alarm clock, the brochures, the sugar packets. If it was there, she threw it in her bag, which

now weighed the same as a small Volkswagen. I begged her to get rid of this crap. I was the one carrying the suitcases.
"Please throw this shit out. "
"No! I need them for gifts."
"Gifts? Who goes to Australia and comes back to say, 'Here. I was in Sydney and I brought you a packet of Equal??'"
The trip was two weeks of living hell. She was a human vacuum cleaner sucking up whatever wasn't nailed down. I was embarrassed beyond words, but I made it, holding on to what was left of my sanity. Cut to the return flight. At this point we're not talking. I hate her and her 398-pound carry-on and she hates me for not being an accountant. We're approaching LAX and we are so close to landing the flaps are down and the landing gear is being deployed. My mother rings for the flight attendant.
She approaches and my mother says, "Can I have a deck of cards?" People, it was the last straw and I go ballistic. Two weeks of pent-up anger comes out in First class.
"A deck of cards?? What the hell do you need a deck of cards for?? Oh, I forgot you stole the card table from the hotel. I'm sick of it, you hear me… sick of it!"
I've pulled off my seat belt and I'm standing in the aisle. And now I look like a raving lunatic. Everyone is diverting their eyes. The flight attendant is trying to get me seated for landing. I can see the headlines: "Comedian arrested on plane." My mother says to the flight attendant, "He's been impossible the entire trip."
We land and I bolt from the plane. I'm the first one at customs. My mother is about twenty people back, and like Damien possessed me I say to the customs inspector, "I don't know if this is anything or not. But see that woman in the black suit? She's been acting suspicious the whole trip." Two and a half hours later my mommy is still in customs. I can see her as the door opens and closes; they have the hotel towels and the alarm clocks (plural) and the brochures and napkins and smuggled fruit spread all over the counter. About thirty minutes later she comes out, suitcase wrapped in masking tape. She rolls right past me and turns, "I will never go to Australia with you again," and storms off to the taxi. I spend the next six months in therapy.

My Fiftieth Birthday

NOW WE ALL KNOW WHAT HELL I went through on the first trip to Australia—it was a nightmare. For my birthday the following year, I think, *I just need some quality time with Judy, besides, it's my birthday. I've been a good boy. I've earned it.* However, about a month before my birthday my mother calls to see what I'm doing on my "special day".

"Oh, I don't know. I think I'll go to see Judy".

I can feel the ice forming on the phone. "Really, Judy. Huh… well I think you should come to Florida and see me!" she orders.

"Mom, it's my birthday and I want to go to Australia."

Long pause. "Okay, then you go to Australia. You do whatever you want, no matter who it hurts."

I have never heard her like this. She has become possessed. It's like the Stephen King novel when the gypsy whispers the curse, "Thinner". I get a chill down my spine. I know my trip has just been cursed. "Oh, don't be silly. What could she do?" you ask. You don't know my mother.

I have enough frequent miles to go to Sydney first class. My friend Dina wants to go with me, so I tell her, "I'll get you a ticket with my miles and then I'll contact one of my flight attendant friends and get a buddy pass (this was before 9/11), and I'll go with her." It's a long story, but I created a company that did plastic surgery for flight attendants and I had hundreds of flight attendant connections. If I may add, flight attendants are the most under-rated class of people flying today. They bust their humps for slobs on airlines and get their pensions revoked as a bonus.

The day we are leaving I put the dogs in the kennel and I close up the house. Dina comes over and I take her to the airport. She takes my luggage and she's off to the warm, sunny beaches of Sydney. My plane leaves in three hours so I drive home and my other friend Bennet Yellin (writer of *Dumb and Dumber*) comes to my house and takes me to the airport. I get to the gate. The flight is cancelled. I call Bennet, he comes back and gets me. Not to worry, there is another flight leaving tomorrow, "We'll get you on that one." The curse is starting.

Next day, same routine. Dogs to kennel, close up house, Bennet to airport. Bad weather. Curse. At this point, Dina is in Sydney with my luggage. My underwear is in Australia. I'm in LA. Next day, same routine. Dogs, house, ride… overbooked. Curse. This goes on for days until I realize that if I left now, I would arrive in Australia the day after my birthday (because of the international dateline) and would miss my birthday altogether. The curse thickens. I call Diana, who is staying with Judy—someone she does not know—and I tell her I'm not coming and to enjoy the vacation she's having with my frequent flier miles. She can't talk… she's going to the beach! Fuck!

I go home. I get the dogs out of the kennel. I fill the house with food. I open the shutters and have myself a good sit on the pity pot. This is the time I watched *Schindler's List* to try to cheer myself up. While I'm watching the movie the phone rings. It's a flight attendant in San Francisco. She tells me the flight to Sydney is wide open—if I can get to SFX I can make it out tonight. Adrenaline rush. The dogs go back to the kennel. I close up the house. I take the food and bring it next door. "Here take this. I beg you, take me to the airport." They are eating dinner and get up from the table to take me.

We get to the airport; the line to SFX is out the door. They've had mechanical trouble and two planes did not take off; these are the people who didn't get on the earlier planes. I think, *how could all these people piss off my mother?* I'm desperate. I find a flight attendant.

"Get me on that plane and I'll get you a free facelift."

"Honey, you'll get on that plane if you have to go as luggage."

The plane to Sydney leaves at 10 p.m., the plane from LAX lands at 8 p.m. We have plenty of time. Oh, you'd think so, wouldn't you? We are held on the runway for one and a half hours. Curse. I land in SFX at 9:35 p.m. We land at gate 6, the flight to Sydney leaves from gate 96. I run like I've never run before. I get to the gate three beats short of a heart attack… its 9:58 p.m. There are fourteen standbys. I'm fourteen. They take thirteen standbys and close the door. The stress of the last three days hits me. I start crying like a five-year-old who just lost his Dancing Elmo.

The counter rep, a huge, doe-eyed black woman sees me crying. She leans over the counter and puts her arms around me. I will never forget this act of love till the day I die.

"I don't know if I should tell you this or not," she begins, "You just flew up from LA, didn't you?"

I nod through my tears.

"Well, honey, there was a misconnect in LA. 138 people missed the plane. If you had stayed in LA, you would have been on your way to Sydney."

I instantly know that God did not want me in Australia on this birthday. "Ok, I'll get back to LA." We have closure. I turned around and the United counter was dark, the American counter was dark, Continental, Delta… the entire airport was dark. No one was flying out of SFX that night. I was stuck in San Francisco. Curse. No wait, this is not a curse. San Fran is a great place to celebrate your birthday. I'll get a hotel room, I'll see a show, and I'll go out to dinner.

I start calling around for a hotel room but there appeared to be a gay horse breeder or a gay cow breeder or a gay goat breeder convention in town and there wasn't a single room available. Not one. Not a Motel 6, not a Marriott, nothing!

Now it's midnight and I'm wandering around SFX. It's my birthday, no one cares. I am exhausted and find a corner to lie down on and fall asleep. That's how I spent my birthday, sleeping on the floor of San Francisco International Airport in my navy blue cashmere rain coat.

As I'm drifting off I hear my mother's voice whisper in my ear, "Thinner."

Vern

THE HOUSE I OWNED before the one in Bel Air was in Northridge. You remember Northridge… 1994 earthquake. Oh yes, that's right, Mr. Lucky bought a house right over the San Andres fault. Why? I couldn't find one in Hell! There hasn't been an earthquake in Northridge in 1,500 years. I move in and Bingo, 8.9 shaker. That's another story for another day. Today I want to tell you about my neighbor in Northridge, Vern.

The day I bought the house, Vern came over to introduce himself. He was a slight man, salt-and-pepper hair, fair complexion. He was Ohio, Utah, and Iowa all rolled up into one. He was your uncle, the postman; literally the guy next door. He was the whitest man I've ever seen. He looked like Mr. Green Jeans on chemo. He was married to Nell. Vern and Nell, E-I-E-I-O. Vern was very friendly; so friendly you wanted to take the gas pipe every time he came over, "So whatcha doin', Stevarino?" Nell, on the other hand, was a little less friendly. Once in a while you'd see her dart in front of a window or open the door to suck in the mail, but it was like living next to The Bates Motel. The mother was there, but she wasn't.

A few years passed and Vern was a royal pain in the ass. Nell was invisible. At one point the other neighbors thought she might be buried under the roses in Vern's garden a la *Rear Window*. I was cordial; after all, they had the house right next door. I had been on the road for a month and when I came home, Vern was standing in my driveway with tears in his eyes, "My Nell has cancer." It was a horrific day and we talked and I told him if there was anything I could do… just ask. It wasn't six weeks later when Nell passed. Wasn't ten weeks later when I noticed Vern had blonde hair. At twenty weeks, he had a ponytail and cut off micro-mini shorts. Vern was coming over more frequently and had been hitting the sauce quite regularly

"Wanna come over and swim in my pool? You could swim naked. Just us!"

I could feel the vomit backing up in my throat, "No, thanks, gee... um... look at the time."

It was no surprise to me, shortly afterwards, when Vern came screaming out of the closet. *Scream-ing.* All of a sudden there was a blonde Cabana boy living in Nell's house and it appeared the little fucker was an alcoholic. My nice quiet neighbor had turned into Steve Rubell of Studio 54. There were nightly parties and loud music and cars and beer and men. Lots and lots of men. It was my own personal nightmare. I buy a house in the suburbs and Boy George moves in next door.

One night Vern comes over shit-faced. I stand at the door not letting him in.

"Can I help you, Vern?"

"Why don't you come over? I've got porn."

Okay, he crossed the line. I slammed the door in his face. I'm fuming. I walk back to my den to finish watching a movie when, without warning, a brick sails through my picture window. It smashes into a thousand pieces and breaks that horrific piece of crap vase my agent gave me. "Vern finally had a purpose." I call the police.

Now I swear to God to you, on my father's grave, this is what happened next. Two huge officers enter my home. I tell them about the cabana boy and the booze and the cars and the brick. There is nothing they can do because they didn't witness any of the events. While I'm asking them what I can do to protect myself, one of the officers enters my den. He turns to the other officer and says, "Hey Stanley, look at this." I think he's found evidence.

The second officer joins him and I hear him say, "Is that fabric on the walls? This place is fabulous."

"Yeah?"

I'm like, "Hello what has this got to do with Sodom and Gomorrah next door?"

"So how do you get the fabric to stick?" the first officer questions like Joe Friday.

The second excitedly adds, "I could do this in my den."

I'm thinking, *why can't they just beat me like they did Rodney King?*

They want to know where I got the sofas, who did the painting, where I got my windows, what's a better design station, HGTV or PBS?

I'm thinking, *should I reach for their gun?*

They leave with swatches to show their "wives". Yeah, right. They probably have an apartment in the Castro, and I'm still left with the Vern problem. I want nothing to do with him. Not because he's gay, but because he's a creep. He's a gay creep. Why couldn't he be hip like Elton John? Why couldn't Elton John move in next door to me in Northridge? Why, because he'd rather have a steel wool enema. I'm stuck with Nell's gay Barney Fife.

I call my carpenter and he comes over the next day, "Don, I want you to build a fuck you fence." I describe an eight-foot fence, the unfinished side facing Vern's house, with space on the top for vines and gun turrets. Don is a master carpenter and builds the fence in four days. It's a beauty. My own personal Berlin Wall.

Now I go to my favorite place, Home Depot, where, "You can do and we don't give a shit." I grab a guy in the garden department and this is what I say verbatim:

"I want a very invasive vine, something that goes deep and fucks up the plumbing. It should spread like wildfire and drop lots of flowers and berries. I want it deciduous so it drops leaves in the fall, and I want six of them."

The guy looks at me like I'm crazy and then says, "Are you building a fuck you fence?"

I nod.

"I got just the thing."

He sells me these plants and they come with magic beans. I get the plants home and couldn't wait to put them in the ground. I bought Vigaro to make sure they took off, and take off they did. I've never seen anything like it in my life. I expected Jack to come down the stalk chased by the giant. This thing covered the fence, the sidewalk, the gate, his roof, his car, and the cabana boy. It was a joy to behold. Six weeks later I put my house on the market.

In escrow, I left specific instructions on how to water the vine and when. Moral of the story: never ever throw a brick through my window.

Return From Hawaii

A FEW YEARS AGO, I had been working in Honolulu. It's one of those jobs God gives you in exchange for taking your mother to Australia. It was a perfect gig. I had a suite overlooking the Pacific Ocean, friends had flown in from LA to see my show, and Judy had flown in from Sydney. It was perfect.

At the end of the trip, we all parted, I got on my flight to LA, and that's when it started. We are seated and waiting to close the doors when the flight attendant comes on and says, "The captain has informed me that we are too heavy for present weather conditions. Two passengers will have to get off." She then stands in the aisle and points her finger, "You and... ah... you!" And two people have to get off. *Wait a minute, how much do they weigh??* I'm panicked. Shouldn't it be more precise than, "you and you"? No one seemed to worry about this but me and we took off. I was a nervous wreck the entire flight. I am not a good flyer. When I fly, to me, everyone looks like they have box cutters. I didn't eat, I didn't watch the movie, I didn't even steal a second amenities kit for my mother. I was frozen in fear.

We were about twenty minutes out of LA when our plane was hit by lightning and I screamed like a schoolgirl. Actually, there were schoolgirls on the plane who were braver. I broke out in a cold sweat, *we're going down, this is it. Shit! My best suit is in the cleaners. They're going to bury me in a sports jacket. Who are you kidding, after this thing goes down they'll bury you in a thimble.*

Soon there's another announcement, "Due to bad weather we are forced into a holding pattern until further notice." To me this is like going up in front of the prison board and not getting parole. I just wanted to get down on the ground and off this plane.

We circled for two hours.

Ring around the Rosy at thirty-thousand feet. At this point my blood pressure was six-hundred over death. No one seemed to be worried but me, and that worried me. Shouldn't someone else care? Then, another announcement, "We have just been informed that we will not be able to land in LA tonight." I think, *we have to circle till tomorrow? I'll get dizzy.* We were diverted to Las Vegas. Huh? Oh wait, that's not so bad. I have lots of friends there. I could see a show, and I could gamble. God is good.

We land in Las Vegas at about 1 a.m. It's raining and there is no one in the airport but us. I proceed to baggage claim. Thirty minutes, forty-five minutes, one hour no bags. It's 2 a.m. I go to an airline rep.

"When do you think the bags from flight 234 are coming up?"

"Oh, they're not coming up. We're keeping them on the plane because we are leaving at 6 a.m. tomorrow."

Slowly I turn, step by step, inch by inch, "When were you going to tell us that?"

She changes the subject, "Why aren't you on the bus?"

"What bus?"

"The bus to the hotel..."

It appears that in my nervous anxiety I had missed the announcement that the buses would take us to a hotel where we would spend the night.

I run up to the buses where 358 people hate my guts because they had been waiting an hour for me. I get on the bus and it's like I'm radioactive. No one talks to me; no one makes eye contact. I'm a man without a country. We get to the hotel in about twenty minutes. I get off the bus and it's then that I see we are not on the strip. We are like in Henderson or Elk Balls or some small town just outside Las Vegas. No shows, no dinner, nada. I look at the hotel and it looks strange. What is it about this place? Holy Shit! It's under construction. They were putting us up in a brand-new hotel that was under construction. I swear to God!

I enter the casino and it's empty of all furniture and gaming machines, except on the wall is written, "Slots Here" or "Kino Board Here". At the end of this football field size room is the check-in desk with one man. One very old man. It looks like we have awakened him from a long nap. Rip Van Winkle is checking us in. Over three hundred people check in at the same time, and he's all alone and slow. He hands out the keys and, person by person, they leave the lobby. The line for keys stretched from the check-in desk, through the empty casino, out to the bus. Guess where

I am. Dr. Fortune has kissed me again; I'm tenth from the end. About this time, I start to notice that people who have gotten their keys are now returning. It appears the keys were put in the boxes today and someone put them in "one slot off" so people went up to their rooms and then came back down. The keys didn't work. Have you seen the pictures of the fall of Saigon? That's what this lobby looked like, people screaming and shoving, Asian women crying, small children hanging from helicopter doors. It was a living hell.

At 4 a.m. I get to my room. Room? Ha! It wasn't finished. There was a bed wrapped in plastic and a phone. In the bathroom, a toilet and no sinks. At this point I am so exhausted I fall on the bed, plastic and all, and I'm out like a light. Within twenty-five minutes the phone rings. "Wake up call. The buses are leaving for the airport." You know how some people can take a twenty-minute catnap and are refreshed? I'm not one of those people. You wake me after a twenty-minute nap and I'm like Donald Trump. I can't focus, I can't walk, I'm incoherent.

I drag myself down to the lobby and crawl onto the bus. Check-in at the airport is smooth; we're on the plane in thirty minutes, and sit there for three hours. No food. No movie. Nothing. Just my delusional self and my sleep-deprived inner voice, *if I had a box cutter I could take over the cockpit and fly this fucker home.*

Finally, after twenty-eight hours, we land in LA. The flight attendant gets on the speaker and says, "Thank you for flying United. I know you have many choices and we thank you for choosing… oh forget it… let them fire me," and the entire plane, including myself, screams with laughter and breaks into applause.

I got $300 for pain and suffering.

My Last Vegas Gig

WORKING IN FRONT OF LIVE AUDIENCES is what I live for. I love the work. Love it. I have more fun in those forty-five minutes on stage than an alcoholic in a brewery. It's the other twenty-three hours and fifteen minutes that make me want to hang myself from the room service cart.

I forgot. I just forgot what Vegas was like. The whole city is one big "cousins who fuck" convention. I've never seen anything like it. Isn't anyone rotating the crops? Doesn't anyone exercise? If Vegas is a cross-section of our country, I can understand how Trump got elected.

Let's start with the hotel room. I live in a big house. It's a house that was featured on HGTV, so modestly I say, it's nice. When I travel it's really important to me that I have similar accommodations. I check in and ask the girl what floor I was on. Fifteen was the answer. I'm thinking view of the strip, I'm thinking neon lights at midnight, I'm thinking Billboard with my name on it. I'm really excited. She called it the "Luxury Tower". However, like everything else in Vegas, reality has its own space and time. The hotel adds ten floors to make it seem grander, so I was not on the fifteenth floor but the fifth. As for Luxury, I was in the Warsaw Hilton. There was still blood on the carpets from the last guest's murder. It smelled like a carton of camels and I'm not talking about the cigarettes. Who picks out the colors, Stevie Wonder? Pink and green? I needed a motion sickness pill to go to the bathroom. Still, I wanted to see what I could see from the fifth floor. I open the drapes and as God is my judge, on my father's grave, I swear to you there are six fourteen-inch air conditioning conduits running right across the window blocking fifty percent of the view. I am looking at pipes; huge, silver pipes. I can see the strip if I drag the table onto the bed and stand on it. The room sucks.

I unpack and head to the showroom where I discover the announcer has been fired the night before and a new one has been hired to make a tape loop for my introduction. Before I even hear the tape, I know what to expect. My name is pronounced Blue-stine like beer stein. The announcer on the tape is going to say "Blue-steen" like Bruce Springsteen, and that was exactly what he did. "Can't we make another tape?" They look at me like I just shot the Pope. Every night when they introduce me, I'm backstage with my fingers in my ears going *LALALA*, so I don't hear my name sounding like some summer camp director.

The shows are great. I was working with Cathy Ladman and Steve Altman. They are two of my favorite people on the face of the earth. We drove up together (so my plane did not crash in the desert). We had a great drive until Baker—where they are repaving the road. Bumper to bumper, five miles an hour, for six miles. I could have gotten out and run to Vegas faster. Cathy has a small child and decides we should play car games. I check the glove box for a gun.

Cathy, Steve, and I are like the Three Musketeers. We do everything together; the most of which is laugh. Three comedians who like each other—this is like finding an Arab who wants to move to Shaker Heights. The hotel gives us free food at the Riviera Club. Sounds nice, no? It's the employee cafeteria, or as we called it, Death's Diner. The hotel sends down day-old food from the "good" restaurants. The employees can feast on shoe leather chicken and cream of the day-before-yesterday vegetable soup. Since I can't cook, I don't mind the swill. But the other two were very picky.

"I want taste."

"This is rubbery." Babies.

During the day, we do what all comedians do on the road. We go to the mall. We usually spend about six percent more than we earn. I found a sports jacket to replace the one from J. Crew, "Take the security tag off, please!" Cathy buys enough children's clothing to keep China sewing for six months and Steve Altman went wild in Structure.

The week was like that; bad food, shopping, fat audiences, sleep. Sounds exciting, no? Then yesterday it happened. What you were all waiting for: the bad thing. I have a bad back. I have bone spurs in my L4 and L5. They are the result of Polio, which required a spinal tap as a child. Every so often, without warning, the spurs cause muscle spasms in my back that absolutely cripple me. One time I was out with my dog and had an attack that left me paralyzed on the sidewalk. I was on the ground for ten minutes unable to move, with the dog still attached to my arm via the leash. A woman walks up to me and straddles my chest.

"Are you ok?"

"No! My dog is taking me for a drag."

Guess who has an attack in the hotel room, alone. I'm in the room and I'm on the floor unable to move because the pain is that great. The maid opens the door and sees me lying there, "Oh! I'll come back later," and she walks out. I'm screaming. About that time, Steve Altman walks by and hears me. He gets them to open the door. He drags me to my bed. I have pills for the pain but I have to do a show. Cathy is out shopping, naturally. I call her and ask her to pick me up a back brace. Steve insists I take the pill. I take one and do the show stoned out of my mind.

The next night we close. The shows sucked. Not because I was loaded, I wasn't. It was Sunday and the audiences were exhausted. It reminds me why I like writing so much. No one from South Dakota is in the room with me trying to figure out what I'm saying. We leave Monday morning. I take two pills to get me through the long drive home, but Cathy needs to stop at the outlet mall to return something she bought. I'm telling you, we are serious shoppers. I am asleep in the car and wake up at the mall. I think we are in LA and get out. I realize that we are still in Nevada and decide to go inside and pee. I am flying like a kite. I get into the bathroom, remove my equipment and return it only to realize the plumbing had not shut off. I am now standing in the men's room with an eight-inch wet spot over my pee-pee and trying to think of creative ways to wet the rest of my pants and make it look like it's supposed to be that way.

I am wearing a hooded sweatshirt and no undershirt so I can't even take my top off and drape it over the leakage. So I pull my sweatshirt down over my crotch and walk out with my hand in the sweatshirt pockets. I get to the car, where Cathy and Steve are waiting.

"It's the perfect end to a perfect week," I say and I lift the sweatshirt. Steve Altman is sipping a Starbucks and does the Danny Thomas spray-take on the inside of the windshield. Cathy is laughing so hard she almost wets her pants. I crawl into the car like Quasimodo and Cathy heads back to LA with her two friends named Steve.

We talk all the way home about a film we want do, about writing together. We just talk. We just love each other. We cannot wait to get booked together again. This is the best week we have ever had on the road! It's then that I realize that back pain and the bad view and the ugly room and the horrible audiences and the mispronounced name really doesn't matter. What really matters is good friends and good times, and I had that this week!

I'm still in a back brace.

The New York Trip Part 1

I KNOW MANY OF YOU THINK I am making this shit up so I want to start by swearing on a stack of bibles that what I am about to tell you is true, it happened, and I am not making up a single detail. It all happened just as I'm about to tell you. This story is long. I'm going to tell it in three parts.

My good friend and publicist, Richard Gordon, called me and asked if I wanted to do a TV talk show that shot in NYC. They would pay airfare, limo, and food plus pay me $1500.

"Are you out of your mind?? Sure, I'll do it."

Now I'm not exactly a household name. "Toilet" is more of a household name than I. I thought it strange that they would offer me this deal. However, I was not looking a gift horse in the mouth and I took the gig, but with a suspicious eye. The day I'm to leave they send a limo to my house. I had asked to fly on American Airlines to get the frequent flier miles (the airline was offering triple frequent flier miles if you flew that month). I got my wish, first class. I got to the airport and a woman was waiting for me. She escorted me to the first-class lounge and waited until the plane took off. All the time I'm wondering when the hammer is going to drop on this farce of a gig.

I get on the plane and sure enough there is my seat. The flight is uneventful and we arrive at Kennedy. I step off the plane and there is a limo driver holding up a card with my name on it. He hands me an envelope and takes me to the hotel. The Plaza! He tells me he'll pick me up at 8 a.m. tomorrow for an 11 a.m. taping. No problem. I write down his name and number. I'm having Interpol check him out.

The next morning I'm in the lobby at 8 a.m. sharp. No driver. No driver at 9, 9:30 or 10. Ah-huh, this is what I have been waiting for! I call the studio, "Is there some mix-up?" What I learn is that the show has been cancelled. Ah-huh! Here it comes. I'm going to be stranded in New York. But I'm told the driver will be over with my check and, "Why don't you keep the limo for the day?" Now I understand exactly what's going to happen. The check is going to bounce. These people are full of shit.

The driver comes with my check and he takes me all over New York. We go shopping at Bloomingdales, we go to the theater, I see friends; it's a whole day of me in a Limo in New York City. When he drops me off at the hotel, he tells me he'll pick me up tomorrow to take me back to the airport. I think, *sure you will*.

The next morning I'm up early and call for a cab. I'm waiting for it when the limo driver shows up at the hotel. Now I'm starting to get worried. I see myself being kidnapped or wearing cement shoes in the East River. But no, he takes me to the airport. What's going on here? He tells me someone will be waiting for me in LA to drive me home. Ah! That's where the murder will take place.

I figure since there is no problem with the limo, it must be the airline tickets. I go to the first-class window and sure enough there are my tickets. I'm still not convinced. I board the plane. I'm not convinced. I drink the OJ. I'm not convinced. Then it happens.

"Excuse me, sir."

Ah-huh! Here it is! This is what I've been waiting for. Okay, honey, let me have it!

"We are sold out in first class and if you move back to coach I'll give you $1,000 travel voucher."

I just look at her

"Okay, two thousand."

I'm dumb struck.

"Three thousand and not a penny more."

I'm sitting in coach reviewing my trip. First class to New York, limo pick-up, hotel, food, limo for the day, limo to the airport, $3,000 in travel vouchers. The check is definitely bouncing.

The plane lands and there is my driver; he takes my luggage and drives me home. He leaves, I tip him, wave good-bye and run inside to get my car keys. I throw my bags on the comforter that no one is allowed to sit on and run to the bank to deposit the check. Six working days later it bounces like a kiddy bouncy hut. I'm not so stupid, with a head cold I can smell bad fish, but in this case, it's not all bad. I had earned 15,000 air miles and $3,000 in travel vouchers. Lemons to lemonade.

The following week the limo driver called me. "Did your check bounce?" I told them yes, and then learned the checks to the airline, the hotel, the restaurants all bounced. The TV show was a scam to the tune of $250,000. I was not the only person who got the royal flushed treatment, many entertainers had been flown out. It was the weirdest show biz experience of my life but I came out smelling like a rose.

I decided to take my travel vouchers and buy a ticket to Paris and this is where it gets good.

Trip To Paris
Part 2

I HAD BEEN GIVEN A $3,000 travel voucher and was about to purchase a ticket to Paris for the dream trip of a lifetime. Then I remembered I was agoraphobic. I can't go to a country where I didn't speak the language— who would feel my forehead to see if I had a temperature? How could I ask where suicide prevention was? Who would cut my steak? I remembered that Bella, my neighbor, spoke French fluently and so I made her an offer, "I'll buy you a ticket to Paris, you take care of the hotel." I had a travel companion, which made me sound like I was an elderly woman in a wheelchair. I didn't care.

The day of departure was very exciting. The dogs were in the kennel, the house sitter was in place, the phones were covered, the bills were all paid, nothing was going to get in my way of having a good time. Nothing but my life! Then, in the cab on the way to the airport, Bella says,

"Shit."

"What shit? What are you shitting about, we're six minutes into the trip, how could you shit already?"

She turns to me, "I forgot my luggage keys."

"Bella! How are we going to get through customs?"

"I speak French, I'll just explain to them what happened and we'll be fine."

Thank you! I now have my thirteen-hour flight obsession: not being allowed into France for lack of keys.

I get on the plane and we have great seats; bulkhead. I am on the aisle. Across the aisle from me is a dark woman with a mustache. I smile, she smiles. I stop smiling and she doesn't. She smiles, and she smiles. Out of the corner of my mouth I say to Bella, "Utna on the aislekay." We take off and Mona Lisa is still smiling and staring at me. They serve the drinks, she's still smiling. I'm so uncomfortable I want to pluck off my eyebrows. Bella has a wonderful sense of humor and loves torturing me so she reaches over me and talks to the woman.

"First time to Paris?"

"I first go time. Me see. Me see," Miss Toothpaste replies.

This now opens the door to a wide area of conversations with Rain Woman.

"I come to book. I see. You see. Book on table. I run with book. Come look at book," and other phrases she's learned at Berlitz. Bella is wetting herself she is laughing so hard. I am on the aisle and must maintain composure, however, it's not working. The more Gunga Din talks the harder it is for me to keep a straight face. Now I start laughing at Miss Malapropism and she starts laughing. That's how I spent the first 6 hours on the plane, laughing with Mrs. Goodbar.

Finally, the movie starts and I'm saved. We land and then I remember about Bella and her keys. She's fine with it as she approaches immigration, "Bon jour" and lots of other French words that I don't understand. She's very composed and positive, the agent is not. I see him take her and her luggage to a private room. She turns to me and says, "They are going to open my bags."

The immigration guy looks at me and says, "Are you with her?"

I nod. I'm in a private room; a room in which they are removing every single thing from my suitcase, including toothpaste which they stick a prod into and my pills, which I had to explain. "This one is for anxiety and this one is to sleep and this one is for anxiety when I sleep and this one is to bite in case I'm captured behind enemy lines." No laugh; I need a pill. They take out every piece of clothing I have packed and shake it, tap it and pat it down and when they are finished with the packed clothes they start on the ones I'm wearing. I am strip searched and given a prostate examination, if you get my drift. The ordeal lasts about an hour and I am cleared.

I meet Bella in the waiting room and see her luggage has been pried open and all her stuff is in plastic bags. She looks at me and says, "There's no truth to the rumor the French are not friendly, look how nicely they packed my plastic bags!" I am not in a good mood. I've been in the country ten minutes and I've already been prison raped… and without dinner and a movie first.

We gather up what's left of our belongings and we head to the hotel. We walk in with shopping bags and suitcases wrapped in masking tape and our hair all a mess and I can't sit. Bella gives the desk clerk our names; he looks up the file.

"Oh. I am so sorry," he purrs in a French accent, "Your rooms are not ready."

"When will they be ready?" I growl.

"Thirteen hours."

"Thirteen hours??"

Bella calms me down. "Let's get something to eat. They'll hold our Baggies."

I have wanted to go to Paris all my life, but so far, it's not what the brochure said it would be. The hotel clerk takes our crap and we go out for pizza. We're in the gourmet capital of the world and she takes me to Shakey's. I am really depressed at this point. Bella can see I am not happy and pays for the pizza. Not spending money always makes me happy.

The pizza comes and we begin to dine. Bella is all up and happy. She's telling me about what we're going to see this week as I take the first bite. I'm chewing when Bella notices the expression on my face.

"What's wrong?"

As calmly as I can, I tell her, "I have just swallowed at $1600 gold and porcelain crown," and open my mouth to show her the gaping hole left in my smile.

She starts laughing, "Oh, don't worry. What goes in must come out."

That was the understatement of the trip; for the very next day, in my Paris hotel room, I am on a treasure hunt.

Trip To Paris
Part 3

THE DAY AFTER THE PIZZA FEAST I get up to do my morning rituals. I tell Bella, "I'm going to the bathroom."

"You'll need something to find your tooth."

She gets the room cart and hands me my surgical equipment: a plate and a fork. I head into the bathroom and she heads down to the lobby. We're going to Versailles; she needs directions. In French bathrooms, there is a toilet and a bidet (A fixture similar in design to a toilet that is straddled for bathing the genitals and the posterior parts).

My ritual is done and I get everything on the plate. Yahoo! I'm a poo wrangler! Then, I start the task of probing. It's like looking for a body in an avalanche. I sit on the bidet and am deep into my work. I cannot believe I'm doing this. Who would believe it? This is not what I came to Paris for.

Did you ever get so deep into your work that all surroundings cease to exist? That's how I was on this treasure hunt. I was working in complete concentration. Then, for no reason, I look up, and much to my chagrin, the maid is standing there. Ashen.

"Monsieur! NO!!!" She runs out of the room. I am now known, by the hotel staff, as The American Shit Eater.

Bella comes up. "What did you do to the maid? I just passed her in the hall and she's crying." I tell her what just happened and Bella starts on a laughing jag that lasts fifteen minutes. Every time she composes herself, she looks at me and starts all over again. "You'll find it tomorrow," she says as she wipes away a tear. "Do you want me to wash your plate?" and she's off again laughing.

We take the train to Versailles and Bella is still giggling. Versailles is magnificent, looks a lot like my Aunt's house on Long Island, only with less gold. We're enjoying the gardens when I say to Bella, "I have to go to the bathroom again."

"I'll get you a plate and fork." I go once a day like clockwork so I am sure this second time is the tooth eating its way out. I get to the men's room but in France they have a woman who sits in the entry.

"I take the plate?" she asks in broken English.

I shake my head no, "I need it." RED FLAG! I'm in the stall and I see two sets of feet outside the door.

There is a tap on the stall door, "Monsieur! Would you come out? *Sil vous plait*." Now I'm trying to explain to the police why I need a plate and fork in the toilet. They're not buying it and we are thrown out of Versailles.

Bella is in her glory. "Oh God, I wish you had found the tooth there... Versailles is the perfect place to find a crown" and she's screaming with laughter. Meanwhile I look like Aretha Franklin with a huge gap in my mouth.

This hunt goes on for the rest of the week. Plate, Bidet, Fork, plate, bidet, fork. Nothing. No tooth. Now I'm sure it's hooked itself onto something in my intestine and it's going to cause some kind of abscess that will explode. I'll need a colostomy bag and will never be able to wear shorts again.

We arrive back in LA and I call my dentist for an emergency session. She makes a temp for me because the next day I am opening in Vegas. I figure I'll make one last ditch effort at home to find the tooth. I take a triple dose of Ex-lax. I am determined to get this tooth out of me. Next morning... it's like my intestines were on vacation. Nothing. Not even gas.

I'm on the plane and we are taxiing down the runway. We're at 350 mph and the nose is just about to lift off when all of a sudden, my stomach explodes. I have never had to go so badly in my life. The seat belt sign is on but if I sit there they're going to have to repaint the cabin. I need to get to the bathroom. Now the plane is in assent and at a forty-five-degree angle as I pull myself up out of the seat and up the aisle. The flight attendants— all of them—start screaming.

"Get back in your seat! The seat belt light is on!"

"If I don't get to that bathroom, we're going to arrive in Vegas fifteen minutes early because the jets on this plane are nothing to what's about to blow out my ass (this was before 9/11)!"

I make it to the bathroom. Lo and behold there is the tooth. I reach down to get it and the plane hits a rough spot. The flap on the toilet bottom gives way and the tooth drops into the tank of waste. I am now screaming profanity like a champion! There is a knock on the door. It's the captain. I'm in deep shit, literally. He sits me down and explains why I have to sit in my seat or will be arrested when we arrive in Vegas. I tell him the tooth story starting with the maid.

"Get back in your seat," is all he said.

Epilogue

I'm at the dentist and I tell her about the plane ride. She says, "Steve, even if you found it, would you really want me to put it back in your mouth?" She's got a point!

My Car Gets Stolen

I JOINED THIS ACTING CLASS my friends Fred and Mary Willard run. I had met the Willards years ago at The Comedy Store and Fred had asked me to join his comedy troop, The Ace Trucking Company. Mary and I were writing partners and worked on several TV shows. Nothing, and I mean nothing, gives me as much joy as seeing Fred's current success. He and Mary so deserve it.

I was in this acting class. I joined because at this point my life was a total disaster. A relationship had just broken up and it was not pretty. I lost a job and I was in a deep depression. Deep. Not even seeing my ex get herpes could cheer me up. Mary insisted I come to class, "It'll be gud faw ya (She's from Boston)."

[God! I just took off my shoes and it smells like a yak died in there]

I was driving a Lexus coupe at this time. It was a white two-door; the long sleek one! I loved that car; it was my baby. I parked it under a street lamp on Ventura Blvd. so it would be well-lit and protected. Ten thousand cars an hour drive by this location, it's not like it was in a dark secluded alley. I did everything the "police guide to saving your car" says. I didn't even give it a thought as I set the burglar alarm. My car would just be there when I got out of class.

I went to class, which lasted about three hours. I walked out, and the space where my car had been was empty. My first thought, *did I drive here?* Then like a bolt, it hit me. My car had been stolen. I ran to the pay phone and dialed 911. I got the dispatch operator.

"Hurry, my car has been stolen."

"Please hold."

I'm on hold for 10 minutes. She's back on line, "What is the nature of your call?"

"My car has been stolen!"

"Please hold."
Another ten minutes and she's back, "911 how can I help you?"
"I need a ride."
"Why?"
"Because you're a moron and by now my car is in Ecuador."
She hangs up.
Needless to say, the Police were of no help. Car theft to the police is just below home burglar alarms. Did you know that the police will not respond to a home burglar alarm unless you are standing with a gun to your head and have witnessed the thieves putting Grandma's silver in a gunnysack? In other words, you have to die before they'll respond, and it's so hard to dial when you're dead.
About a month later I get a call from a detective, "We found your car." I am elated. "Where was it?"
"On the corner of Slauson and Verdugo…. Also, La Brea and Sunset… and Pico and De La Crecenta."
The car had been stripped. They left nothing. I parked a car; the police brought me back a paperweight. Have you ever had to identify your stripped car? It's like going to the morgue. They had the car covered and when I arrived they pulled back the tarp:
"Can you identify this car, sir?"
"Yes, that's my baby," and then you fall into the arms of a loved one.
The next stop is the insurance broker. They offer me $6,000 for a $48,000 car. It's like being robbed all over again. I put them on hold and call my attorney. He tells me what to say; I say it. Now I've got $16,000. I put them hold and tell him what they bid, he tells me what to say. I get $20,000. I tell him what the new bid is and he tells me what to say. I get $26,000. I tell him what the bid is now and he tells me what to say. They tell me to go fuck myself. I take the $26,000.
The one thing I hate in life is buying a new car. I would rather take my mother to Australia. I think all car salesmen should be neutered so they don't pass along that annoying gene. I won't bore you with the details but I bought a Mercedes, which turned out to be the biggest piece of crap that has ever been put on the road. It's like the Germans are still getting back at the Jews but they've found creative ways to do it, "Let's annoy them to death." This lemon was delivered with the battery dead and it went downhill from there. You know you've got a bad car when the receptionist at the dealership recognizes your voice, "Oh it's you, Mr. Bluestein. Do you need a tow?"

The theft of my car began a three-year life slump. One in which everything I touched turned to shit. Eventually things began to turn around, and that's what I wanted to share with you. Life is a series of ups and downs. The ups don't last forever but neither do the downs. Remind yourself that the next time fate hands you the shit end of the stick. It won't last forever; you are not alone!

Maggie

I OWNED AN ENGLISH SPRINGER SPANIEL, Maggie, and she owned me for fourteen years. I got her through divine intervention. I was sitting at the pool at my house on July 3rd when out of nowhere a voice said, "Go to the pound right now," and I did. The first dog I laid eyes on was Maggie. She and I went through two relationship break-ups, three auto accidents, a surgery, and an earthquake together. When I looked into that dog's eyes, I knew she understood me. Only pet owners know what I'm talking about.

At the end of her life she couldn't stand, she peed on herself, and she needed help walking. She was a canine Keith Richards. I could not bring myself to put my beloved friend down. I kept thinking, *she'll get better*, but she didn't. So, one day, I had to bring her to the vet one last time. It was the saddest and most traumatic day of my life. I was crying so bitterly it would have been easier to just put me to sleep. I got her leash and started down the street. This was our last walk. About twenty yards from my house a kid in a passing car threw a full glass of melting ice at me. The ice hit me on my back and was like a slap in the face. It left a huge welt on my back that snapped me out of my depression.

I cleaned myself up and my neighbor, Hadley Arnold, drove with me to the vet. We put Maggie on the table and I started crying so bitterly the vet started crying. Right in the middle of my death scene, Maggie lifted up her head, looked me in the eyes and licked my face. She was saying, "Thank you for putting me out of my misery. I love you." That was it. I was a basket case. If it hadn't been for Hadley I would never have gotten through it. She said something that made it all better. She said, "If Maggie had been out in the wild she would have been culled by the pack a long time ago. You've given her a long and happy life. Now it's time to let her go."

In all my life, I never loved an animal like I loved that dog, and I was sure I could never have another pet. Then came Tori Spelling, the terrier mutt I rescued. I called her Tori Spelling because she had huge eyes and blonde hair and was as stupid as a brick. She's a nervous wreck this dog. "Sit, Tori," and she whirls in a circle and runs into the bedroom. She's sweet and adorable and brain damaged, but she's good as gold. Doesn't chew, doesn't bark, doesn't make in the house. In other words, it's like having a piece of furniture you have to walk. I like Tori; I loved Maggie.

Two years passed after Maggie left and I felt I was ready for another dog. Now mind you, Tori was still here shaking in the corner. I went to the pound. I always get my dogs at the pound. Once on stage I said that and a woman yelled out, "At the pound or by the pound?" I went to the pound every day for a week and found nothing but pit bulls. It's pathetic. People get a pit bull and think, "What a cute dog for the kids," and then the cute dog rips the toddler's face off. The dog ends up in the pound. The owners should be put in the pound, not the dogs. In any case, I kept coming back and then one day, there was this Golden Retriever there. I walked up to him and he sat and just looked at me with pleading eyes, "Hey, dude! Get me out of here." I brought him home that day. I know enough about dogs that I didn't bring him into the house but into the garage where I brought Tori in to meet him. She took one look at him, then looked at me as if to say, "You ungrateful bastard," and ran into the house. She had nothing to do with him.

Sully was a puppy, 11 months old when I got him. The first thing he did when I let him into the house was eat the guest bathroom. I'm serious. I put him in there while the painters were here and when I opened the door he had shredded the towels, the toilet seat, the mat; ate the soap and chewed the leg off the table. It looked like I had a punk decorator.

That brings me to his other wonderful trait. He'll eat anything. So far, he's eaten a sponge, a rubber ball, several toys, a shoe, tissues, paper towels, the first step in the living room, and copious amounts of cat shit. I have never seen a dog like this in my life; he ate $18 worth of salmon, a pork chop, a banana, and a filet mignon and didn't even fart. How does he get this stuff? He simply stands on his hind legs and takes it off the counter. He's almost six feet tall when he stands. I haven't so much adopted a dog as a basketball player that barks.

I have a small gym in my house. It had rubber mats on the floor. Had! He's shredded four of the six mats. He chewed the pedal off the stationary bike. His rapidly moving tail has decapitated several indoor houseplants and his nails have gouged my floors beyond repair. He's a wrecking ball that sheds. That's his other endearing trait, he sheds. I have dog tumble weed blowing through my house.

We haven't even mentioned the cat, Kitty Carlisle. This bitch is a piece of work on a good day; you bring this horse into the house and she becomes Courtney Love. There was a stand-off in my kitchen last week. Carlisle was on the counter and Sully was standing on the kitchen table. The two were frozen. I heard the theme music from High Noon. I was afraid to get between them because I could lose an eye. Tori doesn't mix in. She's was in the bedroom shaking. Finally, I just screamed, "I'm calling the dog whisperer!" and they both went to neutral corners.

Let me tell you what my "leave the house" ritual is: "Tori, get in your bed." She runs." Sully, into the bathroom." He runs. I close him in where's he's out of sight so the cat can… "Carlisle, get into the bedroom," and she runs.

I feel like Siegfried and what's left of Roy.

Here's the good news. I wouldn't trade a single animal for all the tea in China. I love Sully as much as I loved Maggie and I never thought I would ever say that. He's sitting at my feet as I write this. Tori is in her bed and Carlisle is building a car bomb.

Welcome to my world, folks… The Bel Air Wild Kingdom.

The Brady Bunch Variety Hour

My very first job in this insane business was as a writer on what's become a cult favorite: *The Brady Bunch Variety Hour*. That's right, *The Brady Bunch Variety Hour*, starring Florence Henderson, Robert Reed, and a cast of thousands in the pool. My agent set me up for the interview; he didn't tell me what it was for because he knew I wouldn't go if he even mentioned *The Brady Bunch*. I NEVER watched *The Brady Bunch*. Who could relate to that? I came from a divorced home. *The Brady Bunch*? *Lost World* would have been more like it. I walk into the office, I'm meeting with Carl Kleinschmidt and Ronnie Graham (he played Dirt in that famous gasoline commercial). We're talking and joking and they look at a video of my stand-up and it's all good and then I ask, "So what's the show?"

Carl says, "The Brady Bunch Variety Hour."

At that very second a tiny gnat flew right in front of me, as a joke I tried to grab for it. Carl thinks I'm making a comment on the show by making some *Three Stooges* take; what I was really doing was trying to kill a bug. But because Carl thought I was putting down the show, I got hired. He was looking for a group of writers who were hip and could write tongue in cheek. That's the insanity of my business; I had no credits, I had no experience, I couldn't relate to the show; but because I was perceived as sarcastic, I got hired.

It turned out to be the best experiences of my life. The other writers were Bruce Vilanch and Terry Hart. Terry was an advertising executive who had gotten into writing for television; Bruce was the genius who created Bette Midler's attitude. Carl had a list of credits as long as his arm. Ronnie was a veteran of show business going back to the 1950s, and me, Mr. "I don't deserve to be here."

Carl became my mentor telling me things like, "There is no time clock on creativity." Meaning, if I wasn't funny from 9 to 5, it might happen at 11 p.m., and I should be writing then. Those words stayed with me my entire career and through every show I ever wrote on. It saved my ass on several occasions. To give you an idea of how good Carl was to me, right in the middle of production I walked into his office and said, "I'm having my nose fixed on Wednesday, I'll be out a couple of days." He said, "Cool." I had the operation and came back to work black and blue and all bandaged. On the tape above my nose I wrote "UNDER CONSTRUCTION." When I walked in, Carl was the first one to laugh and laugh the hardest (the nose turned out well).

The producers of the show were Sid and Marty Krofft. They were the wunderkind of television that week. Sid was the creative one; Marty was the business one. Sid was, shall we say, odd. His mind thought in ways others didn't. He was in his own Puff 'n' Stuff world and welcome to it, but he created an empire, which still lasts today.

I got to work with many stars on the show: Tina Turner, Lee Majors, Farah Fawcett, Rip Taylor, Rick Dees (this is where our friendship began), Vincent Price, Tony Randall, Milton Berle, and many more. Of all the stories, my experience with Milton is the best.

There was one additional writer, whose name will remain anonymous, who was an incredible pothead. He was stoned the entire time we were in production and had his own office away from the set so he could smoke his evil weed. We were working under a deadline and Carl asked me to go up to this writer's office to work on a scene with him. I wasn't there six minutes when out came the pot. This was the 1970s and everyone was smoking pot, myself no exception. It was a time when we all felt invincible; we have since learned otherwise. I was young and invincible and I partook and partook and partook. This writer always had the best shit! I think he flew it in from Hawaii. I was flying higher than the plane that brought this crap in. We were writing this hilarious scene, or so we thought, when the phone rings. It's my secretary, "They need you down on the set." I could barely stand. In my drug induced stupor I thought, *I can do this. No one will notice,* and I put on a pair of sunglasses and left for the set stopping only to buy candy bars at the roach coach.

I walk into the sound stage and *everyone* is there. Florence, Robert, most of the kids, the network executives, the production staff, and Milton Berle. Bobby is missing, however, and Jack Regas, the director, says to me, "Steve, will you read Bobby's part?"

Panic City! "Sure."

It's a scene where Milton introduces himself to Bobby. "Hello, Bobby, I'm Milton Berle."

I'm supposed to say, "Hi, Mr. Berle." Instead I say "Hi Mr. Berle, I'm Steve Bluestein, one of the writers."

Berle breaks character and turns to Carl, "Look at that, I'm such a good actor the kid thinks I'm talking to *him*." Everyone laughs; I want to die. My heart drops about six feet. I am scared shitless I am going to get in trouble. I look for a friendly face... ah! Carl.

I turn to Carl and raise the sunglasses to show him my eyes. He knows I've been working with Mr. El Stone-o and knows instantly I'm about to audition for a *Cheech and Chong* movie. He rolls off the chair and is so convulsed with laughter he has to leave the stage. That is the irony of *The Brady Bunch Variety Hour*. This wholesome, all-American, family entertainment show was written by stoned freaks who were the hippest writers of that time. See, show business is all bullshit, but I would not change a minute of that experience. Florence Henderson was a joy to work with, Robert Reed, although totally out of his element on this show, was a professional. The kids were great! I loved my fellow writers. I got to meet Witchy-poo and all the Kraft characters. What could be so bad?

Oh! I think it was last year that TV Guide voted *The Brady Bunch Variety Hour* as the fourth worst show in the history of television. Thank you. It was my pleasure.

The Playboy Playmate Awards

ONCE YOU GET STARTED WORKING in show business—especially behind the camera—you continue to work on and on and on, and that happened to me and the other writers on *The Brady Bunch Variety Hour*. Carl went on to write films, Ronnie wrote books, Terry produced TV shows, Bruce won Emmys for his work and became a celebrity. The stoned-out guy went on to get the head writer's job on an ABC Late Night Special, *The Playboy Playmate Awards,* and who did he hire to write on the staff with him? His old smoking buddy, *moi*! Also hired was another writer, whose name escapes me, but he was older, extremely bookish, very intellectual, and had a very dry sense of humor. We have the three writers: I don't deserve this job, dry, and stoned. I see a Pulitzer in my future.

The special is to be shot at the Playboy Mansion and the producers want the writers—that would be the unholy trio—to get to know the place. We are invited to tour the grounds and meet with Mr. Hefner. First the tour: Disneyland with condoms. I have never seen anything like it in my life. Forget the peacocks, the game house, or the grotto; the place had a staff of at least a hundred. That's a lot of undocumented immigrants. It was the details that impressed me the most: the bowls of M&M's everywhere, the pads of paper by every phone, the little touches that made this home feel like a hotel. He lived there but it wasn't a home, it was a publicity machine. In the hallway were works of art by the masters, and each one hung on a hook that was attached to an alarm button. Lift the picture off the hook and the alarm goes off. You know, just like at your mother's house.

We meet with Mr. Hefner, who shows up in his pajamas and velvet initialed slippers. He's a caricature of himself. He sits on a sofa under the bust of Barbie Benton. Not a statue, the actual bust. He's talking and Barbie is looking down on us. All I could think of was, *where do you buy one of these?* You don't go into Macy's and say, "I'll take a Barbie in a 38D." Then, Hef, as we're told to call him, gives us his vision of the show. The meeting lasts about twenty minutes and he has to go upstairs and fuck someone. The stoned writer looks at me.

"Did you understand what he said?"

"Look at the Bust of Barbie Benton," I replied.

The intelligent writer says, "Don't worry, I got it."

We are given an office on the grounds. As I remember it, it was over a garage somewhere, but it was fully stocked with paper and desks and every amenity a writer could need. We start writing at about 10 a.m., we work until about 9 p.m., Hef wants to meet at 11 p.m..... 11 p.m.? We stick around the Mansion and then the director comes up to me to ask if I would do stand-up on camera for the special. Sure, extra money. It would be Jay Leno and me.

Hef walks in with the script under his arm and tosses it on the table, "It's wrong." Now he explains a totally new concept for the show. Not a single point we discussed in the morning meeting is in his new concept. It means a whole new script. It's 11:30 p.m.; we start shooting at 9 the next morning. Hef gets up and says, "My staff will provide you with whatever you need," and leaves. Spin Rapunzel spin.

We get into the office and the first thing the head writer does is get stoned. He really was the *head* writer. The intelligent writer starts musing about the meaning of the show and I call the kitchen for some food, "Can we get some munchies?"

We start writing, 1 a.m., 2 a.m., 4 a.m. I'm on a sofa shouting out jokes, the intelligent guy is typing, the stoned guy is finishing off a three-layer chocolate cake. We have ten pages written. The trucks are pulling up in five hours and we have ten pages written. When I get overwhelmed, I get giddy, and that's what happened this night. I start laughing and I can't stop. The head writer is stoned so he starts laughing. This pisses off the smart writer who only wants to "Get the fuck out of here and get back to the reality of the Valley."

We vomit out another ten pages and it's 7 a.m. What we have managed to do is produce twenty pages of pure, unadulterated garbage. It's one large smelly gastric bypass. The trucks start pulling up and the lighting crew is lighting the set. We have half a script. We are sweating bullets now and start spewing out streams of consciousness that makes Dali look like a paint-by-numbers. The director comes into the office.

"What have you got for me, boys?"

We all sort of chuckle, "What are you shooting first?"

Thank God it was something we had written. That's how the entire day's shooting went. It was my job to run down to the set and see what the next shot was. I would then run back to the office and tell the guys who would madly write it before the script supervisor would ask for it. It was insanity, complete and total insanity.

I'll never forget the feeling of complete inadequacy when Bill Cosby approached the three of us. "I need a joke here," and you could actually hear the *buzz* in the air as the three of us came up with nothing. Bill waits for an answer and none comes, he walks away shaking his head. The head writer turns to me, "I think that went well."

The whole show is shot around a party, which means hundreds of guests, cars, and more confusion. Arnold was there. Bill Cosby and country singer, Barbara Mandrell. Barbara was to sing on the special and I will never forget the image of her standing in the garden as calm and composed as a queen. Around her Rome burned but she did not let it affect her. It was a total mad house, this shoot, but she was a self-confident woman who kept her cool. In the meantime, I was having a nervous breakdown.

Somehow, we got through the day, the other guys churning out literature for the masses. It came time for me to do my stand-up routine. It was to be shot in the living room, with playmates and guests all around me. I was exhausted. I did the set and then wanted to slit my writs. It sucked big time. The whole 'in the living room' was not working for me. The audience was too close; I could see their reactions, which, naturally, I took as negative. Afraid of being judged badly, I grab the director and tell him, "Look, I know we're running long. If you want to cut my set... do." He does. Jay's set airs, mine ends up on the cutting room floor. Jay later goes on to host *The Tonight Show*; I sell knitting supplies on the Internet.

The shoot lasts until late in the evening. I've been up for twenty-four hours, living on chocolate cake and coffee. Somehow it all gets in the can—as it always does—and when it airs, it wins its time slot. Oh. My. God! Tits sell.

The writers and I part ways, never to work together again. I see them at parties from time to time and we console each other over our experience. One of the writers became a famous producer and is occasionally seen as an actor. The smart writer is still writing books. Me, I'm the poster child for unfulfilled dreams and wasted lifetimes. I don't think I'm too hard on myself, do you?

Two Million and No Linen Closet

A FEW DAYS AGO, I happen to pass a housing development that brought back many memories. It all started about thirty-five years ago when I was first breaking into show biz. You don't know poverty until you start out in show business. There is a hunger that burns inside you to be discovered and a real hunger that's caused by lack of food. If you have a great group of friends, you can get through anything. I have been blessed with wonderful friends, like Pat Proft. When Pat first came to LA he had a son and wife back in Minneapolis and was earning $65 a week on unemployment. As I remember it, he was sending half of the unemployment back to his family and living on almost nothing. Pat was one of the favorites at The Comedy Store. He was blonde and blue-eyed and very, very funny in a unique way. I remember one year—I think it was after Thanksgiving—Pat didn't have enough money to eat and I had a turkey leg in my fridge. Two mouths, one leg. Those are actually some of my fondest memories, those days of sharing and poverty. For me, it was actually more fun trying to break into show business than to be in it. I found when some of my friends finally did make it, they changed; some were bitter, some arrogant, some self-obsessed and obnoxious, but mostly distant and unavailable. Not having a real family, these friends were my adopted family so when I would lose one, it was sad, very sad. That's why Pat was special. When he began working, he never changed; he was just Pat, the blonde, funny guy.

Where is Pat today? He did okay. He's the guy who wrote *Airplane, Police Academy, Naked Gun, Hot Shot, Scary Movie 3...* shall I go on? I will not be buying Pat a Turkey leg this year. In fact, he will be buying me a turkey farm or I will sell the pictures of him and that donkey to the

Enquirer. I'm happy to say Pat and I are still friends. You see, some people never change and that makes all the assholes you have to deal with worth it. But, like panning for gold, the good ones remain: Pat Proft, Carole Ita White, Gary Austin, the late Monica Johnson, my little nuggets of gold.

I digress. I was young and starving and living in this apartment building in Hollywood, which would soon be called The Comedy Arms. I was the first one to move in, and then Freddy Prinz, Johnny Dark, Andrew Johnson, Len Wayland, Alan Bursky, assorted comedy writers and managers all moved in after me. Can you imagine the egos around *that* pool?

One of the girls at The Comedy Arms was not in show business, didn't want to be in show business, could care less about show business. Michelle was what we called "a civilian". I had the typical starving actor's apartments. Brick and board bookcase, sofa made from pillows on the floor, director's chairs, plants, and bed on the floor. Everything was on the floor. The nice thing about finally earning money: you sleep above the baseboard.

We're sitting around the pool one day and Michelle says, "I want those Pompadour Grass things for my apartment." These were tall grasses with a puff of fluffy cream-colored balls at the end. They're used as landscape on freeways out here. As luck would have it, I had noticed that they just planted some of these grasses at a new housing development off the freeway. *Ah, finally he's getting to the story.* We decided that we could go there and cut some for Michelle's apartment.

We make the long drive to the Sepulveda pass, where the grasses are growing, and park our car on the steep road that leads to the housing development. Michelle walks down the embankment to start harvesting her crop. I stay with the car. It's not six minutes when an LAPD cruiser pulls up behind me.

"Anything wrong?"

"Oh no, we're just on our way to look for a house when my wife dropped her high school graduation ring out the window." What am I talking about??

Now, you have to remember these were two million dollar homes and I was driving a beat-up Toyota station wagon with a hanger for an antenna. I call out to Michelle, "Honey, the police want to know if you found your ring?" Michelle drops the grasses and scurries up the hill. "Come on dear, we'll be late for our appointment," I say, and pull her into the car. Once out of earshot of the cops I explain and head up the hill to the sales office. The police follow right behind us. They follow us right up to the door of the sales office and then go inside as I fill out an application for a two-million-dollar home. I was working in a Photomat booth at the time.

The cops leave and now we are left with a real estate lady on commission. This is like leaving a cheesecake with an overeater. This bitch is determined to sell us a house and does not stop talking.

"These homes are of the finest quality, only the finest woods and appliances have been used, everything is custom, we pride ourselves in the design and their energy efficiency of your home of the future."

Now she's got my attention, "What type of heating are they using?" Michelle looks at me like I just shit in her purse.

"Why don't I show you?" and the real estate broker has me under the arm and is escorting me to the model. We enter this mansion on the hill, "This is our Savannah. Notice the use of crown molding in all the rooms."

Suddenly I'm on an inspection tour, "Is this what they call a linen closet? My God look at the size of that thing, you can't use this for a linen closet, I'd have to rip the whole thing out and start over again." Michelle sits. Her mouth is open.

"No, that will be quite adequate for linens," the broker says

"Maybe in your house," I reply, angrily.

Now the broker and I are fighting over the guest closet, the linen closets, the bathroom fixtures, the size of the guest room, and the placement of the door from the maid's room to the kitchen. Michelle is still sitting in the living room plotting to get me committed.

The broker and I are really getting into it. "I couldn't live here," you have to remember I'm living in a $165 a month one-bedroom apartment.

"Sir. I don't think this development is for you," says the broker.

"I agree," and I grab Michelle, "Honey, we're taking the place in Malibu," and I storm back to my rusted car.

"Are you out of your mind?" Michelle asks.

"Me? That moron is trying to sell us a two-million-dollar house without closet space, who's the fool here?"

The broker runs after us. "Did I give you my card?" Michelle looks at me and looks at the broker, then back at me. On the fool question, the jury was still out. We never got the grasses we came for.

Howie Mandell

WHEN I FIRST STARTED WORKING and made some money, the very first thing I did was invest in real estate. I had a share in an apartment building and lived there as manager/owner for over a decade. Over the years many people filled that eight-unit building, many who became famous. Kim Fields and her mother Chip, Comedian Bob Zany, Infomercial King Jim Caldwell, Steve Tyler, and my favorite, Howie Mandell and his wife Terry. It was an interesting time in my life, it was right after my divorce. I was doing a lot of stand-up at the time and had to juggle a lot of balls to keep the building going and be on the road, but I did it. Remember, I'm a survivor. I do what has to be done.

Howie Mandell is truly one of the funniest human beings I know. There are comedians who are technicians, who have learned, *if I say this set of words and stop, the audience will laugh.* Then there are people like Howie Mandell, Elayne Boosler, Cathy Ladman, David Letterman, etc., etc. who are genuinely funny people. They think funny because they are funny.

Here's an interesting Howie story, one he may not be aware of. It's because of Howie that I decided I should not pursue a stand-up career. Howie was living in my building when he got the part on *St. Elsewhere*. We were friends at the time since we saw each other daily. He called me one night and asked me if I wanted to go with him to the Improv; he was doing a set.

"Why would you do a set? You're on a series."

"I need to," Howie answered.

At that moment, I knew I would never be a star. You see, I didn't "need to," yet I was in a business of people who did. Those people would do anything they could to reach the top. I would not, and so on that night

I slowly began to withdraw from my dream. At the time, I thought it was a healthy thing, but in retrospect I think that what I did is what I've done all my life: *I'm not good enough. There will always be someone better and they will get the prize, not me.* Survive? I don't know how I did. Let me tell you a Howie story.

Howie and I are walking down Ventura Blvd in Studio City. This is just before he was cast in *St. Elsewhere*. We were deep in conversation and in mid-sentence he says, "Wait. I need to do something," and I follow him into a one- hour photo place. He says to the guy, "Listen, I told my parents I was going on vacation but I spent the money. I need pictures of vacations, any vacation... without people in them." I wanted to die because I know this is a bit. The guy behind the counter barely spoke English.

"You wanna what?"

"I need photos of other people's vacations. Just places, no people."

The guy starts bringing out photo after photo. Howie is going through them, "No, this one has a lady in it. The background is good. Do you have this without the lady?"

"No!"

"Ok, do you have anything of Paris?"

The guy exits to the back room, "No Paris."

"Okay, then what about the Bahamas? But the good side of the island, not where the cheap hotels are."

Howie stays in the shop for a half an hour, all the time I am in the background stifling a laugh. I'm stifling a laugh and staring in amazement that he could pull this off without laughing. I knew then he would be a star. I was right.

Years later, when Howie had moved out of the building, I was out having dinner when Howie and Terry walked in. We waved to each other and I continued to eat. I called the waiter over.

"Did you know that today is Howie Mandell's Birthday?" It was not.

"We'll take care of it, sir," said the waiter.

Within five minutes the entire Mexican wait-staff was singing "Happy Birthday" to Howie in Spanish. Howie laughed and looked right at me, "Touché." He knew!

My Insane Life

IT STARTS AT 10 A.M. I'm driving to a doctor's appointment and I'm on a narrow country road. There is a girl on a bicycle in front of me What is it with bicycle riders and joggers? There is a perfectly clear sidewalk right over there but they think they're in their own personal 10K Marathon and have to jog right in the middle of the street. Add to that, this kid thinks she's in the Tour de France. She's in and out of traffic; she's on the curb and then swings back in the middle of the street. She's weaving like she's making a bedspread for her hope chest. She darts out in front of me and I tap the horn because I don't think she sees me. She gives me the finger. I think, *that ungrateful little bitch!* I start to fume. I get to the red light and she pulls up next to me and she starts screaming at me. Like an idiot, I roll down the window.

"I'm trying to protect you from getting hit by a car and you have the nerve to flip me off?"

"Listen, Pops!"

It's like my entire body shuts down. I hear nothing else but, "Listen, Pops!" Who does she think I am, Arthur Fiedler? She peddles off. *Pops?* She called me *Pops*. I have the neck of a thirty-year-old and she calls me *Pops*. I pull the visor mirror down and take a look at my face. No one has ever called me Pops in my life! My ego is mortally wounded. I think "asshole" would have been much more appropriate here. Don't you? Even motherfucker would have been nice, but POPS?

I get to the doctor and learn my blood pressure is so high I could have a stroke. My cholesterol is even higher. I need to start taking pills, lots of pills. A blood pressure pill, a diuretic, an allergy pill, and Prilosec for the heartburn, which brought me to the doctor's in the first place. In one car trip, I've gone from young stud to Pops on pills. I am so depressed I want to shoot heroin but I'm sure my veins are collapsing.

On the way home, I decide to stop at the supermarket. My favorite place…. Not! I pick up milk and OJ and step into an empty line, so I think. Ahead of me is an old Jewish man. Why is it always an old Jewish man? You never see a Protestant saying, "Why isn't the white bread on special?" The old Jewish man has already been rung up but he's standing with a six-foot long register tape by the bagger shouting at the checker. "Ok show me where the coupon for the Comet is. Where's the two-for-one special on the Preparation H? How come the spinach isn't on special? It was on special last week." I start thinking, *is there a club of these people? Do they stake out my house, 'He's leaving now. Get a unit to Vons.'* I can feel the tension building up in the back of my neck. The checker is being as nice as he can be but my fuse is getting short. Stand back I'm about to blow.

"Can you take inventory later, Pops??" My mouth freezes. This guy is to me what I was to the chick on the bicycle. He turns to me and in a thick Jewish Accent says, "I'm on a fixed income." I can see my future. I'm standing at a check-out line in polyester pants screaming, "You didn't double the coupon on the Metamucil!"

My depression is deeper now. I went from hip comedian to 'Pops' in two hours. I need to buy myself a gift. I need a nice gift. I know, I'll get a new Dustbuster. I head for Bed Bath and Beyond/Grand Central Station. I have never seen anything like it in my life. There must have been two thousand cars in the parking lot and six spaces. Did I know yesterday the 20% off coupon was published? Evidently, I was the only one who didn't get the memo! The place was packed. I get in the store and all of the mideast is shopping. Everyone looked like a suicide bomber. It's 146° out; they are all in heavy woolen coats with scarves. I find my Dustbuster and head to the register. Screw the 20% I just want to get out with my life. Again, empty register, except she's there again. The Persian woman that shops where ever I shop, gets her hair cut where I get my hair cut, comes to my garage sale, buys furniture when I need a sofa, eats at the same restaurant where I eat, buys a casket when I've just killed myself. It's the same woman over and over again.

"Vi can't I haf it for $3.99?"

"Because the price is $6.99."

"I gif you $3.99." She's bargaining with Bed Bath and Beyond. What planet do these people come from?

The manager is there! "Ma'am, it costs 6.99," and the woman starts to cry. Now she's got me interested. I've never seen this tactic used to buy dishtowels. The manager will not budge on the price so Mrs. Haggle buys the towels. The girl rings them up, hands her the bag and receipt.

"I haf coupons." One? No, she's got two that are plainly marked "NOT TO BE USED WITH OTHER COUPONS."

"We can't use both of these," the checker says.

"Vy?"

"Because it says so right here."

"You make special for me."

Now Pops is losing it, "What don't you understand about you can't use two coupons??"

"I not talk to you," and she takes my Dustbuster and shoves it off the counter. The checker and I look at each other in shock.

I say to her, "Lady, I'm buying you the towels. Anyone with that kind of balls deserves a prize," and that's what I did. I bought baba ganoush the towels. The checker gave me 20% off without a coupon. I'm a winner!

Satellite TV

YEARS AGO, I had been having a lot of trouble with Cable. Let's just say, they're morons and their cable service sucked. When they installed the cable in my house they laid the wire down the center of my master bedroom. I swear to God. Not along the baseboards, right down the middle of the bedroom. If that wasn't enough, their programming was awful. How many times can you watch *A River Runs Through It*? I had one channel I called The *Steel Magnolia* Channel. Whenever I turned it on, The *Steel Magnolias* was playing. I had had it with cable TV and I decided I was going to get rid of these idiots and their annoying "for technical assistance touch 1" computer answering service. I was going to go high tech and get satellite TV.

I take myself to Radio Shack. Speaking of morons, where do they find these guys? Is there a DeVry dropout program that places these losers at any Radio Shack I go to? Does the VP of recruitment have cousins he needs to place? Do they run ads, "If you're apathetic and know how to ignore customers, we want you!" I walk in and all the help are wearing Hindu head wraps. Okay, so I don't have to call India, they're right here. This is good!

"Can I help you?" the tall slender man with a black wrap says.

"I am interested in satellite TV."

The guy says, "Me too!" Like we have some newfound bond and are going to meet each other at the satellite TV reunion. I tell him that I am not good at installations and Habib assures me, "I'm tellink you, you can du it. It is simple. They have designed it to make it so simple even a moron can do it." Thank you, I think. I buy the dish and take the three-hundred-pound box home. *I don't want the ship that launched the satellite, I'll just take the dish.*

I get the box home and I'm excited because all I have to do is a simple installation. I open the instructions and read the first line, "Locate the satellite in the northern hemisphere," and I think to myself, *I'm fucked.* I can't find my garage and it's attached to my house; the satellite company wants me to find a tiny satellite in the vastness of outer space.

I call Direct TV tech assistance and the girl tells me, "A lot of people are having problems finding our satellite and my supervisors here at Direct TV have asked me to ask you, the customer, what we, Direct TV, can do to make it easier for you, the customer, to find our satellite." I don't know what to say.

"Ah! Put a bell on it." Silence.

She tells me to take my cordless phone and go up on the roof. I like the way she assumes I have a cordless phone. I guess when you go into Radio Shack to buy Direct TV most people get hit for a cordless phone too, "You'll need it, trust me." Now I'm standing on my roof with a cordless phone next to the dish. She tells me the problem is I'm moving the dish too radically and what I should be doing is tapping the dish.

"Go ahead… tap it."

And I do.

"Tap it again."

And I do.

"Are you tapping?"

"Yes."

"What's the dish doing now?"

I couldn't help myself, "It just ran away with the spoon."

Nothing. Then, "Sir, I'm trying to help you, if you can't take this seriously I'm going to hang up." I'm on the roof at 8 o'clock at night and she's got an attitude.

"Wait. If I'm up on the roof, how do I know when I get a picture downstairs?"

Then she says, with the saddest tone of voice I have ever heard, "Oh, you live alone?"

"I need to get married to install this shit??"

Click! She hangs up on me. I phone back and get another tech, person, woman.

"So, if I'm on the roof how do I know if there's a picture downstairs… I'm single."

The girl says, "Can you put a mirror in the garden?"

They want me to redecorate my back yard! I've been working on this project for hours and did not want her to hang up on me too. I climb down the ladder and drag the mirror out of the guest bedroom and place it in the garden. I can see the TV from the roof. At this point it would just be easier to just get married.

Let's review. I'm on the roof with a cordless phone, tapping a satellite dish while looking at a mirror propped up against two garbage cans in my garden, looking for a signal from outer space. Isn't this the plot for *Little Shop of Horrors*? Mind you, my neighbors are all inside watching cable. Then it happened. *Snow*.

"I've got snow."

"You've got snow?"

"I've got snow. What should I do?"

"Start enjoying your satellite broadcasts," she says.

Excuse me, Einstein, but shouldn't there be a picture, something to watch, words, something moving instead of the reenactment of the great blizzard of '88? It takes me two more hours to get the fucker working. One to re-hang the mirror, put the ladder away, and get the tar off my shoes; the other to fine-tune the dish so I can finally get something to watch.

At last I go to the den, happy my four-hour ordeal is over, and sit down to start surfing my new satellite stations. What do I see? *A River Runs Through It*, coming up next, *Steel Magnolias*. You can't win people... you just can't win.

The Israeli Accident

ALTHOUGH MANY OF YOU THINK of me as a "show biz" type, I do not think of myself in that way. Show biz is just what I do. I try to be normal, it's not my fault I met Tina Turner; it's my job. You work for Subway, you meet the guy who makes the bread; I meet Tina Turner. Life's not fair. Deal with it.

One of my dear friends is Lynn Mitchell. Lynn is a retired singer and one of the most dynamic people I know. She's fun and happy and pretty and has OCD. Lynn has always been connected to show business and hangs out with show folk, so when she started her business at the LA Mart, it was natural she would call on her peeps for help. This includes former Miss America, Laurel Schaeffer; Sandi Johnson, dancer and wife of Jay Johnson of *Soap* fame; and me, the dyslexic comedian who can't spell. It wasn't so much a showroom as the set of *One Flew Over the Cuckoo's Nest*.

It was the end of my first day at the Mart and I was exhausted. I had to be there at 10 a.m. and was on my feet until 6 p.m. Seriously, I don't know how you people do it. I work forty-five minutes a night, once every two weeks, and get pissed when I have to fly to the Bahamas.

I'm on my way home from the showroom, in a coma, stopped at a red light, when I hear a *thud* and realize my car has been hit from the rear. I pull over and look at the damage. It's minor but damaged. I turn and I see an eighteen-year-old kid literally roll out from behind the wheel of the other car. He wobbles over to me and laughs.

"Do you have a driver's license?" I ask.

"I gif you nut-ting," he says in the most arrogant tone.

Sweet Jesus, save me; An Israeli has hit my car. I thought, *let me just set the car on fire*. I ask the kid if he has insurance and if I could see his driver's license. He walks away. Now the second guy gets out of the car, he's older, taller and louder.

"VAT IS DA PROBIM. DERE IS NO DAMAGE."

I'm looking at a fourteen-inch gash in my rear bumper as the two of them walk away. I'm thinking, *when are they going to explode?* I call the police. Try to smell a fart in a windstorm; it'll be easier.

"I need help! I was just rear ended and they won't give me their driver's license and proof of insurance."

"Oh, let me call out the SWAT team," the operator replies.

"Huh?"

"Sir, you're in Los Angeles. We don't have the manpower to send a unit out every time one of you hits each other."

"Aren't you the lady I spoke to when my car was stolen?"

"Sir, we will send a unit out when one becomes available." Subtext: You're on your own, White Boy. I call my insurance company.

"Hello, this is Tanisha. How can I help yous?"

I tell her about the accident.

"Mr. Bloomsteen, get their license plate number and get out of there."

As she is saying this, four cars pull up behind mine. Israelis pile out like it's the Ringling Brothers clown car. "Oh my God!" I exclaim to Tanisha.

"Honey, what's happening?" I tell her who just pulled up. "Listen to me. LISTEN TO ME GOOD!!! Get in your car. Lock the windows and doors... I'll call Homeland Security."

I get into my car. All types of Israelis—big ones, fat ones, tall ones, skinny ones—now surround it. One is tapping on the window. His shirt is open to the waist; around his neck is a gold thing, which to me looks like the head of Yasser Arafat. His chest is thick with black hair and he's tanned. It's January! I roll the window down a crack.

"My friend, we need to talk, my friend," and I see the headlines: "Body of comedian found in deli slicer."

"My friend, we have a problem. The boy has no license, my friend, or insurance, my friend, and we do not want the police called. Did you call the police?"

I shake my head, no.

Tanisha is screaming, "GET OUT OF THERE! SAVE YOURSELF, BABY!"

The Godfather continues, "We fix your car. I own body shop. You give me your car and I take yours." Oh, there's a deal. I'll give him my Lexus and he'll give me his 1968 Plymouth Valiant.

At this point Israelis are screaming at me from all sides. Finally, I say, "What do you want from me? I'm a Jew."

"He's a Jew? He's a Jew! Did you hear, he's a Jew," the crowd murmurs. I kick the ham sandwich under the seat. The crowd parts as a short man approaches. There is silence.

"I am the boy's father." I look at him and think the next sentence will be, "We are going to behead him!" Instead, the man says, "I am very sorry for this. Why didn't you tell us you were a Jew? Here is my card."

I pull away from the curb; it's forty-five minutes after the accident. My cellphone rings, it's the police dispatcher, "You still need us?"

I take the car home and the next day my garage door falls on it. I start a book, and that's how we all met!

The Niacin Affair

IT WAS TIME FOR MY ANNUAL CHECKUP and so I called my HMO to get my appointment. This was my first year there and so I needed to find a responsible doctor, which at an HMO is an oxymoron. My new doctor tells me my cholesterol is high, 229. He wants to put me on meds but I am not a "meds" kind of guy; I want to try to bring it down with diet and exercise, "Is there anything else I could try?" The doctor says, "Niacin", so the next time I'm at Costco I buy a tub of Niacin for $16.99.

About this time, my house has sold. I have to have the house tented for termites, which means I have to rent a storage unit, put it in my driveway, and put all my belongings in it while they murder the helpless termites that consider my house an all-you-can-eat buffet.

I take my animals and stay in a motel for the night. The termite people will be back the next morning to remove the tent and give me the all clear. Suddenly my house has become Chernobyl. When I finally do get inside, it smells funny. I'm a little nervous about breathing air that kills so I open all the doors and windows. Like that will help. I'm such a dufus.

Since I have no furniture, I'm lying on the floor of the den watching a portable TV when all of a sudden it gets very hot in the house. Hot, like a sudden heat wave, and I'm sweating like a pig. I'm fanning myself and mopping my forehead with a towel. It gets so hot I turn on the A/C; it's February. That's not working, so I go into the kitchen and stick my head under the faucet. I'm still burning up. And then I catch a glimpse of my reflection in the window. Oh. My. God! I'm beet red. I look at my arms; they are beet red, my legs are red. I run to the bathroom and look in the mirror. Sitting Bull is looking back at me.

Now this is how my mind works: *I'm having an allergic reaction to the termite chemicals* made perfect sense to me. They tented the house, I was laying on the floor, at this point my tongue starts to swell. *Jesus Christ I'm going into anaphylactic shock.* Not just shock, mind you, anaphylactic shock. If we're going to panic why not go for the gusto! I dial 911. There is a unit at my house in six minutes, they take one look at me and throw me in an ambulance. It's just like on TV. They're calling the hospital with my numbers, and the doctor at the hospital is telling them what to do. Naturally I'm in the bed thinking, *I have no will.* The sirens are blaring and I can feel the car swerve from side to side as they cut through traffic. The sound of the siren gets hollow as we come closer to the hospital entrance. The doors swing open and I'm catapulted onto the loading dock. A new team of doctors is working on me. An intern is asking me all kinds of questions.

"What are you allergic to? Have you taken any drugs? Are you a diabetic?" He turns to the heavy set black nurse next to him and screams, "I want an IV solution of [whatever] and a 100cc's of [whatever] and call the pharmacy and..."

The nurse puts up her index finger and turns to me, "Honey, you been taking Niacin?" I nod yes. She turns to the intern, "This is a Niacin reaction, Dr. Salk," and she walks back to the automatic doors, hits the button and turns as they swing open, "And don't you *ever* tell me my ass is too fat for my own good!"

Turns out some of the side effects of taking Niacin are flushed feeling, bright red skin, swollen tongue. This cost me $385 for the ambulance and $950 in emergency room fees. I wish you could have all been there when I told the HMO doctor what had happened.

"Ah, I didn't tell you about the possible reaction?"

Duh! "No, you didn't, you sorry-ass mother... doctor... sir!"

Unemployment

I HAD JUST COME OFF WRITING a couple of sit-coms and there didn't appear to be much on the horizon, so like all good writers, actors, and comedians in Hollywood, I applied for unemployment. It's the normal thing out here, you stop working you go on unemployment until your next job. There is no stigma; as a matter of fact, it's where you see the stars standing in line at unemployment. I had not collected unemployment in years and was unaware that things had changed; I got a notice that I had to appear for employment training. Employment training? They were going to train me to be a comedian? I get the time and date and show up for my class. I must tell you my attitude was not good. This was a monumental waste of time and taxpayer dollars. I wasn't the typical unemployed person. You just can't train me to find work, it just sort of happens, like a miracle at Lourdes.

I show up the morning of the class and park my car in the lot. As I'm walking to the front door I notice mine was not the only expensive car there. The parking lot was filled with BMW's, Mercedes, Lexus, and Infiniti; every luxury you can think of. I even saw a Maserati. It looked like Jay Leno's garage.

We are shuffled to a conference room and we sit around this long table. I look at the other people and I'm thinking, *I'm such a loser. I'm the only one here from show business and I'm going to be out of place here.* Just then the "team leader" comes in. He's a tall, good-looking black man with a grayish beard and wearing a grey pinstriped suit.

"Good morning class, I'm Harold Roberts and today I will be conducting the seminar on how to find work. Let's get started by introducing ourselves and sharing what our last job was."

Then it begins, "Hello, I'm so and so, I was vice president of Sony Pictures."

"I'm so and so, I was news anchor for channel four."

"I was executive producer of.... I am casting director of.... I am director of..."

Finally, the last woman speaks, "I created and was executive producer of *Buffy the Vampire Slayer*."

I almost wet myself. I am sitting in a room filled with millionaires who are now all collecting unemployment. Harold asks if we knew why we had been chosen for this seminar. I raise my hand.

"Anyone who earns 6 figures or more gets a bonus class?"

"Close. The State has determined that this group has a 99% chance of not being rehired."

A pall falls over the room but I'm in ecstasy! I'm sitting across from the VP of Sony and we are laughing so hard tears are running down our cheeks. You see, the total gross income of the room could buy the building and if Harold doesn't get us out of here by cocktails, we will.

Harold explains the day's course and introduces our first speaker. The door flies open and this woman whirls in like a tornado. I've never seen such energy. You have to picture this woman to understand what made her so funny. She was dressed in a power suit, her hair was piled up on top of her head like the Seattle Space Needle, her voice was high-pitched like nails on a chalkboard, and she talked like she was on speed in a non-stop barrage of sentences that made you want to choke her.

"Okay everyone, so nice to see those smiling faces and let's not be down because you're out of work and everyone you know has a job you too will work again someday. Maybe. You can find your niche in society; you too will be vital productive human beings again and not be a drain on society. Look at me! Why, just last year I was not working and now I have this job." This manic blabber went on for forty-five minutes. When she was done she picked up her briefcase and whirled out of the room leaving a swirl of dust and a trail of dead bodies.

"What did you think?" Harold inquires like a proud Papa.

"Couldn't we just have a root canal?" I whisper loud enough for everyone in the room to hear. The laugh is ten minutes. Harold is not amused and I am asked to sit up front. I'm just happy I don't have to sit in the corner with a dunce cap. Then it's noon and we have an hour break. The cell phones come out. I'm listening to the conversations around me.

"Maria, make sure the groomer picks up the dogs."

"I'm at this stupid Unemployment thing. Did you hear from the studio? Tell that asshole I cannot do that film for sixteen million, I need at least twenty-eight or we're out."

"Phyllis, is my office finished yet? When do you think the carpenters will get the mahogany paneling?"

The people who were not on their cell phones were networking, "I understand you were with Columbia Pictures. Listen, I've got a project in turn around that I think might be good for your people." That is how the entire hour was spent at unemployment, making deals, talking to maids, and confirming work orders.

The rest of the afternoon was spent learning how to fill out forms, learning how to apply for a job, learning to never apply for unemployment again (and I have not). At 6 p.m. we are released and given our certificate of completion along with a "how to find work" kit. Harold has taken a liking to me and wants to hear from me in two weeks to see how I'm doing in my job search. I call him in ten days to tell him I've just been hired to write a sit-com and there is a deep sigh on his end of the phone, "I'm so happy for you, Steve. I'm glad to know my class is helping people." He then pitches me a story idea and asks if I'd be interested in writing a film with him.

There's a reason why Anne Heche was babbling in foreign tongues by the side of the road. She had just come from The California Unemployment Seminar on Job Searches.

Memorial Day

MANY YEARS AGO, like when gas was 38¢ a gallon, I was part of an actor's workshop, which later became a theater group called The Groundlings. Years after I left the group it produced people like Pee Wee Herman, Jon Lovitz, Edie McClurg, Elivra, Phil Hartman, and on and on and on.

One of the people I love from the early Groundling years is Isabel West Davis. Isabel is daughter of legendary actor/producer Bernie West. She now lives in NYC but came to LA on a regular basis to visit her father before his passing. On one of these trips she called and invited me to Bernie's eighty-eighth birthday and said, "There will be a lot of old friends there." When I walked in the very first person I saw was Lynn Stewart. Lynn played Miss Yvonne on *The Pee Wee Herman Show* and has been seen in countless commercials and movies and TV shows. However, to me, she's just Lynn, one of the most loving people I know. Lynn is just a little off-center and when you are around her all you want to do is laugh. I really love her. She, Cindy Williams, and I hung out in the early years; not so much anymore, and so when I see her it's like a birthday present.

Then in comes Groundling Phyllis Katz. Phyllis is one of the most intelligent people I know. Besides being beautiful, she's a brilliant comedy actor and an accomplished writer whose one-woman show was so funny I wet myself watching. Phyllis is so smart she scares me a little. When I saw her sitting in the front row of one of my shows I almost froze with fear. This has nothing to do with Phyllis. It had to do with my fear of being judged. At the show, Phyllis was laughing and supportive and loving *and* she drove all the way to Pasadena to see me. Now that's love.

Then in walks Tracy Newman. To show you how long I've known her, Tracy was performing on stage at The Comedy Store the very first night

I set foot in the place. I was investigating to see if I thought I could be a comedian. Tracy is just good people. She's smart and funny and, to me, is like a warm blanket on a cold night. She was in the Groundlings with me. As a matter of fact, I think it was because of her I got into the workshop. One day her sister joined the class. We only knew her as Tracy's sister; she was shy and rail thin. However, when she got on stage it was like an explosion of talent. There was magic there and you knew she was destined for greatness. Tracy's sister, Laraine—who later went on to SNL fame and lives a stone's throw from me today—remains a friend who is unaffected by fame and grounded by her family.

The treat of the night for me came when Reni Santori walked in. I had never met him before. He came with Tracy. We were all talking, catching up, when I was introduced to him. Now this is an actor I have watched in films and on TV for years, someone I respect and consider a "real" actor. I'm introduced to him and he says, "Yes, I know who you are. You were wonderful on *Make Me Laugh*." *Make Me Laugh*?? That was thirty years ago! There must have been two hundred comedians on it. How in God's name did he remember me? I was so grateful and honored. Right then, for just a few seconds, I didn't feel like a failure. I didn't feel like me.

What I love about these people is that when we get together, all we do is laugh. Not only do we laugh, but we also enjoy making each other laugh. Phyllis said to me, "Steve, tell the story about when you went home to visit your mother." I did, and they laughed, and I thought, *I forgot about that story. I must tell this in my book*, and this is how it goes.

I was going home to Boston and my mother was getting in her obsessive mode. She called me at least twice a day prior to the trip.

"I want to make sure I have everything in the house that you like to eat. What do you like for breakfast?"

"I like raison bran."

"Kellogg or Post?"

"Post"

"Do you like skim milk or regular?"

"Skim"

"Do you like wheat toast or rye?" These phone calls went on for a week. "Do you like chicken or fish? Cause I want to make everything you like to eat when you come home. You're not home that often and I want to make it special."

The day I arrived, it had been a long trip. I get to my mother's house and I'm not there five minutes when she asks, "Are you hungry? I've got everything you like." I was hungry so I asked if she had any chicken cooked. "It'll be out in three minutes," and it was. I sat at the table as I waited for my first home-cooked meal. I put the first bite in my mouth and spit it out.

"Where did you get this?"

"What does it matter?"

"You didn't cook this. Where did you get it?"

"It doesn't matter. Eat it you'll feel better."

"No! I want to know where this comes from."

"What does it matter??"

"Because I want to know where it came from!"

"...I went to the nursing home, they gave me dinners."

You see, my mother is a fundraiser for the local nursing home, and when she knew I was coming home, her idea of nurturing was to get the institutional chefs at the nursing home to cook dinners for me. In her fridge were seven trays stacked one on top of the other, just like the dietitian had just put them there for the octogenarians.

When I finished telling the story my friends laughed long and hard and for an instant it was like being back in The Groundlings and I was twenty-seven again. I stayed at the party for about three hours and then the group began to break up. We all kissed good-bye. I said I was going to have everyone over for a Tony party. It will never happen. As we left we ran into Carole Ita White coming in. Carole played Rosie Greenbaum on *Laverne & Shirley*. She was a Comedy Store regular and friends with all the Groundlings. Carole has always been three hours late to everything in her life, and this is why I love her. She's consistent.

In the car going home I got very depressed. I miss these people very much. I miss being in their lives and having them in mine. When we were younger we all had a common bond, we were all going to be stars. Only a handful made their goal, the rest are working actors, some are not in the business anymore, some just faded away. It saddens me to think how unfair show business is until a friend, not in the business, said, "That's what life is all about, people come in and out of your life. It's not just show business it's all businesses! It's life." I realized he was right, it's not just me, it's all of us.

Childhood Memory

I MUST HAVE BEEN ABOUT EIGHT years old. I had been out playing with friends in the foundation of a house that had just been ripped down. I slipped and fell and opened my elbow. The blood was everywhere. I ran to find my mother; she was visiting with friends. My arm was covered with blood as I came screaming into my mother's friend Irene's house. Immediately Irene, Edie, and Emmy jumped up and brought me into the bathroom. They were washing my elbow when I heard my father screaming in the background.

"Your son comes home covered in blood and you don't get up off your chair!!!!"

"Why do I have to get up? My friends are taking care of it," my mother replied.

I remember this exchange as if it were yesterday. I remember thinking, *why is he so upset? She's right. Irene, Emmy, and Edie are taking care of it*, but as an adult the reality has come home to roost like barnyard chickens after a hurricane. I understand the lack of maternal nurturing that it takes to think like that. I'm beginning to understand the effects it's had on me.

It was my sixth, seventh, eighth birthday; does it matter? My mother had invited all the kids from the neighborhood for my birthday party. I remember feeling so happy, so special, so loved. As the kids came in, one by one, my mother sat them around the table. This is five minutes after they arrived, "Okay, it's time for cake." They sang Happy Birthday and my mother said, "The party's over." The entire party was ten minutes. One of the mothers said, "What a good idea. Get them in and get them out," but I remember feeling so sad, so un-special, and so unloved.

Then there was the time right before the divorce and after my father moved out of the house that he came back unannounced. He wanted in, she wanted him out. I remember my mother was pushing furniture up against the door. He held his hand on the buzzer as she stood on a chair unscrewing the doorbell. Two can play this game; my father was outside taking the hinges off the door. He pushed the door in. Furniture went flying and he grabbed my mother dragging her into the bedroom where he slammed the door shut and locked it. I was left outside pounding on the bedroom door. Twenty minutes later he came out; she was undressed. I never could understand why I hated *Father Knows Best*. There was no reality there for me.

Then another funny story was when I had gone to sleep-away camp. It was the last day and we were being driven to the drop-off point in the camp bus. I stood at the depot waiting and watching as mother after mother came to pick up their kids. I saw their excitement as they kissed the children they hadn't seen all summer. My mother never showed up. I waited an hour. Finally, I walked home dragging my suitcase behind me. The funny thing here is I wasn't upset; this was just how my life was. I walked the mile from the drop-off point to our apartment. I opened the door and saw two people making love on the sofa. I recognized the gold wedgies, they were hers, so I closed the door. I went down into the laundry room and waited for about forty-five minutes. My mother came out and found me there. She never asked how I got home. She never asked what I was doing in the laundry room, she never asked because she just didn't care.

I swore to myself that I would never share that story with a single living soul. It made my mother look bad. Quite frankly, I don't care how it makes her look anymore. After my IBS attack last night, I'm sore, I ache, and I'm fed up. The damage that has been done to me, the ones that breed these feelings of inadequacy, failure, and not being good enough to love are directly related to these stories and what happened to me as a child. I wish I could make them funny, but to me there's nothing funny about them. At best, they're sad. I'm sharing them to finally release them. Maybe the demons will go away.

Kathy Griffin

MANY YEARS AFTER I had left the Groundlings, I went back there for a refresher course. It felt good to be at the Groundlings again and be involved in the creative energy of that place, and it was great to be introduced to the "new" Groundlings. There is a very strict structure to the Groundling Theater. You have to take classes, and then, if they consider you good enough, you're moved to an advanced class. Then, if you're popular enough, voted into the Sunday Show, and finally—if you're political enough—voted into the main, Saturday show. It's very cutthroat and an ego crusher but if you make it through the process the rewards can be enormous.

The Saturday show is the top rung on the ladder, when you're in that show you are showcased for the entire industry. Because of that, the best of the best are in that show. During my period of reentry into the Groundlings I would go to watch the Saturday cast. There was a young girl who was incredibly funny—she stuck out like a sore thumb she was so funny—yet she was as homely as sin. This girl was not a looker in any way, shape, or form. It didn't matter what she looked like, you could not take your eyes off her and her funny won out.

At some point, I was introduced to her and I was amazed at her personality. She was as shy as a mouse. Shy! A wallflower; not a "look at me" bone in her body. I was not surprised since many actors are like that; Bobcat Goldwaith is so painfully shy he's almost invisible. Hard to believe that someone who is so open on stage can be so introverted, but it's true. Kathy was shy and nice and very talented.

My claim to fame in the Groundlings was my connection to Beverly Hills Plastic Surgeon, Michael Churukian. I'll be the first to admit I've had some work done—nose, chin, lipo—and each time I would have something done, a Groundling would approach me for the phone number of my surgeon. At one point, at least ten or fifteen Groundlings were having plastic surgery with Dr. Churukian. I was the connection and everyone came to me to put in a good word so they could get an appointment. Kathy approached me one day and asked if she could get the "doctor's" number. I gave it to her and she had her nose done. It's remarkable what a nose job can do. It can change the entire appearance of a face. And that's what it did for Kathy; she was cuter after the surgery.

I detest doing stand-up. The traveling, the club owners, the egos of other comedians just take all the fun out of the work. In the late 80s/early 90s I could see the writing on the wall. The Comedy Club circuit was shutting down. TV had taken its bite into the business. No one came out to see comedy; they watched it on The Comedy Channel. At the same time, the quality of the acts began to fail. By then, anyone with a suit was a comedian. The clubs spawned a generic kind of comedy that was centered on the crotch and never went any higher. Instead of bringing the audience up to the comedian's level, the comedian was sinking to the audience's level. Comedy suffered. While acts like Ed Murphy and Richard Pryor could make sex topics funny and insightful, most comedians just made them vulgar. It was during that time I decided to move away from stand-up and closer to writing, a move I never regretted.

During this period, this shy, not-so-pretty actress with Annie curls, Kathy Griffin, came up to me all excited, "Steve, I'm going to do stand-up!" The hairs on the back of my neck stood up. Why? Every actor in town was "doing stand-up." Why? It was a way to get noticed. It had nothing to do with the art of stand-up; it had to do with them becoming famous.

"Oh, God, Kathy, why? Why would you want to be a stand-up? It's hell out there and there is no work anymore."

"I just want to."

I shrugged my shoulder, kissed her and walked away. That was the last time I saw her in person. Years later I'm flipping through the channels and there she was on Bravo. Oh my God! What had she done to herself? She looked beautiful! And that personality, where did that come from? That material, it was blisteringly wonderful. I watched and listened and I laughed. My words came echoing back to me, "Oh God, Kathy, why?" Only this time I came up with my own answer. "Because, I'm going to be famous and a star, Steve. I'm going to do something that no one else is doing and I'm going to do it better than anyone could imagine. *That's* why."

While I do not like the life of a comic, I do respect her ability to live it and carve a niche for herself. I'm happy for her. Just one side note. She started going to another plastic surgeon, one who is famous for being famous, and she is starting to look a little done. She looks nothing like the girl I knew from the Groundlings. That girl is dead and gone. In her place is that powerhouse of a comedian who has her own show on Bravo. Good on ya, Kath, as they say in Oz. Good on ya! I was happy to be 100% wrong.

The Duck Story

I HAD BEEN VISITING FRIENDS in the valley and was on my way home through Laurel Canyon when out of nowhere a duck fell out of the sky and landed on my windshield. It was a mallard and bounced nicely. I have to be clear about this: I didn't hit this duck; it fell out of the sky onto my car. My initial thought, *a duck comes down, I must have said the secret word* (Okay, that's a reference that is so old it's on Medicare. Ask your parents).

I look in my rear-view mirror and I see the duck shaking its head by the side of the road. It's not doing well. It's walking around in circles. I couldn't leave it there and I pull over and walk back to it. It lets me approach it. *This must be someone's pet*, I think, *why else would it let me approach it?* In retrospect, the answer is *because it was in a coma, you asshole*. I go to pick up the duck and it throws up. Have you ever seen duck vomit? Sort of like Pâté you definitely do not want to eat. I think, *I can't touch this thing. Who knows where it's been.* I find a newspaper on the side of the road, lay it on the ground next to the duck and then sort of roll the duck over onto the newspaper with my foot. I'm a real woodsman. When the duck is on the paper, I pick it up by the edges of the paper and have a duck sling, which I am now carrying back to my car.

I lay the duck on the front seat. It's looks dizzy. The eyes are rolling back in its head and it's making this sort of duck moaning sound that I never heard before or since. I decide to take it back to my apartment. What am I going to do with it when I get it there, give it mouth to bill? I can't leave it in the street.

I'm driving through the canyon and I look at the duck. It's worse. How good would *you* be doing wrapped in newspaper? Now I'm rushing to get it home. I'm doing 50 MPH in a 35 MPH zone and naturally I heard the telltale sound of a siren and see red flashing lights in my rear-view mirror. I pull over and a motorcycle cop walks up to me like it's High Noon.

"License" is all he says.

"Officer. I know I was speeding but I have a prize duck here and it's going into labor. I am rushing it to the vet."

The cop looks in my car and the duck vomits on cue. The cop looks at me and then back to the duck. "Do you need an escort?"

"That would be nice," so now I'm racing down Laurel Canyon with a spewing duck and a Police Escort. He never gives me a ticket!

I get the duck home. I run upstairs, with the duck in its newspaper gurney. I have to sneak it into my apartment because the manager doesn't allow pets, and that bitch can smell an animal at fifty paces. I get the duck into my house and it start quacking to beat the band, but I need to shut it up because "no pets allowed". The thing isn't there ten minutes when my phone rings. It's her, the bitch from *Wild Kingdom*.

"Do you have a duck in your apartment?"

"Who me?"

"I have reports of a duck in your apartment."

Reports? What did she do, put out an APB on me? I do some fast taking and convince her it was the TV because, "Who would be stupid enough to bring a duck home?" Hello, you're talking to him.

I get off the phone and the duck is failing. The noise it created was not a sign of renewed vigor; it was a desperate cry for help. It faints. Okay, so I panic. "My duck is fainting…. My duck is fainting!" I run into the bathroom and splash water into its face. Nothing. Then I look down and see the standing water in my toilet. Ah! Duck. Water. Perfect. I put the duck in the toilet. Nothing. It rests its head on the porcelain rim. I think maybe it needs stimulation. I flush. Nothing. I think maybe it's hungry. I rush to my kitchen and open the cupboards. Nothing. A box of matzo. I take the matzo and crumple it up; I run back to the bathroom and try to feed the duck by tossing matzo crumbs at it like we were at the lake. At one point, I stop as I see myself in the mirror. Do you realize you're throwing matzo crumbs at a duck in your toilet? If anyone walked in I would have been taken away.

Okay, so what happens next is the God's honest truth. I swear to God. The phone rings, it's my agent. I need to get over to Universal "right away," but I can't leave the duck running around the apartment. I don't know what to do, so I close the lid.

I leave the apartment and go to the interview. I come home about two hours later. I run to the bathroom and my wife is out cold on the bathroom floor. I grab her up and shake her. Her eyes open a crack.

"Honey, are you okay? What happened?"

"I had to go to the bathroom. I sat down on the toilet and something quacked."

At that point, I see the humor and start laughing. This pisses her off. She thinks she's just shit a duck. We have a huge fight and right in the middle of it, the duck drops dead.

"Are you happy now?" I scream at her, "You've killed my duck." I pick it up and leave the room. We don't talk for five days.

Here's a P.S. to that story.

I'm opening for Donna Summer at the MGM Grand in Las Vegas. Buddy Hackett is down the street at the Sands. His son, Sandy, is a good friend and comes to my show. After the show, he takes me back to Buddy's dressing room. Sandy says, "Steve, tell Dad the duck story. He loves duck stories." I start telling the story to Buddy and he starts laughing. He's laughing so hard that at one point he rolls off the sofa. He's crying he's laughing so hard. I finish the story and Buddy Hackett says to me, "That's the funniest fucking story I have ever heard." I'm beaming from ear to ear. I just made Buddy Hackett laugh.

Here's a P.P.S.

Ten years later when I start my writing career, I call Sandy because I have a play that I think would be great for him and his father. Sandy calls his father while I'm there, "Dad, remember the guy with the duck story?" He does. He agrees to read my play. He loves it but didn't want to do it so he sent it to Charles Durning, who did. That was the start of my career as a playwright.

I love that duck!

Mary Travers

AFTER GRADUATING FROM COLLEGE, I fled from Boston and my family. At graduation, I threw my cap in the air, by the time it landed I was on a bus to New York. I landed a job at United Artists in the international film division. I have visions of myself flying to Brussels to the latest work of some unknown director. Instead, I pushed papers. Lots and lots of papers. I hated the job and it hated me but it allowed me to earn enough money to rent a one room flat on 58th Street. This place was small; when the toilet seat was down, you couldn't close the bathroom door. There were six tiles on the kitchen floor. It had one closet! I paid $156 a month and struggled every month to eat and pay the rent, but it was on 58th Street, midtown Manhattan. I was two blocks from Sutton Place.

Walking to get pizza one night I noticed Mary Travers of Peter, Paul and Mary walking by my flat. It was the first of several sightings. I thought, *she must live in the neighborhood.* Finally, one night, I saw her enter a brownstone just three doors up from my building. It was a magical time for me, on my own and living in New York City next to a legend. I would walk by her town house and you could see the gold records hung in the front room. My God, Peter, Paul and Mary. I wish I could be her friend!

15 years later

I'm flying to Denver to open for Mary Travers. It was during the period when Peter, Paul and Mary were not working together and she was doing a solo act. I had no idea what to expect, who she would be, or how she would accept my act. Turns out she is one of the most down-to-earth, honest, sincere, wonderful, loving, kind, generous people I have ever had the honor of working with. We opened and after the first show she came into my dressing room.

"You are one funny mother fucker."

"Me?"

"Yeah, you. We're going out for coffee after the show, wanna come with us?"

Mary Travers and I went out for coffee every night after the show with her band, we laughed, we joked, she told stories of famous people I could only hope to know and I felt genuinely accepted.

One night after the show someone had pot, and we all sat around Mary's room smoking. The laughter was uncontrolled, we were stoned and soon we were hungry. Mary says, "Let's go to the coffee shop," and we all pile out of her room to get ice cream and cake. This hotel was connected to a Howard Johnson's and there was a long, enclosed walkway from the hotel to the restaurant. Mary throws on her full-length mink coat and we proceed down the corridor. We are screaming with laughter and suddenly Mary stops and puts out her hands. "Wait! We have to compose ourselves. After all, those people think of me as Puff's Mother." I wet myself laughing. The truth of the matter is, I was with Puff's mother. Try that thought some night on acid.

The gig ended and, as happens in show business, you lose track of the people you worked with. Mary made sure she gave me her phone number and told me to call her the next time I was in NYC. Well, as luck would have it, I was in New York about a year later and I did call, "Steve, you must come to the apartment." The irony of all this wasn't lost on me. The icon that had lived two doors down, was now inviting me over to visit. How had I done this?

She was now living in a huge apartment at like 57th and 7th. It was the biggest apartment I had ever seen in New York and it was filled with things from her career. Her daughter was the spitting image of her mother and just as nice. I got the tour of the place and was made to feel at home. I did.

Mary and I talked and talked and talked and I told her about my feelings of failure (even back then) and she said, "Do you know what my greatest fear is? That someday I will be pushing a shopping cart down 7th Avenue."

I couldn't believe what I was hearing, I tried to comfort her. "Mary, how can you say that? You have worked so much. Records, movies, Carnegie Hall."

"Oh, that's no big deal."

"But to stand on the stage of Carnegie Hall!!"

"It's nothing," she says and she pulled my hand and said, "Come with me."

We ran down the street and soon were at the stage door of Carnegie Hall. The door was open and Mary walked in with me. The man at the stage door greeted her like she does this every day. Maybe she does, but not with me. We walked down a short hallway and Mary took my hand and pulled me out to the center of the stage, "You have just stood on the stage at Carnegie Hall. See, it's not so hard to do." I stood there looking at the rows and rows of seats as they soared to the roofline like some giant manta ray that was engulfing the building. I imagined the seats filled with people and me telling jokes. What it would be like? It was honestly one of the most magical moments of my life and I had Puff's mother to thank for it.

Mary and I didn't see much of each other after that meeting. Maybe five years later we did a TV show together. When she saw me, she gave me a hug and the phone number where she was staying. I called and she invited me over. However, this time it was not so magical. Did you ever go over to someone's house and you knew they were being polite and marking the time until you leave? That's how it was. My magical time with Mary was over.

This is not an indictment of Mary Travers; it's just how my business is. Better yet, that's just how life is. You work with someone for a week, become very tight with him or her and then never see him or her again. I had more than that with Mary, I had Carnegie Hall and for that I will be grateful to her until the day I die.

Wish I had a mother as hip as Puff's.

Todd

RIGHT AFTER GRADUATING COLLEGE I moved to NYC. Well, actually I moved to Bayside, Queens. See if you can follow me on this because it's complex. My college roommate was Jon Stierwalt; his fiancé was Ronnie Adler. Jon was half a semester behind Ronnie and me. I wanted to live in New York. Ronnie wanted to stay in Boston. I lived in Boston; she lived in New York. I moved into Ronnie's house with her mother and Ronnie moved into my house, with my mother. I got the better end of the deal. Trust me. Years later Ronnie told me that she moved her wedding date up so she could get away from my mother. When Ronnie told her mother how my mother was treating her, things changed for me. Suddenly I was asked to move out because, "We're painting." Naturally I took it that there was something wrong with me, but the reality was Ronnie's mother was treating me like her own son and my mother was treating Ronnie like an intrusion in her life. There was resentment and I took the full brunt of it.

I moved to the sofa of a secretary at United Artists. I remember feeling lost, abandoned, and hurt by my sudden lack of housing. I remember thinking it was entirely my fault, never realizing the wheels had been set in motion by that little lady I called Mom. I found this one room apartment on 58th Street and was happy to get it. How I was going to make the $156 a month rent was beyond me, but I took the place.

I wasn't there a month when I bumped into Todd Kashden, who had graduated Emerson College with me. Now Todd was special. Very, very special. For the older readers, you'll remember Chatsworth Osborne Jr. on *Dobie Gillis*. Todd was Chatsworth. He talked with the clenched jaw. He dressed in turtlenecks and a double-breasted navy blue blazer. He *was*

Chatsworth Osborne, Jr. (Years later I would meet Steve Franklin, who played the character on TV, and tell him about Todd. He smiled).

Todd was fun to be around and great to make fun of. I mean, how could you not make fun of this millionaire kid from Great Neck. Turns out, he wasn't a millionaire at all. He was just a middle-class kid from a middle-class home who was hiding his pain behind a millionaire's facade. When I learned this, I immediately became his friend. Why? Because I knew the kind of pain he was hiding and I could relate to him. One day I run into Todd outside my building.

"Todd, how the hell are you?"

"Fabulous," he said like a Vanderbilt.

"Where are you living? Are you in the city?"

He points to the building across the street from mine, "I live there."

We both went to Emerson together in Boston. We both moved to New York City without each other's knowledge. We move across the street from each other in a city of ten million people. There must be a reason.

Todd invited me over that night and I meet his roommate. Now you have to remember we were twenty-two years old. In NYC that's the only way you could afford to live. I met the roommate and immediately did not like him. There was something wrong there. I couldn't put my finger on it, but I just got the creeps when he walked into a room. However, Todd was dating Janis and she was like a breath of fresh air. She was beautiful, charming, and easy to be around. Janis lived with two roommates in a one bedroom flat just down the hall from Todd. We all became friends, Todd, Janis, Amy, Cheryl, and me. I am happy to tell you that Amy, Cheryl, and Janis are still amongst my friends even if we don't see each other but once every ten years.

The six of us, Todd, the girls, his roommate, and I hung out and did lots together. I didn't think anything of it when Todd invited me to go to a bar one night. I think we got there at 1 a.m. The place was a converted church and it was jammed with people. Now this was the 60s and before my encounter with smoking pot. I looked around and realized freaks surrounded me. Everyone was a hippie. Everyone was longhaired and wearing the weirdest clothes I had ever seen. I felt like the freak because I was in saddle shoes and a tennis sweater. Todd and his roommate seemed to fit right in and immediately began drinking. Now I had known Todd for years in college and had never seen him drink. It was apparent he was making up for lost time. We stayed at this bar until about 4 a.m. Todd was totally wasted, as was his roommate. I had not had anything to drink,

I didn't drink then, and so I shepherded them home. I remember Todd falling into his bed and telling me, "I don't feel so good." He immediately threw up. I ran to the bathroom for towels. He was out of it. I wiped him up and helped him get out of his vomit-soaked shirt. He flopped back into bed and was out cold. I will never forget that moment in my life. I remember thinking, *he's going to die.*

The next day he called me and asked what had happened. I told him and he laughed. I said, "Todd, I think you have a drinking problem," and he poo-pooed my worries. That was the first of many nights I saw Todd so drunk he could barely stand. It was a nightly occurrence with him and his roommate; soon the drinking lead to drugs. There was a desperation in Todd's use that frightened me.

New York was becoming oppressive. My friend Susan was moving to California and I would follow her. The trip across country with my dog Crosby is a story in itself; getting set up in an apartment and finding a job also a story. Naturally I kept my connection with my New York City girls. It must have been a month after arrived in LA when I got a call from Amy.

"Todd's roommate shot himself."

I heard the words but at twenty-three your friends don't die so it was surreal. "How? Why?"

"He committed suicide."

"How's Todd?"

There was a long silence, "Bad."

I can't say I was surprised. The roommate was always emotionally charged. I blamed him for Todd's downward spiral, but I was not prepared for the next phone call a few weeks later. It was a college friend, Larry Sobol.

"Steve. Todd is dead."

"No, he's not, Larry, I just spoke to him last week."

"Steve, he's dead. He overdosed."

When I hung up the phone my head spun with memories of Todd at the Senior Class Prom, Todd on Jr. Class weekend. I shared a thousand memories with that insane man. Now he was gone. How could this happen? How could such a good person be gone so young? It was my first introduction to life and I didn't like it.

It's forty years later and I still think of him. Still think about what he could have become, what he would have done, where he would have gone. Chatsworth Osborne Jr., my friend, Todd. Life can be so cruel, y'all. It can be so cruel.

Vegas Dribs and Drabs

I WAS OPENING FOR DONNA SUMMER at the MGM Grand. It was a very high-profile gig and my face was everywhere. My name was on billboards on the strip ten feet high and with blazing letters. It's what I had dreamed of seeing all my life. I stood in the parking lot of the MGM looking at the marquee thinking, *Bluestein. It just doesn't look like it belongs up there.* It gets worse. I'm on stage telling jokes, the audience is laughing, and while they're laughing I'm thinking, *I don't know what I'm doing. If they find out I'll be run out of town.*

The whole time I'm in Vegas I'm feeling "not enough". There are people on death row with higher self-esteem. One night after the show I was standing in line waiting to grab a bite at the coffee shop when the head waitress saw me, pulled me out of line, and put me in a private booth with like two hundred people waiting to be seated.

I'm sitting in my booth, which is at the very back of the restaurant, and everyone is turning around looking in my direction. I'm waiting for food and they're looking; I'm waiting, they're looking. Sweat starts to roll down my face. I become self-conscious. I can't sit, I can't eat, and I can't pick my nose. I think everyone hates me because I got a booth and they all had to wait. The food is taking forever. The crowd is looking and turning and looking and pointing. I can't stand it another minute. The food finally comes and I say, "I can't eat." I stand up and realize I have been sitting under the Kino Board. They weren't looking at me; they were looking at their effing numbers. Duh! No paranoia in my family, huh?

Another time I was sitting at the counter at the Dessert Inn Coffee Shop. A woman sits down next to me. I look at her hand and she's wearing the biggest diamond I have ever seen. I say aloud, without thinking, "I've never seen a ring that seats eight." I look up, and it's Bobbie Gentry. She laughs, "Yes, it is rather large," and she tucks her fingers into a fist so the ring cannot be seen.

We chat, she knows I'm working on the strip with Barry Manilow and when we got back to LA, Bobbie and I saw a lot of each other. We were friends, nothing more. I enjoyed her company and she liked to laugh. I can't tell you what the occasion was but Bobbie called and asked if I wanted to go to some social function at Chasen's. As I remember it, it was a movie opening. I said yes and we went in the limo provided for her.

We got to Chasen's and cameras clicked. We're inside and seated at a round table right in the middle of the room. The two seats next to me are vacant. I'm talking to Bobbie and feel a tap on my shoulder. I look up and Sammy Davis, Jr. and his wife are standing there, "Are these seats taken, man?" I almost shit my pants. Sammy Davis, Jr. is about to sit next to me. He says, "I'm Sammy Davis, Jr." like I didn't know who he was and extends his hand.

"I'm Steve Bluestein."

"The comedian?"

I turn to Bobbie, "He knows me."

Bobbie is laughing. I'm like a country bumpkin in the big city for the first time. Yee-haw!

I'm sitting at a table between Sammy Davis, Jr. and Bobbie Gentry and all the time I'm thinking, *what did I do to deserve to get here?* The evening was not long enough for me. Sammy was as warm in person as he was on stage. He loved to laugh. He laughed with his feet. When I would make a joke, his feet would go up and down in a machine gun motion. I can honestly say if I dropped dead at that moment I would have lived enough.

One or two months after Chasen's I get a phone call from a reporter, "Is it true that Bobbie Gentry is getting back with Jim Stafford?"

"Huh? Who is this?"

He's from some rag magazine. I hang up. Why in God's name is he calling me? Then, my phone started ringing, "Steve you're in the *Enquirer* with Bobbie Gentry." I run out to the newsstand. Sure enough, there is a picture of Bobbie and me with the caption something like "Bobbie Gentry recently split from Jim Stafford arrived at Chasen's with comedian Steve Blaustein, who she's dating." (Please note: Blaustein) Dating? Wrong name, wrong information, just friends. I call Bobbie, "If you expect me to buy you a ring like the one you have on, I'll have to sell my stamp collection."

I don't gamble. When I work in Vegas the casino is just the place to walk through when going to the dressing room, but this night I was so bored I was sitting at the Roulette Table just killing time. I had ten dollars that was itching to be lost. I only play red and black. If you win, it doubles. I win a few, I lose a few and I'm up like ten bucks. I have a stack of chips eight inches high in front of me and, quite frankly, I was bored to tears.

A friend sees me sitting at the table and asks if I wanted to get a bite to eat. Anything that would get me out of the hotel after the show is a Godsend. I jump at the opportunity. Without thinking I take the entire pile of chips and just push them out on to the table... you know, like Lucy did in Monaco. I'll be God damned if the number doesn't hit. The guy pushes back a pile of chips that looked like the Enchanted Castle at Disneyland, and in thirty years that is the only time I've ever won. Except when Gallagher and I were stoned out of our minds walking through the Casino and I was using ESP to determine which slot machines were going to pay. No, I wasn't fucked up in those days.... Not... at... all.

There are more stories; stories that I just can't get myself to share. Why? They are too disgusting for me to think about. Those Vegas years were my most destructive and yet my most successful. I still don't think "Bluestein" looks right on a marquee.

Oh, by the way, the next time you read in the *Star* that Cher is dating her exterminator or that Ethel Merman is haunting the gift shop at Cedars... get a life, will ya?

Streisand

MY DEAR COUSIN has been in ill health for years. She's had all kinds of problems that no person should ever have to deal with in their life, but she's been quite brave about it and she's a trooper so we all rally around her. One of her illnesses was quite serious; melanoma. I've got to tell you I made quite a few deals with God on that one.

She calls me from Boston one night about twelve years ago, "Steve, Streisand is going to do a concert in Los Angeles, (cough). I have always wanted to see her (cough). And I was wondering (cough) if you could (cough) get me tickets (cough) so I could see Streisand. I don't know how much longer I have (Cough, cough, cough)." Well my heart broke and my determination focused. I knew people who knew people who were the luckiest people in the business so I made it my job to get us tickets to see Streisand.

I started with Richard Gordon, my publicist and friend of twenty years. Richard has one of the largest Streisand collections in country, knows Barbra, and knew her mother. He's been to every concert Streisand has ever done. I call him.

"Ritchie can you get me comps to see Streisand."

"No."

"What do you mean no? You have more connections than AT&T."

"I mean there are no comps to be had. Barbra won't allow it."

I call my agent. He's a good agent, however, not too sharp. He got excited because he just got call waiting. He didn't even know there was a concert but he asks me if I could get *him* tickets. Now I know why I have no work. I called every person I could think of to get comps. No one had them nor did they know where I could get them. I called Make a Wish

Foundation. My cousin is too old for a wish. I called the American Cancer Society, "We fight Cancer not make reservations." I called foundations and fan clubs and friends of friends. Nothing. Not a single ticket to be had.

It appeared I was going to have to buy two tickets. Now, when you are in show business, you don't buy tickets. It's like paying your mother to cook dinner or paying your sister to have sex with you. It's just not done. You just don't buy tickets, you get tickets, you're given tickets, you go with friends who are given tickets. You have friends who have friends who have friends who are given tickets; they can't go and they give you tickets. It's just how it is. After ten days of using every contact in my address book, Streisand has forced me to buy two tickets. She's brought me to my knees; she's made me a civilian.

I call Ticket Master, "Are there any tickets left for the Streisand Concert?"

"Yes"

"Okay, I need two, up front. Any available?"

"Yes, we can do two, row six, center. What night?"

"Opening."

"Okay, that's two tickets for Barbra Streisand, sixth row, center. Opening night."

"Yes"

"Anything else?"

"No, that'll do it."

"How would you like to pay for these?"

"With YOUR Visa."

Long laugh as I give her my card number. She repeats the number back. I verify and she says, "Okay, we're all set. I'll be charging your card $1,875 plus tax and handling."

Both my balls hit the floor, "No, no, you don't understand. I don't want Streisand to come to my house to sing, we'll go down there to see *her*."

I make her verify the price again as I pick up one ball. I cancel the tickets. The next time I pay someone two grand to sing, it will be at the pearly gates and they'll have wings.

Now I have to figure out what lie I'm going to tell my cousin. Streisand was sold out? She cancelled the show? There was a fire at the arena. I know! "Sheila, you're gonna die without seeing Streisand." I told her how much the tickets were and with the plane fare out from Boston it would have been a three-thousand-dollar concert. Sheila says, "Besides, the DVD will be $14." Surprise, Sheila, the DVD was eighteen.

I am happy to tell you twelve years later Sheila is still with us; she battles her daily demons but she's is on the road to recovery. We love her and support her and keep her in our thoughts, but I'll be damned if I'm going to spend $1,875 to see Streisand sing.

Jan

I WAS PLANNING TO GO on the road with Fred Willard and The Ace Trucking Company, but my wife was eight-and-a-half months pregnant with our first child. I didn't want to leave her, but we needed the money. Her parents were coming out on Monday to be with her while I was on the road. I would leave the next morning. We picked up my in-laws at the airport; they were pleasant, small-town folks who thought of themselves as Cosmopolitan. They were Cosmopolitan like I'm African.

We were renting a town house at the time and three minutes after we walk into the unit, my wife says, "My water is breaking," and runs to the bathroom. Her parents are here twenty-five minutes and her water breaks. *Strange,* I think. Her mother was a smoker, as was my wife, and they both began puffing away like a steam wheeler going down the rapids. It must have been ten minutes later when the first contraction came. I got on the phone and called the hospital, "We're coming in." I called our friend Sonny who had just had a baby one month prior, "I'll be right over." We all sat around waiting for the contractions to come every five minutes.

It wasn't twenty minutes when Sonny showed up. She was all excited and was telling Candy what to expect. Just like a scripted movie, it followed the same course as Sonny's delivery. The contractions were coming more frequently and were more severe. Candy and I had done natural childbirth class. I was her birth coach.

"Breathe, honey."

"You breathe. I want drugs."

It was time to get to the hospital. Candy and I were in the front seat, Sam and Sybil in the back seat, and Sonny was way in the back, where the groceries go. Sam, Sybil, Steve, Candy, Sonny. If anyone had a lisp we would have been drenched. Sonny was like a Magpie she was talking so much. I can't remember a word she said with the exception of, "This is the longest day of the year." I thought she was referring to the amount of effort it took to have a child, a long day's work. Later I would learn that, in fact, it was the summer solstice and the longest day of the year. I thought it was fitting that my child had been given more time to enter the world than anyone else.

We get the hospital and the contractions are like three minutes apart. They rush us up to the delivery room where Candy is put into stirrups and prepped for the birth. The nurse points and says, "See that? That's your baby's head." In a classic neurotic father's reaction, I look at the one-half inch of visible baby skull I can see and say, "Does it look normal?"

Within three hours it was all over. I had a five-pound-four-ounce baby boy. He was early and small, a factor later determined by his mother's two-pack-a-day cigarette habit. They handed him to me wrapped in a white blanket and Candy picked her head up off the delivery table to ask, "Who does he look like?"

I remember thinking, *what a strange thing to ask*, but I answered, "He looks exactly like you," and he did. He had her pouty lips and narrow nose but the question seemed so out of place. Not "Is he normal?" or "Does he have all his toes?" But, "Who does he look like?"

They took the baby from me and cleaned him up. I ran to the phone to call relatives back east, "It's a boy!" Everyone was over the moon with happiness. I was walking around like I was in a dream. I had a son. Jan. I wanted to name him Zack Michael but the nurse said, "Zack. You can't name a child Zack." She said, "Jan is a great name." I had a friend in college Jan Seeburg and so Jan it was.

Before I left for the road, I stood at the nursery window looking at my son. The picture of him in the crib is burnt into my memory forever. I can even see the baby next to him. "Cabeza" was the name. I remember seeing my son and thinking, *I'm a father; me, worthless, unimportant me. I'm actually a father.* Liz Torres shows up and we laugh over the Cabeza baby. Cabeza means "head" in Spanish and all that baby had was a huge head and a mustache. But my baby was beautiful; a perfect specimen, the finest child ever born. My son, Jan. I remember making him a promise, standing there at the nursery window, "I will be there for you. I will be the father I never had. I will love you. You will never be alone."

One year and two months later I learned I was not his father; that my wife had been having an affair; that my best friend had been sleeping with my wife. My world didn't shatter it exploded in a nightmare of torture. My sanity was put on permanent hold. My drug and alcohol use escalated. What ensued was a bitter divorce battle that cost me everything financially and emotionally. My attorney was Howard Weitzman of O.J. fame, "No court is going to make you pay child support for a child you are not the father of" (I had gone to College with Henry Winkler. Henry was married to Howard's ex-wife, Stacy). Howard did a magnificent job defending my position but California law was unbending thirty years ago and I was forced to pay child support for eighteen years. I did. I never missed a payment. Not one.

Each month I wrote that check it reminded me that I failed in the most important job of my life, fatherhood. I was a shell. In the next four years, I would become a raving alcoholic. So much so that a friend finally said, "I'm taking you to AA."

That friend said that twenty-five years ago. Jan's birthday was thirty years ago. My agent Gary's words were with me, "Time heals all wounds." I remember thinking, *I don't want to hear that bullshit.* Thirty years later I'm here to tell you, as in everything, Gary was right.

Frankie Avalon

WHEN YOU'RE A NEW COMEDIAN, and I was once upon a time, there are two things you need: material and stage time. To get these you drive anywhere and stand on anything that resembles a stage. I did that one night about thirty years ago. I was breaking in new material, which for me is the hardest thing I have to do. I don't know if what I've written is funny and I don't know where the laughs are. It's like walking in a field of land mines. Torture.

I found the most out-of-the-way place I could find to break in new material. It was a place on Lankershim, way out in the San Fernando Valley. It's to the Sunset Strip what Fargo is to Paris. No one goes there but locals. It was perfect. I could break in new material and if it bombed, who'd find out? Maybe a farmer.

I get to the club and there are only about twenty people in the audience. Actually, this is even better for my purpose. Just standing on a stage and saying the words gives me some idea where the laughs are and with a small crowd my fears of judgment are reduced. The show begins and I watch as comic after comic goes into the toilet. The audience just was not responding to anyone. It's my turn. The laughs are thin, very thin, but I don't care because I'm only there to break in new stuff. About halfway through my set a couple is seated center audience. I can't see their faces but I see their silhouettes. I abandon my act and start drilling these people for coming in late. "Man, what kind of a shit life do you have to come late to this dump? Lady, if this is a first date run for your life." The audience is laughing. It was on this night I started to develop my improvisational style of talking to the audience between fixed pieces.

The couple loved it. At one point, I cover my eyes like an Indian scout to see who these latecomers are, and I say, "Holy shit. It's Frankie Avalon. Who are you sitting with, the head of NBC and William Morris? That would be my luck, I'm bombing in the valley and these assholes come to see my show." The audience goes wild. They are laughing and screaming. I go on my tirade, "I can't believe this. There isn't even a beach within fifty miles and Frankie Avalon shows up?" Frankie is screaming louder than anyone.

The show ends and I don't do so badly. I'm exiting the stage Frankie reaches out and pulls me closer to him, "Really enjoyed you." I thank him and run for my life. Why? I am embarrassed and I think I've bombed. Who judges me badly? Me.

About two years later I'm working at The Show Biz, owned by Murray Langston, the unknown comic. It was more of a show biz hangout than a real club. Frankie Avalon comes in with his wife, turns out Frankie was a friend of Murray's. He sees me and comes right to me, "Man, you are so funny. We told everyone about you. How you took a dead audience and brought them to life." Huh? Me?

I do my set and it's really strong. Frankie congratulates me. He can't get over how I've grown and how much funnier I am. Two months later my agent gets a call, would I open for Frankie Avalon at the Blue Max in Chicago. With great honor, I accept the gig.

The Blue Max was in the Hyatt Hotel at the Chicago Airport. It was a wonderful hotel for travelers, a nightmare for entertainers. Why? It was so far out of Chicago you could do nothing. There was no transportation, no movies, no shops, nothing. You were stuck in no-man's land but the club was wonderful. It was a little Vegas show room a la the hay-day of Vegas. It was run by guys in Tuxedos and was extremely professional.

The day I arrive I run into Frankie in the lobby. I shake his hand, "You know this is surreal for me. You see me bomb and now I'm opening for you." Frankie could not have been nicer. He tells the story to whomever was standing with him and tells them, "I knew this kid was gonna be someone."

We open that night to a packed house and rave reviews. Frankie is happy, as am I. Because we were stranded at this hotel, Frankie and I hung out a lot. I learned he was just a normal guy with a great sense of humor and a very small ego. Let me tell you a story I witnessed with my own eyes. Frankie was being interviewed by one of the Chicago papers. They sent a limo for him and he asked me to come. Now you have to understand, this is not done. The headliner does not take the opening act along on *his* interview. This is *his* time to shine, not the opener, but that's how Frankie is, a very giving man.

We're standing in the restaurant lobby waiting to be seated and a woman rushes in from the street. She takes her coat off and hands it to Frankie, "I'm late for my reservation. Henderson party of three," and she stands there. Frankie smiles and says, "Let me see what I can do," and goes to the hostess. The woman gets seated. Where do you find people like that in show business? You just don't.

On the same gig Frankie asks me if I wanted to go to a wedding with him. A wedding?

"Yeah, the boys invited me to a wedding."

"What boys?"

"The Chicago boys."

He had been invited to a Mafia wedding in Chicago and that is an invitation you don't refuse. Two guys pick us up. Guys? Gorillas. They must have been eight feet tall, and yet they had a gentle side. They were the Sopranos. We're in the back seat and the goons are up front. Frankie is chatting with them. I'm being very quiet. Frankie is joking and says, "You ever whack anybody?" My face must have blanched because Frankie kicks me. The guys up front look at Frankie in the rear-view mirror. We never got an answer but I knew it was "yes". After writing this I will be found in the witness protection program.

We get to the wedding and it was like nothing I have ever seen. The people were wonderful. I danced with an elderly lady who swore I was a *"pisone"* despite the fact I told her my last name repeatedly. The images of this wedding stayed with me for years and then I saw *The Godfather*. I said, "Holy shit. I was at that wedding." The movie had recreated the scene to a "T". It was then I recognized the genius that is Coppola.

The gig ends and Frankie remains my friend. I'm out to his house a couple of times. I get to know his wife, Kay. It's truly a great experience. There are moments when I have to pinch myself. I'm sitting in Frankie Avalon's house. Again, he was just a guy who happens to sing and be in movies. He's not an egomaniac, he's just Frankie.

I guess it had to be sometime later when Frankie invited me to his country club. It was an exclusive club in Burbank in the shadow of Warner Brothers, and I think it was the Fourth of July. It was Frankie, Kay, and I. The club was magnificent and Frankie was taking me around introducing me to people. We were standing by the pool when a guy comes up to

Frankie, "Hey, Frank, how the hell are ya?" Frankie greets the guy and we stand there a beat. Then, out of nowhere, the guy says, "Ya know why I love this club? No [N-word], No Jews." Frank whips around to me. I do not know what to do. I have never faced this kind of bigotry head on. I just smile. I can tell Frankie wants to die as he shuffles me away from the guy. "Asshole," is all he said.

As with all my celebrity friends, our friendship dwindled. I don't think I ever saw him again after that day. I never blamed him for the country club incident nor did I ever mention it. We just drifted apart as people who work together do. Frank's musical conductor stayed in contact with me for about fifteen years until one day no Christmas Card. That's just how it goes. Life, not show biz. People come into your life for a bit and then pass through. It used to upset me, now, as I grow older, I understand it.

Oh! Just in case you think I only think nice things about people. I did know some prick headliners, real assholes. They were dyed-in-the-wool bastards with an ego the size of a Humvee. Those stories, along with the one about who's hung like a moose, I just don't feel comfortable telling. Those people sue.

Albert Hammond

I HAD AN APARTMENT in Hollywood with a central pool and communal living. That first apartment was the foundation for so much of my life in California. For instance, the day I'm moving into my new place, my neighbor Michelle pops over. She's blonde, perky, and beautiful. She had this airhead quality that instantly endeared you to her, yet she was no dope. This building wasn't like New York where no one spoke to you; in this place everyone just came in, introduced themselves, and plopped down on your sofa. On move-in day Michelle plops herself down on my sofa and wants to know all about me. We're talking and I ask her if she's going to lie out by the pool. She says, "No, this is my year for no sun." She explains that she only sits in the sun every other year. For some reason, I think this is the most brilliant idea I have ever heard and immediately take this as gospel in my life. By the way, not a line in my face, thank you very much, Michelle.

This apartment building was filled with all kinds of characters. When I first moved in, there were no comedians there, not one, but there were show business people. After all, it was Hollywood. Dave Madden of the Partridge family had the unit right over the pool. Len Wayland, the actor, was right below me to the right; Sandy Shire was directly below me. Sandy was David Shire's brother who was married to Talia Shire from Rocky. There were two songwriters from England, Mike Hazelwood and Albert Hammond. They had been brought over by an American producer because they were hot songwriters at the time.

We were a tight little family, this insane building group. I'm forever grateful to them for getting me into show business. Here's how it happened. Gail Lerher, a top fashion model, was living there as well. Gail was fun and perky and Israeli. There was no nonsense with her; she told it like it is. At the time, I was working at the May Company and hated it. Gail said, "Here's what you do. You get yourself fired and collect unemployment. Then you'll have your days free to break into the business." I was appalled. Can you imagine doing such a thing? How horrible. I would never collect unemployment. *Never*. Gail was on me to get my nose fixed too. She was insane! I'd never get my nose fixed.

In the beginning, I was very shy. Still am to an extent, I just hide it well. There was a lot of pot smoking going on in those days and put a joint in me and I'm hysterical. We were sitting around the pool one day and I'm making everyone laugh. Dave Madden says to me, "Steve, you're funny. There is no doubt about it. You could be a comedian. There's a new place that just opened up on The Strip called The Comedy Store. You should go in there and try stand-up." I thought he was insane, however, Albert Hammond is sitting there as well and agrees with him. This starts me thinking, but I soon put those thoughts out of my head. How could I leave a good job at a department store?

Sometime later I'm in Albert's apartment. He's pushing the idea of me becoming a comedian. I say to him, "But what if I don't make it?" Even back then I had these fears of not being enough and of being judged and failing. This shit never leaves you; you just learn how to deal with it. Albert says, "Steve, you can make a living in show business… if you only try." He tells me he'll go to The Comedy Store with me the next night. The next night, he does. I watch the comedians on stage and think to myself, *I could do that*. The seed has been planted. However, I am not leaving my job at the May Company. No way.

God has a strange way of making things happen. Must have been two weeks after my first trip to The Comedy Store when I'm called up to personnel. I was flat out fired. Why? My boss felt my heart wasn't in the job and she needed someone with more fire. I had now been fired twice in four years, once from United Artists (office job), and now The May Company (office job). It was like God was saying, "This ain't for you." Gail's words came back to haunt me, "Collect unemployment so you can break into the business." This option was starting to look very good.

I got back home that day and everyone was around the pool; Gail, Michael, Albert, Len, Michelle, everyone. I announce to the group that I had been fired and a huge round of applause came up. They threw an instant party. Albert says, "Now you can do what you were meant to do." Dave is pushing me to go back to The Comedy Store and Gail is making plans to bring me to unemployment. My head is spinning.

I made the transition very easily. I guess I had always wanted to do comedy but never had the nerve to try. My mother was, shall we say, less than supportive and remained that way thirty years later. In any case, all the ducks were in a row. I got the unemployment, I got into a class and I started hanging out at The Comedy Store. The very first time I got on stage I got laughs. When I got off stage Sammy Shore, the club owner, came up to me, "You come back, kid. You've got the sound." I didn't know what he meant but I do now. There is a sound a performer has, an ease on stage, a naturalness that makes them set apart from an accountant who stands on the stage, and I had it. Those few words of encouragement were all I needed. If Sammy hadn't said them to me I would have walked out of the club and probably gotten another job in retailing.

Now here's where it gets good. A couple of months go by and I'm doing my best to break in to the business. It was January and we have horrible rains in January in California. Horrible. I'm sitting in Albert's apartment and he's looking at the rain telling me it reminds him of the weather in England. I say, "It never rains in California but when it does, it pours." The next day Albert plays me "It Never Rains in California". He had just gotten a record deal and was recording his new album and decided to include that song in his first American release. He asked me if I wanted to go to the recording session, and I did.

I'm sitting in a chair at the studio and Albert is in the booth. He's singing the words to "It Never Rains in California" and when it comes to the part where he sings, "Don't tell the folks back home I never made it." He points to me. He was singing about my fears of failure. I was over the moon. Can you imagine what I felt like when it became a hit? Soon after, Albert and Michael moved out. I saw Albert once, ten years later and we talked about the building and my being a comedian and naturally, the song. That was the last time I saw him. I never saw Mike again.

After thirty-eight years Albert and I have been reunited. Michael has passed away. Albert had gone on to be a huge recording star and was entered into the songwriter's Hall of Fame; he's also earned an Emmy. When I told him the "Never Rains" story he said, "Steve, it couldn't have happened that way. I wrote that song in London," but it's how I remember it and I'm sticking to my version.

The building would change tenants several times. Since I was now entrenched at the Comedy Store as a regular and a member of the Comedy Store Players, comedians were hanging out in my apartment. Soon, comedians were taking apartments as they became available: Freddie Prinze; Liz

Torres; Johnny Dark; and The Burksys: Helen, Herman, and Allan. Allan was the youngest comedian to ever do the Tonight Show at that time. His mother was like the mother of all comedians and could tell you who was on the road, what joke was written by what comedian, who was making what deal and how much they were getting. More importantly, the Burskys were the hub of comedy at that time. The Burskys' home was the hang out. Herman passed away about ten years ago, Allan is now an agent but does stand-up sometimes, and Helen, Helen is exactly the same. I spoke to her yesterday and my love for her is as great today as it was thirty years ago.

The other tenants all passed through my life like I've learned people do. I ran into Gail about fifteen years ago in the lobby of my plastic surgeon's office on the day I was having my nose fixed. She was laughing hysterically because I always swore I would not have it done and there I was, "Going Hollywood." Michelle got married and moved to Pasadena. Maybe twelve years later I learned that her kids were going to school with my best friend's kids, the Churukians, and I reconnected with Michelle. Michelle turned into a wonderful mother. They left California for Vermont and that is where they live today.

Man, I haven't thought about those people in years. Now I'll be depressed all day. I hate the memories. I hate change. I want it to always be as it was, but as I'm reminded time and time again, that's just not how life is. All I want to ask is, *why?*

Post Script

On the day I got fired from the May Company, I sat in my office totally crushed. My assistant came in; let's call him Hal. Hal wanted to know what I was going to do and I declared to him that I was going to be a comedian. I said, "If I don't try I'll spend the rest of my life wondering if I could have made it." It was my declaration of independence. He wished me well and told me he would look for me in Vegas.

Flash cut twenty-five years later. I had been fighting with the idea of getting off the road and doing what had become my love, writing. I had done the stand-up thing for years and was making quite a bit of money but it wasn't creatively fulfilling to me. I had been booked for six months of gigs and I told my agents not to book me anymore. I was done with the road. They were not happy. I was not happy either. I wasn't sure I was doing the right thing. I kept looking for a sign of divine guidance.

My very last official gig was in Hawaii at the Hawaiian Comedy Club on Oahu. When I arrived, the owner of the club asked me if I would like to do a private gig, $1000 for one show. One show! I never do private gigs. I hate them, but a grand for one show, how could I turn it down? The show was the Christmas Party for a local department store.

The night of my Department Store gig I'm sitting in the room they had provided me and a woman approaches.

"Steve, our store manager would like to say hello. Can I bring him in?"

"Sure."

She opens the door and standing there is Hal, my assistant from the May Company. There was my divine guidance. I absolutely freaked out. My career had come full circle. "Did you know this is my last show? Did you? You were there in the beginning and now you're there in the end," I blabber on. "Wow," was all he could say and he tells me he's followed my career and how he tells everyone about that day in the office when I declared I was going to be a comedian.

I didn't do stand-up again for about five years. I don't do it very often any more. Writing, that is my love. To sit alone in my office and create words that inspire and make readers laugh. That's what I love.

The Old Man In the Mountain

I THINK IT WAS RIGHT AFTER my parents' divorce when my father wanted to take me on a trip through New England. We were going to see the White Mountains and stay in a motel and see the Old Man of the Mountain. What's the Old Man of the Mountain? It was a famous rock formation, which created a profile that looked like an old man. It was famous in New England, like a personality, and everyone either talked about it or went to see. I was finally going to see it.

However, like everything with my parents, nothing came easily. Mom didn't want me to go. There were rules and times and distance restrictions. She would drill me on what it was going to be like, "You'll be alone a car with him for hours. Do you want that??" I had witnessed horrible acts of violence by that man. He was a monster, or maybe I should say he was driven to be a monster. As an adult, I know the frustration that is my mother, but as a child, being around him made me uncomfortable. I loved him and yet I kept him an arm's length away, not allowing him to get too close to me. I was simply too afraid.

They finally came to some kind of agreement. Most kids just went out with their fathers, with me it took a NATO Treaty. My father would be picking me up at 9 a.m. At 8:45 I was on the porch waiting for him to come. "Come inside," my mother would scream, "I don't want him to see you waiting for him." This was a ritual that went on every time my father would come to get me. I would be on the porch and she would scream at me for anticipating his visit. She hated him so much she wouldn't even give him that, and as always, I suffered the consequences of her wrath. I was not allowed to express to my father the little love that was left in me.

He did finally arrive and we were on our way but not before she had her dramatic good-bye scene. It's always about her. Always.

We got on the road and the interrogation began, "Is she seeing anyone? How much money is she making? Does your grandmother give her money?" My parents were to child psychology what dynamite is to glass. They fought their divorce through me.

"Tell your mother I want..."

"Tell your father he needs to...."

It went on for years until a shrink finally told me, "Tell them to fight their own battles and leave you out of it," and I did. On this day, the interrogation was going long and hard. I was nine. I remember wanting to crawl out the window to escape with my life, but it didn't end there. When the interrogation was over it was followed by the tirade, "Do you know what your mother did to me?" This went on for hours. He complained to me about her and her family like I could do something about it. It was, for a child, an absolute nightmare. I had no rest. I came home and she was downing him. I went out with him and he was downing her. If you think about it, maybe that's why I have no self-esteem. If I came from such bad parents then how could I be of any worth?

We stopped along the way to eat. My father was addicted to food, to the smells, the textures, and the colors. To me it was a way to fill my stomach; to him it was an experience. I made it through the first day, and when he quieted down with his tirades and inquisitions, the trip was quite wonderful. The hills of New Hampshire were green with maple trees and pines. The air was fresher than in the city and certainly better for me. I saw deer. I saw cows. I saw things I only had heard about. We'd stop at a roadside stand to buy fruit or pulled off the road so I could swim in a lake. This was, after all, my very first road trip and he wanted me to see it all.

On day two we were heading to see the Old Man of the Mountain. My dad was talking about I don't know what, and I was gazing out the window as trees and rock formations whizzed by. At one point, I saw a grey Pontiac pulled off to the side of the road. A man had his hand on his front bumper. He was bent over and was retching out a steady stream of white liquid. We must have been doing 60 MPH at this point and the scene passed in an instant. A little bit later I said, "Did you see the guy throwing up by the side of the road?" My father immediately looked in his rear-view mirror. "No, I didn't see anyone." He was slowing the car down to make a U-turn as he talked. Soon we were heading back in the direction we had just come from. I pointed out the car to him. The man was still there. My father pulled up next to them.

"My son says someone is sick here."

"Yeah, got a little car sick."

My father turns off the motor and opens our trunk, "Here. Try this." He hands him a bottle of soda water, "This will settle your stomach." The man takes the soda, shakes his hand and my father was back in the car in two minutes.

I never gave that incident another thought, but years later, in therapy, it came up. The shrink said, "Do you realize the kind of kindness that took? The kind of empathy your father must have had? He could have continued on his journey with his son but he chose to go back. Steve, he couldn't have been the monster you remember. And if he was a monster, what made him one?" It started me thinking; maybe the shrink was right. Maybe my father wasn't so bad, and if he wasn't so bad maybe I wasn't so bad.

Here's the twist in this story. Later that day we made it to the Old Man of the Mountain. I remember standing at the observation point and looking at that profile, so strong, so mighty. It was a good day, a day in which there had been no fighting, no drilling, no idle mother-bashing. We were just a father and son out on the road. Later we went to a ski lift and I got to ride up the side of the mountain with him. Our feet dangled from the lift seats; his arms were tightly around me. From the top of that mountain I saw vistas I have never seen before: hills and valleys, peaks and magnificent cloud formations. We could see for miles. I was only a child and danger wasn't an option; I started to run down the side of the mountain on my own. He reached over and scooped me up! "No," is all he said. He was laughing at my absence of fear but at last I felt protected.

The next day we were headed to Maine to see the coast with its famous lighthouses. We stopped at a motel. I can see that room like it was yesterday with its knotty pine walls and single bed and red bedspread. The room was dark and dank and had lampshades that gave it an amber glow. It was right out of a Stephen King novel. I think being alone with him in that single room triggered some childhood fear. The fear mushroomed into a full-blown illness and soon I was so sick I couldn't move. He just stood over me not knowing what to do. I wasn't faking; I had a migraine. I threw up. He just stood there, frozen. He was not good at childhood emergencies.

Early the next morning I wanted to go home and he was so scared that he had done something to make me sick he agreed. We ended our trip without seeing Maine. My mother wasn't home when we returned. We learned she was playing cards with her friends Edie and Emmy at The Pines, a small town by the sea. They were in the back yard around a card table as I walked in. My mother was surprised and began to cry.

"Why are you crying?"

"I'm glad to see you."

I shrugged my shoulders and wondered why she was acting this way. You see, in private she screamed at me and told me what a piece of shit I was, but in public she showed these buckets of tears. How could I believe her? How could I believe anything she said to or about me? She ran hot and cold like a faucet.

The memory of my father's kindness to that stranger remained with me for years. When I was looking for a shred of evidence that would make him a viable human being, I kept going back to the side of the road and him handing a stranger our last soda. It was a memory of an act of kindness that changed my life. He wasn't a monster. And if he wasn't a monster then I wasn't the son of a monster. I was the son of a kind man and if I was just like my father, as my mother would scream at me daily, then maybe, just maybe, being like him wasn't a bad thing.

Post Script

After hundreds of years the rock formation that formed the Old Man of the Mountain gave way and the profile was obliterated forever. For me it was like a death in the family. This formation was so much a part of my history, so much a part of my childhood, and now it was gone. The lesson of "life equals change" is being taught to me daily. I'm really glad my father took me on that trip, I would have never seen that profile nor would I have had my other happy memory.

Jenny Jones

I'M BOOKED AT SPELLBINDERS in Houston. This is a club I've worked quite a few times. It's well-run and I like the owner, Lynn, a lot. My agent calls with the airline stuff and I ask him who is my opening act. "Some blonde," is all he could come up with. I know I'm working with either Marilyn Monroe or Lassie.

The "comedy condo" is usually a shit hole. In Houston, it's a little nicer; it has glass in the windows. The driver picks me up at the airport and dumps me at the condo. Literally dumps me, doesn't come in, doesn't say goodbye, just leaves me on the curb with the keys. I let myself in and that is where I meet my opening act, Jenny Jones. She's lying on the sofa and says as I walk in, "I can't get up, I've pulled out my back." For the entire week we are together, she's bent like a pretzel.

I unpack and go out to meet "the blonde," who I did not know and who had never been in TV at this point. I'm a horrible person when it comes to meeting new people. I like or dislike you in exactly three minutes. I liked Jenny in exactly two seconds. She's just a warm, sincere, sweet, quiet person. She had worked in Vegas as a showgirl or a magician's assistant, I just can't remember. What I do remember is someone who was a real person, who didn't have the comedian's ego, and who was fun to be with. To her, each comedy job was an adventure. By this time, I was so tired of working these clubs that any freshness was viewed, by me, as insanity. I couldn't take away her winning personality, it just bubbled out of her.

Jenny was eating dried papaya on the day we met. I had never seen it before. She had it in the fridge and offered me some. It's like someone introduced me to heroin, a snack food that's sweet like candy but without the raw sugar. I went insane for it. Years later it's still my favorite snack treat, thanks to Jenny.

Jenny and I get dressed to do the show. The club gives us a car. Car, ha! It's a wreck with wheels. I think the Clampettes drove under the credits of The Beverly Hillbillies. Understand the club is not being nice, they give the comedians a car so they don't have to pick us up every night. To club owners, comedians are sort of less important than the beer they sell.

This night I'm driving and we find our way to the club. We do the shows. I don't watch Jenny, I never watch the act in front of me but I can tell from the audience's mood when I get on stage she had done well. I do my show, we hang out at the club for about an hour, and Jenny and I get into the car to go back to the condo and her dried papaya. Now, for this booking, the Condo is new and we had never stayed in it before. I get behind the wheel and start driving from memory only I'm driving to the old condo.

Jenny says, "Where are you going?"

"To the condo."

"It's not in this direction."

She was right. I was headed in the wrong direction. I turn the car around and say, "What's the address of the new condo?"

"I don't know."

"What do you mean you don't know?"

"I don't know. They dropped me off and left me there."

Okay, no problem, we'll go back to the club and they'll give us the address. We get to the club. It's closed. This was before cell phones, there was no way to call from the car. We find a pay phone; I call my agent; he's not home. I call the office; I get the service. I call the travel agent; no answer. It's two in the morning and we are in a strange city with no way to find out where we're staying.

Jenny is laughing. I'm in full panic mode, which means I'm furious. The madder I get the harder Jenny is laughing. There is no way to figure out where the condo is but to drive up and down the streets of Houston until we find it, and that is exactly what we did. In the middle of the night, pitch black, in a strange city. We saw a lot of Houston that night, a lot. We knew the general area the condo was in so we just drove up one street and down the next, up one street and down the next, up one street and down the next. Have you ever done that? When you're lost all the houses look the same. I felt like Hansel and Gretel. I would stop and run out and try the key here or a key there. No luck and no trail of bread crumbs. We're in a crappy car going ten miles an hour trying to get into a condo, any condo. I'm surprised the police didn't stop us.

After about two hours Jenny screams, "There it is!!!" She was right, the crappy little condo on the corner revealed itself. I ran up to it like a long-lost friend and hugged it. I ran inside, "Honey, I'm home." Jenny and I were exhausted but we both knew we had stories to tell on stage the next night. The rest of my week with Jenny was uneventful. The shows were great and I loved being in the condo with her because she remembered where it was. We had fun. Usually it's a living hell with the opening act but this week, it was a joy.

Years go by and Jenny and I bump into each other from time to time. Then, I read about her all-women nightclub show. No men allowed, and I think, "brilliant." You see, in this business it's all about marketing yourself and she found a niche. I never felt there was anything to market in myself. In reality, I just sort of trod along making a living and never felt I deserved more success than what I had at that moment.

When Jenny got her TV show I felt it was a natural extension of the work she had done in the clubs. It's always good to see one of the nice ones cross over into the big time. It's when the jerks make it that you want to slit your wrists. I never watched Jenny's show. It wasn't what I watch, but I knew she was doing well, and then a guest on her show killed another guest. My heart broke for the stupidity of the act but more so for Jenny. I knew they were going to throw her to the wolves.

When a show is produced, many times, the star gets the script at the very last minute. In a show like Jenny's there are so many levels, so many hands the guests have to go through that it's understandable that Jenny would not know what was going on at the bottom of the ladder. She was at the top. While some of you may say, "She should have known," I say, unless you've seen first-hand how one of those money machine shows works, you just don't understand. It's ratings above everything and the lower echelon in these situations are cutthroat. Why? They are pushing their way up the ladder and trying to impress whomever. When I saw Jenny on the witness stand I knew she was telling the truth. I had spent a week with her and I knew the woman. 'Nuff said. It saddened me to know how hard she had worked only to be brought down by someone else's stupidity.

Years after her trial I was walking down the street in Beverly Hills. A man taps me on the shoulder, "Are you Steve Bluestein?"

I nod.

"Jenny Jones wants to say hello."

He points to a sidewalk café about twenty feet back. Jenny had been eating lunch, saw me walk by and sent this man to get me. She had a hat pulled down over her face and no make-up. It was easy to miss her. We laughed about Houston and I told her I was still addicted to dried papaya. We exchanged numbers and parted. Now, if she was a real jerk, she would have just let me pass without saying hello, but Jenny is not like that. She's a warm, funny, career-driven person who really got the shit end of the stick.

Crosby I

WHEN IN YOU LIVE IN MANHATTAN, the one joy you have in the summer is getting away from Manhattan—away from the hustle and bustle and humidity. I would do that as often as I could. One day we were driving out to the beach in my cousin Harvey's car. We were on the Cross Belt Parkway talking about who-knows-what when I noticed a dog running around in circles. He was a shaggy dog, hair in his eyes, black and white coat. He was filthy and matted and looked like a refugee from the pound, and he was definitely lost. I have been rescuing animals since I was a child and today was no different. I screamed at Harvey, "Stop the car!" I ran out onto the parkway and called "Here boy," and that dog ran to me like I had raised him from a puppy. He jumped in the car and looked at Harvey, "Floor it." We were off. The dog was all over me, licking my face and putting his head on my shoulder. It was like we were meant for each other.

There were no houses on that stretch of road. It was out in the middle of nowhere. There were no lampposts to stick up a sign, no local papers, and no way to find the actual owner. I took him home, to my one room apartment where the bathroom door won't shut if the toilet seat was down.

The first thing I did was give him a bath. Things jumped off that dog from the first century. I rubbed him down with one of my good towels and he licked my face until we were both dry. I had to give him a name since he did not have a collar. Let's see, I found him on Cross Bay Blvd. Cross Bay… Cross-by… Crosby. I'll call him Crosby, and he took to that name like he had been waiting for it.

I brushed him out and he looked like a show dog. He was a wonderful dog. I slept on the sofa in my flat. It was a sofa bed but I was too lazy to pull it out every night, so I slept on it closed. It was Naugahyde, and after years sleeping on it and exposing it to my body heat, the fabric turned shiny black and was as hard as a rock (just a little side note if you ever plan on sleeping on Naughahyde). I crawled into bed that night and that dog crawled right up next to me and put his head on my shoulder, and that's the way we slept till the very end of our time together.

The next day was Sunday and I wanted to show off my new dog, so I ran down to the supermarket picked up some dog food and a leash. I headed for Central Park, the "Sunday get-out-of-the-city place" and began my walk. I wasn't walking ten minutes when a woman came up to me.

"Is that a Puli?"

"A what?"

"A Puli, a Hungarian sheep dog."

"I don't know."

"I have one and yours is a beauty."

It turns out that I had rescued a Puli from Cross Bay Blvd. Who knew?

This dog and I were inseparable. He adored me, and I, him. We went everywhere together, and when I was at work, he would stay in the apartment and just wait for me to return. No problems, no chewing, no barking. He was the perfect apartment dog. Now about this time, my college friend Larry had been over and left me a hunk of hash. He wanted me to keep it so if he needed to smoke something it would be midtown and he wouldn't have to go all the way back to the Village. I'm telling you, it was the 60s and we did our fair share of drugs. Okay, so I take the hash and wrap it in tin foil. I take the wad and stick it in an empty mayo jar and screw the lid on tight. I placed it on my dresser.

The next day I'm off to work. It was a late night and I didn't get home until 9 p.m. I open the door and there is no Crosby. My heart sinks. I call for him. Nothing. Now, you have to remember, this is a one-room apartment, maybe twelve by twenty feet. It's not like he could go run up to the servant's quarters. I called and looked behind furniture, in the bathroom, then the kitchen. He was gone. I opened my closet door and all my clothes were gone. The entire closet was empty. Shit! I've been robbed and they took my dog. Then my eyes drop down and I see every piece of clothing I own in a huge pile on the closet floor, a mound two feet high. Under my winter coat a tail is wagging. I pull the coat back and Crosby is lying on his back with a shit-eating grin on his face. I yell, "What have you done?!" He pees himself.

At this point I notice the broken mayo jar on the floor and a piece of tin foil hanging off Crosby's mouth. The dog had jumped up on the dresser, knocked the jar off the counter, it shattered and he ate the hash. I was panicked stricken. I was sure he was going to die. I call Larry. I tell him what happened.

His response, "It's all gone???"

"For crap sakes Larry stop worrying about your drugs, my dog is going to die." He was there in ten minutes.

We are both looking at the dog lying on his back, laughing. The dog was laughing, not us; he was making sounds I had never heard him make before. We try to stand him up. He stands for a second and then falls over like a tree. Timber! Larry says we have to take him to the Vet. I am scared shitless, "No, how do we tell them he ate hash?? They'll arrest us." You have to remember I was such a nerd in those days. Larry was sure we would not get in trouble and picks up the dog. I'm screaming for him to wait, I need to call an attorney. Larry is out the door. I run after him and we're in a cab.

We go to an animal hospital on the east side. It's about midnight. Larry is doing all the talking. A doctor comes out; he must be about twenty-nine, long hair, jeans, and peace sign around his neck.

"Man, this is bitchin'".

"What's bitchin'? What?"

"I've never seen a dog so stoned. How'd you do that, blow smoke in his face?"

We tell him about the mayo bottle. He checks for shards in the dog's mouth and tells me, "Walk him home, by the time you get there he'll be fine. No charge," and he leaves the room. Larry is laughing and of course I'm feeling like the worst human being on the face of the earth. How could I let this happen to my dog, my buddy, my closest friend? The doctor was right; by the time we got home Crosby was himself and he was hungry.

Crosby and I were even closer after this episode. I think he had a doggie trip and saw life clearer. When I finally moved out of the City and drove to California it was with Crosby by my side. When I got my first apartment in Hollywood, Crosby was there. When I got my job at The May Co., Crosby waited for me when I got home. Until, one night when I got home and he was in bed and wouldn't get out. I tried to coax him with a bone but he was too sick to move. I ran to the vet this time. They found a mass in his intestine, cancer. I could not bring myself to put him to sleep and so I carried him home and put him in my bed. I kept him there for a couple of weeks and then one night he crawled up next to me and made the most mournful sound I have ever heard. I knew it was time to say goodbye. I picked him up with tears streaming down my face and carried him to my car. It was over in an hour. When I got home I remember standing in a corner of my apartment with my face to the wall just wailing. The apartment manager heard me and knocked on the door. She held me like the mother I had always wanted and invited me over for dinner.

The next night we had a memorial service for Crosby with all the tenants in the building. It was a fitting goodbye to a wonderful companion. He was my very first dog, my very best friend and the last dog I owned for almost ten years.

Crosby II

AFTER I HAD GOTTEN MARRIED we lived in my one plus den apartment for about a year. It was a typical Hollywood apartment with a central courtyard that held a kidney shaped pool surrounded by palm trees and tropical birds of paradise. All the units opened up to the pool area creating a communal lifestyle. We were young and I loved it; people came and went. They were in and out of each other's apartments, there were barbecues and parties and gossip. Tons and tons of gossip. I loved living there back then, today I would sue anyone who tried to get me into one of those buildings. Who needs that shit?

My ex and I are having dinner one night on our balcony and a shaggy dog runs into the courtyard from the street. He's a brown version of Crosby right down to the hair in the eyes, the weight and eye color. I say to my wife, "Look, it's a Puli!" The dog hears me and runs to our front door. The door was slightly ajar; the dog pushes it open and runs into our apartment. I look at my wife and she looks at me, "I think we're adopting." The dog comes over, gives us a smell and lies down at my feet. I'm in shock. The wife says, "Do you know this dog?" and I shake my head no.

A little later, friends came over to see the dog. He's romping and playing and someone says, "This dog belongs to someone. You have to let him go." I know he's right. I open the door and say to the dog, "Go home." The dog bolts. Everyone nods in agreement that we've done the right thing. The guests stay a few hours and then filter out to their own units. The place is still as we shut the lights for the night. I'm just about to walk into the bedroom and I hear scratching at the front door. I open it and there is the dog. "Hey fella, you need a home?" and he jumps into my arms.

I carry him to the bedroom "Look who came home, Lassie." We both fall madly in love with this dog instantly. It wasn't hard for me, he reminded me so much of my Crosby. "Can we keep him?" the wife nods. We were instant dog owners; it wasn't a problem in that building, ownership had changed and they now allowed pets.

Well, this dog was a carbon copy of Crosby and so I named him Crosby II. Why not? It worked the first time. The dog was no problem, didn't chew, didn't bark, didn't poop in the house. He was just the perfect pet. We must have had him about six months when two friends came over, Rick Granat and Jim Caraso. They were a musical comedy act called "Junkman and the Carpenter." Jim had been in the original cast of *Hair* on Broadway and Rick was a hoofer. They did musical comedy parodies and were very popular for about fifteen minutes in the early 70s. Interesting side note here, Rick's brother dated Mavis, who would later become Mrs. Jay Leno.

Rick walks in and I say, "Wait until you see the dog we found," and I call him, "Crosby!" The dog comes running. Both Rick and Jim's face go ashen.

"Bock! You found Bock."

"What are you talking about?"

It turns out that their friend had owned my Crosby aka Bock and lived the next street over. When they moved the dog ran away. My eyes filled with tears and I begged Rick not to take my dog away; I had already lost one Crosby, I couldn't lose another. Rick and Jim swore they would keep our secret and they did.

Must have been about two months later when my darling wife announces she's pregnant. My world was set upside down because I was not ready to be a father, financially or emotionally. It put a strain on the relationship, to say the least, but I finally came around and was happy that I was going to be a father. We got through the pregnancy, we move into a town house in the valley, we have the baby and Crosby comes with us every step of the way.

Having had a child, I can say there is nothing more difficult for parents than a newborn. There's no sleep, you are always on guard, and you can never relax. Gallagher says it best. He throws out an anchor on a chain and says, "No, we can't come, we have the baby." My ex had never thought about anyone but herself her entire life, and now she was a mother. It was killing her. I did all that I could to help but I was in and out of town doing comedy. When I was in town I was writing on staff and that was a sixteen-hour-a-day job. Life was hell but our one constant was the baby and Crosby, he was always there and he adored the child. He would sit for hours while the baby slept. My wife was tiring of the dog. It had to be fed, it had to be walked, it needed attention and my wife was at her max with the baby.

One week when I was on the road, she called Rick and told him to tell Crosby's owners that he had been found. Rick did, the people were thrilled and came and got the dog. Shortly after that, I come home and my dog was gone.

I say to my wife, "Where's Crosby?"

She tells me what she's done.

I hear the words but they don't sink in, "You gave the dog away without asking me?"

"Well it was the right thing to do," She mutters as I fall into a chair. I can't believe that she has done this. The betrayal was beyond words, but her ability for betrayal went far beyond giving the dog away. I would learn later that year when I was told my son was not mine.

I remember sitting in a chair and making a decision. You have a son. You can either chose to fight over the dog or accept what has happened and move on, so that is what I did. At that moment in time, a little bit of the love I had for that woman died. It would be laid to rest when the whole thing about the baby was revealed.

I guess it was a year or two after my divorce and nervous breakdown that I ran into Bock/Crosby again. His owners owned a theater on Melrose Ave and I went there one night to see a production. As I walked out, I saw Crosby asleep in the office. I opened the door and said, "Crosby?" He lifted his head and growled at me. I backed away as I had backed away from all my feelings up until that time. He didn't remember me and it was almost fitting because at that point in my life, I didn't remember who I was either.

It's a horrible feeling when you feel you have no rights, when your dog is given away, or you learn your child is not yours, or you lose a job, or get robbed, or drop your keys down the storm drain. You just accept it. It would take years of therapy to make me understand I have choices and that I didn't have to accept the shit end of the stick any longer. In many ways, the breakdown was the best thing that ever happened to me. I remember sitting in a hospital bed saying, "Everything you have done in your life has led you to this point. If you get out of this bed and do it the same way, you're an idiot." I made a vow to change my life. It took several attempts before I found the right formula but I did do it.

Honestly, I should have kept the dog and given away the wife. It would have been a lot easier.

B'Hai Story

IT MUST HAVE BEEN the summer of 1969 when I was living in New York. My college friend Susan Herzberg calls me and says, "Get dressed, we're going to the Village." Susan and I were very close during this period; we had gone to Emerson together and I had gotten her a job as a singer-waiter with me in some small dive as well as a job in Summer Stock in Morristown, TN. Yee-haw! We were close, after all, we were both going to be stars.

She drags me down to the Village to see a brand-new group called Seals and Crofts. I remember it was at the Village Gate but not the main room, it was either upstairs or downstairs but it was not the main room. It was a room, as I remember it, not as big as my den today. The walls were bleak, cream, rubbed with years of cigarette stains and the black soot that only New York City can produce. The stage was a wooden platform and I'm almost positive that the audience was seated on the floor.

When we got to the room, I could not believe how many people were there. The place was packed. It was kids our age and I wondered how all these people knew about this group that I had never heard of. Susan was working at IFA at the time and she discovered them when their manager Marsha Day was shopping the group trying to get an agent. All Susan said to me was, "Wait until you hear them."

The guys came on stage and I had never seen anything like them. Dash had long black hair and was male model handsome; Jimmy was bearded in an artistic way, and wore a cap—the same cap that would make him world famous. They tuned up and began their first song. I had never heard harmonies like this before. It was a high nasal quality that seemed to mesmerize you. They sang song after song to thunderous applause.

They had an encore and then they were gone. Susan pulled me through the crowd, "We're going backstage." Backstage was sort of a storage room. The guys were very nice, we chatted and left. Susan said to me, with the strangest look in her eyes, "I'm going to work for them someday."

"As what?" is all I could say.

She began this long story about Marsha Day and the B'hai faith and how these people were going to bring peace to the world and unite us as one and how she wanted to be part of it. My reaction: "Whatever."

From that point on Susan's life revolved around Seals and Crofts and the B'hai faith. And what Susan's life revolved around, so did mine. I was going to B'hai functions and hanging out with Jimmy and Dash, but I never wanted to convert. Ever. I am not an organized religion person. I feel you carry God around with you in your heart; it's not necessary to go to a church or a mosque to find him. The more I resisted B'hai, the more Susan pushed, till she finally pushed my back to the wall and I refused to go to any more B'hai things.

One day Susan called and said, "Marsha offered me a job"

"No!"

"Yes, and I'm moving to California. And you're coming."

"I am?"

Within a month she and I were on a plane to LA for a look-see. I got off the plane and felt I had lived there all my life. It's like I was having an out-of-body experience. Places I visited for the first time I knew I had seen before. The people were incredibly warm and the drugs, oh my God, the drugs. Wait, maybe that's why I thought I had been here before. I was tripping.

Susan had made up her mind she was moving but I had this really good job at Alexander's Department Store that I hated. Hated is a strong word, let's say detested. Susan moved in a month and the memory of the palm trees and the warm summer nights were calling to me. I walked into Alexander's personnel department and gave them my notice. I called Susan and told her I was coming out. I needed a ride to get my stuff there. Within twenty-four hours she had hooked me up with a B'hai guy who was moving to LA and driving out in his van. I packed a trunk of clothes, an eight-inch TV, and a crappy old stereo, and this guy, Crosby, and I headed west. I sold my apartment and its contents for a tidy profit and had money to start anew in LA.

We must have driven a couple of days when one night this guy says to me, out of the blue, "I'm not happy." He wanted to see the country not the highway. He was turning around, heading back to drive the side roads and see the country. That's exactly what he did; he turned the van around and began pulling off on country roads to see Texas. I was being held captive but I wasn't in danger. I was just not getting to LA at the speed I wanted to go. I hadn't washed or shaved for four days when we got to Amarillo. We passed an Avis office and I screamed "Stop!" and I got out with Crosby and my trunk, marched myself to the Avis desk, handed them my credit card and rented a car. I asked them if they had a shower I could use and they did. I washed and shaved. When I walked out, I will never forget the woman behind the counter. "Honey, y'all clean up good," and she upgraded my car.

I left the hippy B'hai guy in Amarillo. Crosby and I drove the rest of the way to California by ourselves, Crosby by my side the entire trip. I will never forget coming in on the 10 Freeway and rounding that curve to see the LA City Hall, or for you older people, the Daily Planet Building in *Superman*. It was a feeling of accomplishment that I can't even explain. I had made it across the country all by myself. It was the start of something new.

I had two friends in LA. Susan and Jan Seeburg (whom I would later name my son after). I called Jan on a Wednesday, stayed with him one night, and the next day found the apartment where I would meet Albert Hammond and Dave Madden. The day after that I heard about a job at the May Company, went down, applied and got it. In three days, I had an apartment and a job.

Just a side story here. The first day at the May Company I walked into the office and one of the assistants had her back to me. She turned around to reveal she was one of the most magnificently beautiful black women I had ever seen. She had light cocoa-colored skin and was about 5'11" with light brown hair she wore in a short Afro. She was Sheila Washington and she was breathtakingly beautiful. I introduced myself to her and we chatted. At lunch, she told me she had just moved into a new apartment, 1535 Laurel Ave. I just stared at her. "What. What's the matter?" I had moved into 1545 Laurel Ave. I had moved across the country, gotten a job in two days, and the girl I'm working with lives two doors down from me.

I digress. When we got to LA, Susan got deep into B'hai. Deep. She converted and she was determined to get me to convert. I went to every B'hai function there was. They were wonderful, loving people. I had no interest in converting. I wasn't a good Jew; I wasn't going to be a good B'hai. What I did get to do was meet Marsha Day and her gorgeous daughters.

They all were singers; one was married to Dash. They were a musical family and the girls backed up the boys on the road and on their records.

Years roll by. I leave the May Co. and become a comedian. All the time, Marsha and that insane B'hai clan are my friends. I wouldn't let any of them come to see me because I wasn't ready to be seen as a comedian (fear of judgment), but we were all close and they followed my career. Let me tell you how poor we all were at this point. It must have been August, and Billie—Dash's wife at the time—was pregnant with their first child. Susan was working for Marsha and I was on unemployment. It was one of those hot summer nights when it's 89º at midnight. Susan calls me. They are dying of the heat and none of them had air conditioning. I did. The entire clan comes to my one bedroom apartment for the A/C. Must have been about twelve people. Jimmy and Dash were on the road and Billie was about 8 1/2 months pregnant. She was a beautiful woman but during the pregnancy had put on quite a bit of weight and let herself go.

The A/C was not working because of all the body heat in the room. It was hot and disgusting. We were sticky and wet and in a coma from the heat when all of a sudden, Billie jumps up in her short shorts with her belly sticking way out. She begins to rub her stomach and purrs in her sexiest Marilyn Monroe voice, "I know every man in the room wants me." You know how it is when you're a kid and someone farts in church. That's how it was in that room when Billie sat down. We laughed for about forty-five minutes.

It wasn't too soon after that that my first agent Gary Weinberg signed me to ICM, the same agency Seals and Crofts were signed to. The guys were just an act at the agency until *Summer Breeze* hit and hit big. Suddenly, overnight, Seals and Crofts were *huge*. Then came the string of hits and the money was rolling in. I was wondering how these B'hai were going to handle all this sudden wealth. They bought a recording studio in San Fernando and they all moved out there. San Fernando? Why didn't they just move to hell?

The guys' career went gangbusters for years. Then, as in all music acts, they began to slow down and the hits were few and far between. I honestly think it was the B'hai stuff that was a turn-off to so many record promoters and radio stations. Remember, this was the era of drugs, sex, and rock and roll. Seals and Crofts were preaching the antithesis of this. Bookings became harder to get in the rock world. Not that they were hurting, their royalties and music publishing were bringing them in tons of moola.

I'm with Susan one night and I hear Seals and Crofts are going to work the MGM Grand in Las Vegas. She says to me, "Would you like to middle for them? They need an act between themselves and Maureen McGovern. Marsha just signed her." This was my first big Vegas gig and I was scared shitless, but I said I would love it. It was all arranged. Now, here's the good part. I need constant reassurance; it's the same with the audiences when I work. I need them laughing all the time. At the MGM Grand, when I stepped out on the stage, there must have been three thousand people there, seventy-five of them in Marsha Day's party. These are all people who I knew, who had been to my apartment, who invited me to their wedding, who had gone to the beach with me. These were my friends and these people whopped and hollered for me the moment I stepped out on stage. I knew someone in that crowd loved me and that's all I needed. It kept me going and as I told jokes my B'hai family screamed with laughter. The reviews were good. Seals and Crofts were a huge hit and we all went on the road together.

I have to tell you, going on the road with Seals and Crofts was the best experience of my entire career. Why? It wasn't like going on the road with strangers, these were friends that I had known for years and we were all living our dream. They gave me respect and they loved working with me. I loved working with them. They let me live *my* dream. One night in their grand finale, they dragged me on stage and let me sing backup. It was one of the most exciting experiences of my life.

The Last New York Story

I WAS WORKING AT ALEXANDER'S DEPARTMENT store in the late 60s. I was hired for the men's department, actually, the Tomorrow Shop. I didn't realize it then, but The Tomorrow Shop was where the good-looking, young, hip people were put to give the store a trendier image. I didn't know I was young, hip, or good looking. Me, trendy? One day the VP of marketing came into the shop and looked at me, "What are *you* doing here?" She pulled me downstairs to where the men's fashion show was being held. She grabbed a suit off the rack, threw it at me and said, "Now get out there." She thought I was one of the models.

"Ma'am, I'm a salesman."

She took a beat, looked me up and down and said, "Not anymore." She put me in the show and used me to model in their catalogue until I left for California.

I actually liked working at that store. It was like a family. We fought, we loved, we talked about each other behind our backs. It was just like a family. Here's a funny side note: no one in that store had a last name. Like, I was Steve from Tomorrow; made me sound like I was from Disneyland. There was Rosie from Receiving and Gail from Dry Goods and Phil from Shoes and Nancy from Jr. Petites and Arnold Goodman, the Coat King. Arnold worked in coats, looked like Eddy Munster, was as masculine as Ellen DeGeneres, and as funny as Joan Rivers. He had the thickest New York Accent ever and was a fixture in the store. He was the Coat King then but today he works in Furs and is the Prince of Pelts.

We all would eat lunch together in the cafeteria: Arnold, Rena, Gloria, Steve Leest, Rosie, me. Over the years we experienced deaths and weddings and bar mitzvahs and firings and rehirings sitting around that cafeteria table. It was the strangest collection of people ever. We came from all over and yet we were one. I remember once we had a party at a restaurant after work. People would look at our group trying to figure out what the connection was. Why was that black woman sitting with that white boy, and why was the skinny Puerto Rican girl talking to the fat Russian lady? We were an odd mix but it was the oddity that kept us together.

I remember one woman in particular, Evelyn. She sat by herself and wasn't part of our group. She was short and frail and worked in children's wear. She was Evelyn from Children's Wear. Most of the women in the store were fashion-conscious, Evelyn wasn't. Most had their hair colored. Evelyn wore hers grey like a badge of courage. When she would come into the café it would grow silent and I never knew why. Then, one day as she passed, I heard a whisper, "She lost her son. Twenty-four years old. Vietnam." Now I understood. They were giving her space to grieve.

Sometime later I remember Evelyn coming into the cafeteria and seeming out of sorts, more distant than normal, more alone. I watched her as she peeled her orange. She slit it from the top to the bottom in four sections like a beach ball, and then she would peel back the skin to reveal the untouched meat inside.

"I wish I could do that," I said almost not knowing I was talking aloud.

"It's simple, come here, I'll show you." She produced another orange and peeled it for me. When the rind was off, she shoved it across the table, "Nuh" (Yiddish for "here"). It was then I noticed the tattooed numbers on her arm. I had never seen them before; she always wore long sleeves. I had lived a very sheltered life in Boston. She saw that I saw and she just tugged at her sleeve. I wanted so desperately to reach out and take her hand but I didn't dare. She was a very private woman. Suddenly she burst into tears. "One year. One year today," is all she said. I knew she was referring to her son. It made me feel guilty. I was alive; her son was dead. I had no reason to feel that way but I did. I slid over to a seat next to her, "I'll be your son." She took my hand and squeezed it just a little, just enough to say thank you.

We never spoke of that moment again. I was too embarrassed to mention it. I think she just wanted to forget, but it created a silent bond between us. She'd bring me a cookie or peel me an orange. I would always make her laugh, "Stevie, such a funny boy." I had always considered her frail but she showed me how strong she could be one day when Gertie came in and had a nervous breakdown.

We were seated around our table in the café. There were long tables all lined up like a prison dining room. Their yellow Formica tops were discolored with years of misuse and half-hearted attempts at cleaning. I was with a group talking about an impending sale when Gertie runs in and plops in a seat. She announces to no one.

"I need to talk. I've got to throw her out."

"Who?"

"My Judy"

"Why. What happened??"

We all knew Judy was Gertie's pride. The first to go to college, she was Gertie's only daughter, the reason she worked, the sun rose and set in that girl. Now she was throwing her out?? She tells us that the night before, her beloved Judy had taken LSD. Gertie came home and Judy was sitting in the middle of the kitchen floor stark naked, sitting in a box of kitty litter, playing with it like it was water. Gertie told the story like each word was a knife cutting into her throat, "I screamed at her, 'What are you doing??' And she laughed at me. She just laughed." With that, Gertie broke down and began to sob. This was not like Gertie; Gertie was a tough cookie. Gertie was the one you called when your ad merchandise was stuck in receiving and you couldn't get it out. Gertie was the one you called when the buyers were giving you a hard time. Gertie was not a crier, Gertie made *you* cry. My heart broke for her as she pleaded with us to tell her what she should do. We sat there like dummies. What did I know? I was twenty-three. Opinions were being offered left and right. Suggestions were a dime a dozen and then quietly, from her table, Evelyn gingerly raised her hand.

"Gertie, go home and hug your daughter."

"What?"

"Go home and hug her. She needs it." Then, without saying a word, she picked up her tray, walked over to the trash and dumped her milk carton, "Hug her, Gertie. There may not be a chance tomorrow." She slid the dirty tray into the slot to be washed, "I know." She left to go back to the selling floor shaking her head all the way to the swinging doors by the long line of time cards.

The group was hushed and stunned. Then Rena said, "You know, she's right." Gertie sat there staring out into space, not crying, not blinking. I think she was processing the information. The next day Gertie couldn't wait for our group's gathering at noon. She was the first one sitting at the table. She had good news. She had talked to Judy. She had laid down the law. No more drugs. Evelyn walked by and Gertie yelled, "Evelyn did you hear?" Evelyn nodded as she sat by herself peeling an orange. She looked at me and winked!

I loved those people at Alexander's. There were a million stories in that store. A million? Ten million. I never thought I would ever think of them again, but I guess it all went into the computer between my ears. I'm sure I'll think of other stories, funny ones, but when I thought of Alexander's and New York and my life back then, the first thing I thought of was Gertie and Judy and the day she told us about the Kitty Litter. Funny, huh? What your mind lets you remember. Now, where are my car keys?

Chicken In the Projects

MY FATHER WAS A COLLECTOR OF CRAP. He'd be driving down the road, see a sofa, bring it home, and in three days he would turn it into an entertainment unit with running water. I can do the exact same thing. I'm a dyed-in-the-wool trash picker and proud of it. My mother had no artistic sense. She had good taste, she knew what looked nice, but she couldn't create it. When my father would bring home crap it always started a fight, which usually ended with the SWAT team staying for dinner.

One day, my father was visiting friends in rural Massachusetts and took me along. He passed a sign that said "Live chickens," and like a junky that's found the fountain of smack, a gleam came to his eyes, "I need to stop." We're walking around the chicken farm and my father meets the owner. The one thing my father had was a personality. He could charm the pants off a mannequin. He's joking with the farmer and the farmer is laughing and next thing I know my father is walking back to the car with two live chickens under each arm. I must have been seven at the time. I was in heaven. New pets.

Back then we lived in a two-bedroom apartment in the VA housing projects. My Dad walks into our tiny home with a gunnysack. My mother goes on the defensive.

"What's that?"

"Chickens" is all he said.

The bag opens and it's the phone booth scene from *The Birds*; attack chickens are flying everywhere. She screams like Tippy Hendren and grabs for a broom. My father is yelling, "Don't! You'll break the drumsticks." At this point I think she would have bitten off his neck al la Ozzie Osbourne if she could have caught him.

We finally got the chickens corralled in the kitchen. He's created a pen by taking her best folding chairs, the one she uses when the "women" come over to play canasta and he's got them in a corner with the chickens penned behind them. She's spread newspapers like we're training a puppy. I'm in seventh heaven. My own chicken farm right here in the projects. I get every kid in the building to see my new pets. These are city kids, not one of them has ever seen a live chicken. "Where do the eggs come from?" one kid asks. My father picks up a chicken, flips it over, and exposes its ass. Childhood Nirvana! Chicken ass in the kitchen.

The next day I'm up to feed the livestock. My mother is in a foul mood (Pun. Thank you). She's slamming dishes and throwing pots. She wants them out. He wants them in.

"We can use the eggs."

She slams her fist down, "I will not live in an apartment with live chickens. You call Gopen or I'll break *your* drumstick."

In those days, we lived in a small town. When you needed groceries, you'd call Promisels. "Are the grapes good today? Okay, send me a pound of grapes. I need a box of corn flakes and make sure the box isn't crushed like the last time," and then Promisels delivered it to your door! They were way ahead of their time. Ralph's does that today via the Internet but it's not the same. It's not bicycle-delivered by a kid named Billy wearing a white apron. We also had a bread man, Toni, that delivered rolls and pastry; milkman for milk. Then there was Gopen, the butcher. DA-DA-DA-DUM!

Next day, no chickens. I ask my mother, "Hey, where are Sadie and Jake?" Evidently, we had Jewish chickens. "They got lonely and went back to the farm," she replied. I was seven; this made sense to me. I didn't question it. The chickens were back on the farm. I guess they flew.

Then my father comes home with the corpses... ah... packages wrapped in brown paper. I go out to play and my mother makes dinner. About 7 p.m. she calls me in. It was Friday night. You know what that means? Chicken. I swear to God, I never made the connection that dinner could have been clucking in our kitchen the day before. My mother couldn't eat. "I feel like a cannibal," and she takes her plate and dumps it in the trash. My mother is not from the high rollers. This woman saves Tropicana Orange Juice Bottles by the thousands. My dad sort of pushed his meal around on the plate with his fork. Meanwhile I'm sucking up white meat like there's a chicken shortage.

We never spoke of those chickens again. Why should we? The next week he brought home a lobster. I'm not making this up, it filled the entire bathtub. We couldn't bathe until "it went back to the Ocean." He brought home birds and fish and eels, and at one point I thought he was building an ark. There was a place in New England called Cherry Hill Farm, a working dairy farm. I loved to go there with my Dad. He took me one day and as we walked out the door my mother screamed, "Don't come home with a cow!"

Penny Marshall

PENNY MARSHALL AND THE LATE CARRIE FISHER had birthdays very close together, so every year they would throw this party with their combined guest list. Monica called me up, "Do you want to go to Penny's birthday party with me? It's always fun." She's been invited to them all since she was a producer on Laverne and Shirley. Now, you have to understand that I have never heard about this party. I'm like the kid from the small town going to the city with his sophisticated friend. I'm thinking "party", you know, like *we* have a party: the deli platter from Costco and the Lipton onion soup dip. Wrong.

Monica comes to my house looking drop dead gorgeous. I'm in jeans. She says nothing. I drive, and on the way to Penny's house Monica fills me in, "It's the last year they're going to do this bash and I'm really sad because I love this party." She's excited for me though. Bringing me to the party is like her gift. I'm asking her all kinds of questions and all she said is, "You'll see."

We drive up a long windy road to Penny's house in the hills. There's a line of about fifty cars and valet parkers running to get everyone's car handled. "Jesus," is all I could say. Monica chirps like my spiritual guide, "You've seen nothing yet." We give the keys to the valet and head down the driveway. I can see the front door is wide open and the place is packed with people. As we enter the house, Monica turns to me, "Ok, honey, here you go," and we're in the foyer. The very first thing I hear is James Woods saying, "Owen Wilson, have you met John McEnroe?" Folks, that was just the beginning.

I have never seen so many A-List celebrities in one place in my life, ever. Not at the Emmys, not at The Comedy Awards, not at the Golden

Globes, no place! The house is a huge two-story mansion. You enter on the top floor and walk down to the backyard, as the house is built into the side of a mountain. The entire backyard is a swimming pool and gardens. However, it's not a swimming pool and a garden like your Aunt Fanny has, it's like a swimming pool and backyard at The Hilton Resort on Maui. This pool is packed with people. If a bomb went off that night, Omarosa would be hosting the Academy Awards.

We're standing by the pool and I hear, "Steve!" I turn and Richard Lewis is standing there with his girlfriend. I've known Richard for about twenty years. We talk briefly. Garry Shandling joined us, also a comedy friend. While we're chatting, George Lucas walks by. I look past him and Francis Ford Coppola is eating at a table with Magic Johnson.

I'm like, "Look... a Laker."

Richard says, "You mean Lakers," and he points. The entire Laker team is seated at tables around the pool. Then Monica takes me inside to see Penny's collection of Sports Memorabilia. It looked like the back room of the Smithsonian. I've never seen so many signed baseballs, basketballs and footballs in my life. Each one is in its own Plexiglas case. I say, "Who dusts all this crap?" Monica just stares at me. While I'm ogling the collection, Laraine Newman comes over and just stands there. I don't recognize her at first. She finally says, "Steve?" and I come out of my coma. She's standing with Lynn Stewart and Cindy Williams. I see Tracey Ullman; I've gone to comedy heaven.

The room is packed so Monica takes me upstairs, "That's the table John Belushi passed out on." I'm starting to freak out. This is Hollywood like you think Hollywood is supposed to be. When I tell you every single name in town was there, I wouldn't be lying. It looked like the Players Directory had exploded and landed in Penny's back yard.

Here's how I think. With this huge crowd, I'll bet things are going to get stolen. I immediately look for "perps". I'm at the biggest party of the year and I'm looking for shoplifters. I think I see someone putting something in his pocket; it's Barry Diller. Fuck, it's Barry Diller. He was putting Warren Beatty's card in his pocket as Annette Benning watched.

Now I start seeing people I see at the Willards' party: Michael McCheon and David L. Lander (*Lenny and Squiggy*), and Michael's wife, Annette O'Toole. Peter Boyle walks by, "Hey Steve."

Monica has written most of Albert Brooks's films. We chat with him. Jim Brooks is standing talking to Jim Belushi. I'm freaking out. I turn to Monica,

"Why didn't you tell me it was going to be like this!!!"

"I tried, honey, would you believe me?"

No, I wouldn't have believed her, this is the kind of party that you only hear about on *Extra*. Michelle Pfeiffer is joking with Jon Lovitz when I spot Tom Hanks. Now, Tom's wife Rita and I were in an acting class together. Rita Wilson waves at me. Monica says, "You know Rita Wilson?" At this point in the evening it starts becoming blasé. "Oh look, Danny DeVito and Rhea Perlman." Yawn.

Like in any party the people split off into groups, only these groups were like Saturday Night Live Stars, A-list film directors, and People with Oscars. It goes on like this for hours. At one point, I just sit down and watch as the parade of stars pass by. It becomes surreal, everywhere you look there is someone you know from TV, Film or Sports. And I'm not talking about supporting players. I'm talking about Stars. I'm introduced to Carrie Fisher and Penny Marshall; they looked really beautiful. I wish them both a Happy Birthday as they look past me to more important guests.

Monica and I stay about three hours and we've had enough. Our group of friends is leaving when John Travolta walks in with his entourage. We duck out. In the car I say to Monica, "Now I can die happy." And Monica says, "Don't die yet Steve. Maybe they'll have the party again next year."

We lost Monica to cancer about a year ago. There is not a day that goes by that I do not think about her and her insane sense of reality. She saw only the good in people, except for the ones she hated. She would be the first to buy this book and she would be so proud that I finally got it published. I miss her a lot.

Mike Douglas

THE DAY AFTER I LEARNED that I was not the father of my child (Nice opening line, no? Makes you want to go running through a field of land mines), my managers decide that I should be kept busy working. God forbid he misses his 15%, and so they booked me on *The Mike Douglas Show*. I had done the show several times; it was an easy booking and in theory it was a great idea, "keep him occupied." In reality, it was the worst thing they could have done. Why didn't they just give me a toaster in the shower? I was falling apart. All you had to do was look at me and you could tell. A man who cries when the light turns red is not someone who should be flying. Charles Manson had a better grip on reality.

I tell my agent I'm worried about this gig because I won't be able to sleep on the plane. He gives me a pill. I needed a straitjacket; he gives me a pill. I never learned what the little beauty was but was told to take it when they announced boarding. This was the first mistake; you don't send a nervous breakdown to LAX with instructions.

That night I'm sitting at the airport. My head's in a good space, I'm like, *I could throw myself into that jet engine. I don't think they'll mind.* I'm overwhelmed with all kinds of emotions, anger, fear, anxiety, hate. Aren't those the seven dwarfs? I've lost what was supposed to be the ideal life and now I'm supposed to make the world laugh on TV. I hold on to the pill for dear life. Suddenly there is an announcement: "Ladies and gentleman. Flight 266 nonstop service from Los Angeles to Philadelphia..." I get up and take the pill, "... has been delayed two hours."

Fuck. The clock ticks away and I feel nothing. The pill has not worked. How emotionally shut down do you have to be to have illegal drugs not take effect? I think I'm going to sit up all night and then have to do a TV show, which, in reality, was the last thing I wanted to do. What I wanted to do was lie down on the San Diego Freeway and let rush hour kill me. One hour and forty-five minutes later there is another announcement.

"We are ready to pre-board flight 226 non-stop to Philadelphia…. And now our first-class passengers…"

That's me. I reach over to get my shoulder bag from under my seat. Suddenly the ceiling is where the floor should be and vice versa. Then my legs fill with Jell-O and my fingers turn numb. I flop over on the floor like I've been shot with a tranquilizer gun. The pill worked.

I'm flying and the plane hasn't even left the gate. There are no two ways around it. Finally, my agent came through. I have to pull myself together or else they won't let me fly. Being a comedian I make a joke about "rough seas". I get myself up and focus, *you're ten feet from the loading ramp. You can do this!* I turn on the stoner's autopilot; it guides me to my seat. I'm on the aisle. That's all I remember. I got to my seat and I'm out.

About three hours later I wake up. The woman sitting next to me says, "Well you're a sound sleeper."

"Huh? Why?"

"My husband had to go to the bathroom and we tried to wake you. You didn't move. We called the stewardess; she called the Captain. We thought you were dead."

"Oh?" Is all I could get out, "I was really tired" (and totally stoned out of my mind). I later learned I had been introduced to my first whole Quaalude, an introduction that would lead to many, many nights asleep on the kitchen floor.

I get to Philly; the limo driver picks me up and notices something is wrong. Maybe it was the drool. They all know me because I've done the show before, only this time I'm very quiet and to myself. As I remember, we drove right to the studio and got into make-up. The segment producer goes over my material and okayed it. I'm holding it together by a thread. I'm in wardrobe and we're ten minutes from air. It's live. I'm opening the show after Mike does his monologue and first segment. I'm standing backstage, my heart is pounding, and I'm running lines in front of the curtain. I have to go out there and make this audience laugh; my heart is breaking and I'm on the residual effects of the finest drug Tijuana ever made.

Mike has started my intro when the segment producers comes up to me and puts her arm around my shoulder, "Here we go." I straighten my suit jacket. Then she innocently says, "Aren't you going to kiss your baby's picture?" Up until that day, my ritual before I went on stage was to kiss

Jan's picture for good luck. She didn't know about the paternity and so was asking a logical question. However, what it did was hit me in the face with a shovel ten seconds before going out in front of the cameras.

"And now, here's Steve Bluestein."

I have the videotape of the show on a reel somewhere. I walk out of the curtain and it's like I'm about to burst into tears. I'm doing my routine while fighting to hold it together. The audience is laughing and I'm crying. It was one of those moments that they write in movies and people say, "Shit like that doesn't happen." Oh, guess again Gunga Din.

I got back to LA that night and continued to work in the weeks that followed. The powers that be felt I needed to be kept busy. They were taking care of the outside; I needed them to take care of the inside. I began a downward spiral that ended with me in the hospital, probably the best thing that ever happened to me. I had to stop and reassess my life. All these years later, I can tell you everything happens for a reason. I needed a good kick in the ass and that hospital stay was it.

Okay, so now that you're all happy and up from that rollicking romp through TV memorabilia, let's all make a pact to meet for the suicide prevention convention. I am remembering things that I haven't thought of in years. I'm getting them all out and hopefully put in a place where I won't have to deal with them ever again. It's all as it should be.

Candid Camera

I WENT TO EMERSON COLLEGE with a lot of people who became famous, Henry Winkler and Andrea Martin just to name a few. There was also Vinnie DiBona. Vinnie was two years ahead of me but we hung with the same crowd. Emerson is like a mafia family; once you're in it, you're in for life. When you meet someone from Emerson, it's like you've met a long lost relative.

Vinnie had a lot of success locally in Boston and had come out to LA to try his luck in the big time. It was about the time Henry was "Fonzie" and was world famous. It was also about the time I found out Jan was not my son and I was eating pabulum through a straw. I don't remember how, but Vinnie and I connected and I told him what had happened in my marriage and he said, "It's a movie". I had never thought about it like that, it was just too painful, but he was right. It was a movie. I sat down and wrote a treatment called "Men Cry Too." A few weeks later, I gave it to Vinnie. He loved it and immediately started taking it around town.

I think I've said this before, but there is something really wonderful about starving in show business with your friends. You're all hungry and the chance to break through to the big time is exciting, it's like a carrot on a stick. It propels you forward. Vinnie pushed hard for this movie on so many levels. He liked the story, he liked the writing, but mostly he wanted to produce this because he felt it had so much heart. That was Vinnie; he had a heart as big as all outdoors. He would sit with me for hours and tell me how sorry he was that this was happening to me but that we were going to turn lemons into lemonade with this movie.

Months pass. We take it to Henry; he is not in the position at that time to do anything with it. Vinnie is like a pit bull, finally someone at

ABC reads the treatment and loves it. She calls us in, "It's not a story about paternity, it's a story about what makes a father." The woman got it. She was bringing the script to the next level. Vinnie and I were thrilled. This was our big break. While we awaited a verdict from the next level, the woman was fired at ABC and that was the end of the project. Vinnie had spent months on it and could no longer spend any time and I, feeling that anything I could produce would be worthless, just let it drop.

Years pass. Occasionally I see Vinnie socially but for all intents and purposes I lost contact with him. He had had some success with a few TV shows, nothing earth shaking, maybe children's programming, but I'm not sure.

I had to be up at ABC for a meeting. I'm walking down the hall and I see a sign on the door, "Vinnie DiBona" so I go in. Vinnie is glad to see me. We sit and talk. He says to me, "Want to see my latest pilot?" He sits me down and shoves a video in the VCR. I watch and instantly know it's a hit.

"Vinnie, this is a winner. I can feel it in my bones."

"From your mouth to God's ears. I find out next week if we're picked up."

I spend some more time with him and we part. The name of the pilot: *America's Funniest Home Videos*.

More years pass. Vinnie has become a powerhouse in Los Angles. I hear through the grapevine he's earning seven figures a month. I had just come off writing a show for Fox called *Totally Hidden Video* and hear Universal was starting production on a new *Candid Camera*. The head writer from the Fox show was going over to *Candid Camera*; he asked me if I wanted to go with him, "Sure!" I had to meet with the producer, Vin De Bona. I walk into Vinnie's office and immediately notice the nameplate. Vin Di Bona. Ah. It begins. Vin and I meet and he's all business. It's like we don't know each other. I'm trying to find the old Vinnie but he's gone. In his place is a very successful producer who has a job to get done and he's trying to assess if I can do it. A few days later I learn I got the job.

Candid Camera

I get to Universal on my first day and it's like a reunion. All the people from *Totally Hidden Video* are working here, but there's a new guy, Max Mutchnick. Max was young and balding. He was the kind of guy I liked to hang with: funny, hip, smart; he was just a lot of fun to be around. I really liked him and looked forward to working with him.

Max had a cubicle next to mine. I would hear him on the phone talking to this one and that one about making this deal and that deal. I called him the little hustler. Max and I developed a love-hate relationship—we teased each other without mercy. He was balding; I had very long, thick hair. As a joke, he would say to me, "You're old and it's over for you."

I would stick my head over his partition and say, "Yes, but can you do this?" and I would flip my head so my hair would bounce like a Clairol commercial. It would make him laugh.

Working on *Candid Camera* was a living hell. I used to call it Auschwitz with typewriters. It was a non-stop churning out material to be sent to producers in the field. The working conditions would have made Norma Rae spit blood. The office was filthy, they had ants and gnats, the A/C didn't work, it was noisy and crowded. Basically, we were writing comedy on Skid Row. In the back of my mind always was the idea that I was working on the show that Allen Funt had created. Allen was the warm, loving, sweet man that came into my living room every Sunday night. He and Derwood Kirby were a childhood memory that I cherished. As luck would have it, I became close friends, and still am, with Randy Kirby, Derwood's son.

One day we are informed that the writers are going to meet Allen Funt. I cannot tell you how excited I was. I'm going to meet my idol. Now both Randy Kirby and Joan Rivers had told me how tough Allen was, but I thought, "How bad could it be? This guy's like a father figure to the nation."

We're all crammed into this small room at a restaurant in the valley. I'm seated right next to Allen. I'm in seventh heaven; he's an icon from my childhood. Max is seated across the table from me. Allen begins the meeting.

"Okay, I've got a life vest here, what can we do with it?"

"How about we do a fashion show where we get people to wear the vests," I suggest.

Allen cuts me off before I can finish, "That's the stupidest fucking idea I've ever heard. Where in hell did that come from? People, we have to come up with better ideas than that stupid one."

I look over at Max, he's laughing so hard he can barely sit. He can't just burst out laughing so he's suppressing it. I see Max struggling and I start to laugh but I'm seated right next to Allen and cannot be disrespectful. I can't laugh; I can't even show any emotions. I'm laughing so hard on the inside tears are filling my eyes. Every time I get control I get a glimpse of Max and we're off again. Max is sliding down in his chair with his hand over his face. I'm about to wet myself.

As the meeting progresses, Allen is getting meaner and angrier with every suggestion, but he's taken a particular dislike to me. I'm so beaten that I simply give up and become a child. It's now my goal to make Max laugh out loud during the meeting. If I'm going down, Max is going with me. Every time Allen looks away I make a face behind his back, he turns around I go back to normal attentive Steve. Max is watching and laughing. I'm making faces, Max is laughing. Allen is ignoring me. I'm making faces. Allen is oblivious. At one point, I start to doodle. I draw the Dallas Book Depository with Allen in an open car. I shove it across the table to Max and another writer Nonie Breen. Nonie sees the sketch and laughs out loud! All eyes turn to Nonie. She's pretty and Allen thinks she's laughing at something he said. He's pleased. Max and I are up for grabs.

The meeting ends and I say to Max, "I think that went well," and we're off again, only now we're outside and screaming as loud as we can. Max did not let me live down that meeting. At the drop of a hat Max would bring up Allen's dislike for me, "We need to get a script over to Allen. Why don't we let Steve bring it? Allen likes him." It became common knowledge on the show that Allen hated me. He wouldn't meet with me again, to Max's delight. Max would remind me daily of my banishment. I would flip my hair. I can honestly say that if it hadn't been for Max Mutchnick and Nonie Breen I would have lost my mind on that show.

I guess I was working there three or four months when I learned the show had been cancelled. Big surprise, it was a piece of shit—nothing like the original show—and Dom Deluise was so wrong as the host it was not even funny, and it wasn't. I had one last meeting with Vin before we closed down the office. I said to him, "Vinnie, maybe now, with your clout, we can get 'Men Cry Too' made."

"Excellent idea. Here. Call my development person," he said.

I called, had the meeting with the development guy. The development guy hated the idea. Hated it. I'm sitting there thinking, *Vinnie loved this idea when he was no one but now he's gotten so big he has people who he can hire to hate stuff he used to like. What the fuck has happened to my life?*

There is so much bullshit in show business that if you lay it out on a football field you could grow dead roses. People, whatever your job is, wherever it is, go in and kiss your boss, because if you think my job is glamorous and rewarding, I've got some Enron Stock I'd like to sell you.

Post Script

Nonie went on to play the Sister in *Late Night Catechism* and tours all over the country. Max went on to create and produce a little show called *Will and Grace*. I couldn't be happier for him. He's worked hard and deserves all his success. Me? I will be working at a 7-11 in Little Rock and happy to get that.

Mac Davis

RIGHT AFTER THE DIVORCE, my managers decided I must be kept working, basically because I was calling the office and was depressing the staff. It wasn't so much they were trying to get me work as they were trying to save their own sanity. My manager also managed Mac Davis; Mac was going on tour and needed an opening act. There was an opening at Hutchinson Kansas State Fair and I got it. Now this gig was going to be amazing. It was held on a racetrack and the stage was set up in front of huge bleachers. Naturally the tapes in my head began to play: *they won't like you.... You're not country*, and other assorted things my mother may have told me.

Right before I left to work with Mac, I had to do a TV show. I can't remember which one but one of the guests was Minnie Pearl. We were sitting in the green room and began talking. I told her how nervous I was about doing the gig with Mac and she said, "Honey, they'll love you. Here's a joke you can open with." She gave me the following joke:

"A man with eleven children goes to the county fair. He wants to see the prize stud bull but he doesn't have enough money because of all his kids. The ticket taker looks at his line of children, 'Are those all kids yours?'

"The man says 'yes'.

"'Hell, wait here, I'll bring the bull out to see YOU.'"

Now, this joke is not me. It's a joke, and I don't tell jokes, I tell long stories—much like I'm telling in this book—but I thanked her and knew I would never use the material.

The week before we left, I was wondering how I would get to Hutchinson, Kansas. It's not exactly a hub. I mentioned that to Nancy Henson from my management office. Let me tell you about Nancy. You know how I told you managers don't care and they're only out for their 15%? That was *not* Nancy. She was the exception to the rule, a caring person. The day I found out my son was not mine Nancy ran over to my house to sit with me. I can see her face in front of me as she just listened. I don't boo-hoo cry. Once as a child I saw the "ugly cry" in the mirror and said, "Boy you look stupid." From that moment on, I never ugly cried again. My crying is looking deadpan and just having tears stream down my face. That's what I was doing with Nancy, just talking deadpan while tears streamed down my face. She just listened and was there for me, the only one from the office. There is a special place in my heart for Nancy.

A few days later Nancy called me and said, "I've arranged for you to fly to Kansas with Mac in his private plane." I was in shock; this just wasn't done. She added, "Just be careful what you say to him. He's from Texas." In other words, his neck has been permanently painted red.

The day of the gig I drove myself to a private airport in Van Nuys. There were about seven people on the flight. Mac sat with a young lady who was one of his back-up singers and I sat by myself. We landed in Kansas and were picked up in Limos and taken to the dressing rooms, which were the men's room for the racetrack. Mac and I shared a room. I pace before I go on, it's how I get myself in the mental state to do comedy. I think this pissed him off.

"Man, what the hell's wrong with you?"

"Just nervous I guess."

"Well cool it."

Thanks for understanding, I thought.

The show starts and I step out on the biggest stage I have ever stood on in my life. The audience stretched for as far as you can see to the left and as far as you can see on the right and it goes back a couple hundred yards in tiered bleachers. Ten thousand people are sitting in the audience. Ten thousand! I begin "Good-evening… evening… evening." Fuck, an echo, a nightmare for comedy. It threw me for a second and then I remembered Minnie Pearl's joke and I told it. The crowd screamed. I have never heard a laugh like that before or since! That huge laugh propelled me and gave me the courage to go on. I simply did my act as if it were the Comedy Store. They loved it and I got thunderous applause. I can still hear it to this day.

After the show, I was more relaxed and Mac was a lot nicer. Many times, the headliner won't talk to the opening act until they see what the opening act can do. Then, if they are good, the headliner warms up. That's what happened to Mac and me. He said to me, "Why are you so nervous? You're good." Like a punctured vomit bag, I told him the story of my son and my divorce. He just looked at me, "Let me tell you a little story. Lunt and Fontanne were appearing on Broadway. The reviews came out and they were brilliant. The reviewers said, 'Lunt gave a performance that will go down in theater history. His characterization will be remembered for generations to come. His lips are a little thin but he uses it to his best advantage in creating a real character with depth and history. And the reviewer goes on to rave and rave. Fontanne puts the paper down and said, 'Congratulations, darling.' All Lunt said was, 'My lips are a little thin, huh?'"

Then Mac looked at me and said, "Boy, in this business everyone cares about himself. Nobody cares about what's happening to you. How would you like to have your divorce in every newspaper in the country and have your best friend steal your wife? [His own divorce] Just go on and don't bore people with the details 'cause they don't care." At that moment, I realized he was right. No one cared and I was going to have to change. It was an eye opener from a redneck.

We get back and Nancy tells me the reports of the show are good, "Do you think I'll work with Mac again?" She just laughed and mumbled something about Mac and Jews. I did not work with him again, but I think I got something more than a job that night, I got a direction for my life.

About five months ago I was filling my car with gas when I looked up and across the island saw Mac Davis doing the same to his car. Do I talk to him? What the hell.

"Mac, I opened for you at the Kansas State Fair and you changed my life."

"Really, what's your name?"

I told him; we shook hands and he finished pumping gas as if I just told him the sky is blue. I guess he was right; no one cares.

Jim Bailey

ONCE I GOT WORKING on the road opening for big name acts, I worked nonstop for years. I was at the top of my game and nothing frightened me, so I opened for Jim Bailey. Who? Jim Bailey. He was the first drag queen to do national TV. Carol Burnett discovered him and put him on her show. The public had never seen an act like this before and so Jim worked a lot doing his illusions of Judy Garland, Peggy Lee, etc.

They book him in Evansville, Indiana. Evansville, home of the cow pucky. Evansville, a small town in the middle of nowhere, filled with people who date their cousins, and now a drag queen comes to town. Do you see where I'm going here? Cows, these people knew from cows. They had a Marriott or a Holiday Inn, which had a showroom; a showroom in Evansville, Indiana! These venues don't work in New York, Chicago, or LA, but some builder decides to put a showroom in Evansville, Indiana. There's a developer I want to meet, "You know what we need? A place where farmers can see men dressed as women." I want some of his drugs.

Let me explain how Jim worked. The show is in three parts. Jim opened the show with Judy Garland, then the comedian comes on while Jim changes his costume, and then Jim came back as himself (wearing more makeup than the real Judy Garland).

It's opening night and I want to see his show. While I never see my opening act, I always see the act of the headliner. I'm sitting in the audience and Jim is on stage as Judy Garland. The illusion is incredible; it's like watching the real Judy. I'm seated in front of two elderly women with grey hair who have just finished rotating the crops. They both look like Superman's mother in little floral print dresses clutching their brown leather purses.

I hear the first lady say, "What a wonderful show."

"I don't know why but I thought she was dead," the second lady responds.

"Don't be an idiot, that's her daughter."

Now I know my usual jokes won't work. These people did not have a clue. Jim finishes his first set and I run backstage and do my thirty minutes. I now knew my audience and homogenized my set. Huge laughs. Jim comes back out and I run back to the women to see what they're going to say now.

"Who's this guy?"

"I don't know," she shouts, "Bring back Liza!"

It took every ounce of strength I had to get out of the showroom without screaming in the middle of Jim's set.

That's how it went all week. The shows were good; the days were a nightmare. Even without make up, Jim looked like he had makeup on, and you can't go to the mall looking like that in Evansville, Indiana. Not without a lynching party. We stayed very close to the hotel. Ha! Hotel! I called down for extra towels and was told, "We'll get you some as soon as Becky gets back from the depot." I was in Hootersville.

Now it starts to get good. A waitress at the showroom develops a crush on Jim. Honey, try hitting on dead people, you'll have more luck. She had a full-on crush, brought him flowers, sent him love notes. I was sitting at the table when she came over in tears, "Why won't he answer my letters?" Ah, because he takes it up the old chocolate highway? The girl was a raving lunatic. Finally, it was up to me to break the news to her.

"Jim is married."

"Oh, I thought something was wrong with me?"

Duh, you're falling in love with a drag queen... red flag... red flag.

This goes on for a week. It's closing night or thereabouts. Jim does his Judy Garland and I follow with my thirty minutes. I'm just about to say good-night when I see Jim's orchestra leader in the wings doing the "stretch" sign. I do another fifteen minutes; he's still stretching. I do another fifteen; he's still stretching. I've done an hour and fifteen; he's still stretching. Now I'm doing every knock-knock joke I've ever heard, I'm doing jokes I remember from college, I start telling jokes my father told me. He's still stretching. I was at almost an hour and three quarters when I looked at the audience and said, "How long does it take to get out of a dress?" They screamed. Then I said, "I've done my show and every joke in the Joel McCrea songbook. I'm finished but they want me to stay on stage so I'll stay on stage." I looked over and there was a magazine on the piano. I picked it up and began reading; I flipped the pages in true comic fashion. They were laughing long and hard. I rip out a page, look at the audience, "Coupons." I do everything with this magazine but fuck it and finally I get the "get off" signal. I close the magazine, look off stage but say into the mic, "He's ready?" and nod. I turn to the audience and as big as I could say, "Thank you, the time just flew!" I get a standing ovation.

As I'm leaving the stage, Jim passes me, "Sorry. Judy was giving me a hard time," and I play the Looney Tunes Song in my head.

David Copperfield

I WAS WORKING AT The Turn of the Century in Denver with Lola Falana. To give you an idea how old this story is, they are both no longer working. Lola was a joy to work with; sweet, charming, and lots of fun off stage. With the luck of the draw, she contracted MS. Another career cut short. We were closing in a couple of days and David Copperfield was opening after us. I had never heard of him and probably would not have if the owner of the club had not said to me, "Hey, Steve, look at this," and he holds up my 8x10 and then next to it holds up David's. We looked exactly the same in the photo; same Tuxedo, same pose, same hair. Now in real life we look nothing alike, but those two photos made us look like brothers.

The very next night, David comes in to the club to see our show. He comes backstage and we joke about being related. David has come to Denver a few days early to receive his shipment of illusions. He has free time and we hang out the next day. He's like an old friend; we immediately click. He's just a nice normal guy and there is no show biz bullshit. To prove that we are not the same person we take a picture together both doing the same magic pose. We exchange numbers and say we'll connect in LA.

When I get to LA I give him a call. He invites me over to his place. At that time, he was living in the Hollywood Hills on or off a street called Tower. It was called Tower because the only way you could get to his house was via a tower, which held an elevator. It's been used in several films. David has just broken up with his girlfriend and the place is almost empty: mattress on the floor, sofa, and TV. That's all. Rather stark surroundings for an up-and-coming star. What I've learned is the real stars become stars because they are fixated on their careers and nothing else. I was always collecting art or buying houses. David was looking for new illusions. I was once told that if I spent as much time on my career as I did on my homes, I would be a star. They were probably right.

On stage, David is this handsome, sophisticated, suave illusionist. Off stage he was like your old Jewish cousin. He walked slumped over and he dragged his feet in sort of a shuffle. Off stage, he's the kid you used to beat up after school. On stage, he's the matinee idol women faint over. I once said to him, "I could ruin your career with one call to the *Enquirer* because this debonair, crafty magician is actually a schlep in real life." He laughed. David and I remained friends for a few years but as happens, our careers took us in different directions and we drifted apart. We liked each other and phoned every so often. Then I get a phone call from him one day.

"I'm doing a special, got any ideas?"

"You're such a classy act why don't you make a Rolls Royce or a Limo or a Ferrari disappear," I say to him.

There is quiet on the other end and all he says is "Thanks."

Later that year I hear he's done just that. To be fair, I don't know if that conversation spawned the illusion, but in my mind, it did. The following year I get another call from him.

"Steve, got any more ideas? I'm doing a special in New York."

Without a beat I say, "Why don't you make the Rockettes disappear?"

"The Rockettes? Hmm."

Next special he makes the Statue of Liberty disappear. I take full credit for that. Not.

David becomes a huge star. He's a bankable draw in Vegas. He's dating international models and flying here and there to do shows to sold-out houses. He's crossed over into the big time. I see him interviewed on TV about his warehouse of illusions. He collects vintage illusions and has millions of dollars in equipment. I'm happy for him because you always want to see friends do well.

Then comes Rick Marcelli's wedding. At one point, Rick had managed both David and myself so I knew I would be seeing David at the wedding and I was really happy. I hadn't seen him in years. I arrive at the wedding and sure enough, there is David. He's standing with a gorgeous blonde and three or four men. I go over to him.

"David. How the hell are ya?"

He looks over, "Hello, Steve."

"How have you been, David?"

The man standing next to him says, "David's been fine."

Huh? "Are you in town long? When's the next special?"

The man says, "We're opening in Vegas next week and the special doesn't shoot for a month."

I'm beginning to understand what's going on. David does not talk anymore. One more try, "Where are you staying?"

The man says, "We're at..." and he gives the name of the hotel.

I've had it. "Ok, David, nice to see you again."

The man says, "Thank you," and I walk away. The magic is gone, trust me.

I just don't know how people change that much, but they do. They change and it upsets me. I have been taught that I am no more important than the person who cleans my toilets. As a matter of fact, that person is probably a lot more important cause I sure as hell ain't sticking my hand in the crapper. I have seen it time and time again; people who have achieved stardom become aloof and distant. I just don't get it. When you're famous is when you're supposed to be the most open. It's the time when you're making big bucks and should be happiest, but in some cases, they appear to be inward-driven and closed off. It's a very sad commentary on show business and those that inhabit it.

Charo

IN MY JUNIOR YEAR, Emerson offered college credits for classes taken in Europe, so I went to school in Rome and London for a summer. I was in Rome having dinner at Piazza Navona and I noticed this couple walking by about a hundred feet in front of us. The man was dressed in a white linen suit with a Panama hat and the woman was wearing a tight-fitting floral dress and spike heels. I thought, *look at that old guy with the young hooker*. As they approached, I realized it was Xavier Cugart and Charo. That's all that happened. I saw them, and they walked by. I didn't go up to her and say, "coochie-coochie," I just saw her walk by.

Two years later, I'm working at Alexander's Department Store in New York City and Charo comes in. She walks right up to me and asks for assistance.

I'm helping her and I say, "I saw you in Rome two years ago."

She says to me, "Ja know, I lookin at ju and I know I know ju but I don know fram where."

Now this was bullshit because we never met, but she was just being show biz polite. It was my first experience with the sincerity of show folk. She buys her sweater for $6.99 and leaves.

Five years later, I'm writing the *Brady Bunch Variety Hour* and Charo is a guest on the show. I say to her, "I waited on you at Alexanders in New York."

She says, "Ja know, I lookin at ju and I know I know ju but I don know fram where."

I'm thinking, this sounds familiar, must be the only sentence she learned at Berlitz.

About three years after that, I'm working in Las Vegas with Barry Manilow. I'm invited to a party for all the acts on the strip. Ron Galella, famed paparazzi, asked if he could take my picture, and he pulls me over to a group of headliners and stands me next to. Charo. I say to her, "I was one of the writers on the *Brady Bunch Variety Hour*."

"Ja know, I lookin at ju and I know I know ju but I don know fram where."

Oh, fuck you.

About three years later, I'm working the Honolulu Comedy Club. Charo is working the Hilton. I'm out shopping and bump into her. I say, "I was at that party in Vegas. Ron Galella took our picture."

"Ja know, I lookin at ju and I know I know ju but I don know fram where."

You're kidding! This bitch has been in the country twenty years and that's all she can say?

Ten years go by. My friend Gary Bernstein is in Cedars Hospital having back surgery. I'm sitting with his mother in the waiting room and Charo sits down across from me. She's crying. Director Tito Romero is with us. He speaks fluent Spanish and goes over to her to see if there is anything we can do. She wants to be alone because her mother is gravely ill. She looks over at our group and I wave. Tito tells me she says to him, "Who is dat man? I lookin at jim, I know I know jim but don know fram where."

That was the last time I saw Charo, however, this is where the Forrest Gump connection comes in. I'm watching *Extra* and they say, "Happy Birthday Charo, January 15th". My birthday is January 15th. We share a birthday only each year she gets younger and I get older. That's why she doesn't remember me. With her age reversal, we haven't met yet!

Judy Garland

My friend Larry was getting married to Francine in Montreal. I was living in NYC, as was Henry Winkler. Henry and I decided to drive up to Canada in Henry's father's car. Once we were there, Larry made sure that I was well supplied with grass. I think he gave me an ounce or something, sort of a "thank you for coming to our wedding" gift. I put the dope in my suitcase and Henry and I headed back to NYC after the wedding. He throws his bag into the car and slams the trunk lid; only to realize the trunk keys are in his suitcase. I start to panic.

"Henry, what are we going to do when we reach the border? If we can't open the trunk they'll search it and find the dope."

Henry was very calm about the whole thing. I was a nervous wreck. His calm made me worry even more. We drive all the way to the border; I'm smoking all the way. Henry does not. He says to me, "Make sure you have nothing in the car." Like a scene from *Around the World in 80 Days* where the balloon is losing air and they have to dump sand to make it lighter, I start dumping shit out of the car windows. It's in my pockets, my pants, and my shirts. I finish the last of a joint and toss it out the window. We open the windows wide to air out the car as we head for the border crossing. I can see the guard by the time we do this, that's how close we were.

I'm freaking out, "We're going to jail because we can't open trunk. Why did you lock the keys in the trunk??" Henry is calm and in control. I'm screaming. Henry is calm. I'm deciding which federal prison I want to be sent to. I say to Henry, "Whatever you do, don't mention the trunk." He just looks at me and nods.

We get to the guard station.

"Evening Gentlemen, what business brought you to Canada?"

In his most charming voice, Henry says, "We went up to Montreal to go to our friend's trunk. Wedding." I hear Henry make the Freudian slip and measure my wrists for handcuffs. He shoots a look at me like what should I do, then back to the guard. "We attended a wedding at the Ritz Carlton."

The guy says, "Minute please." He leaves us and goes into the guard shack. My heart is pounding through my chest. This is during the Vietnam era and Americans were flocking to Canada to avoid the draft. They checked everything. The guy comes back and hands Henry his driver's license.

"Okay, welcome home, gentlemen," he lifts the gate and we drive on through stunned. Now you know how terrorists enter the country.

We start our drive again and we're sharing. I was telling him how much I wanted to be in show business but that my mother was being non-supportive. Henry consoled me by saying, "How do you think I feel? My father is begging me to take over the lumber business but I want to be an actor." We really understood each other's pain.

I got to know Henry on that trip to Canada. I've got to tell you, the man you see today is exactly the man I went to school with. He has not changed a single bit—maybe he's gotten nicer. I'm really happy when my friends make it big. When I was in college, I used to wonder how I would feel if my friends became stars but I was nobody. I got to see how that felt as friend after friend crossed over into the big time. It's not so hard to take if you enjoy shoving bamboo under your nails.

Henry dropped me off after getting the spare key. I didn't see much of him after that until we both moved to LA and he called me out of the blue. He wanted to know where he could find an apartment. There was one across the street from me and so Henry moved in and was my neighbor for about six months. Do you remember when Henry Winkler was dating Cindy Williams for about five minutes? Guess who introduced them? That's right, me, Forrest Gump.

I digress; back to that night we drove across the border. As we drove home that night, Henry turned on the radio. We heard that Judy Garland had died of an overdose in London. We talked about what show business was going to be like without her. I felt very sad, but you have to know this about me; I get sad when I take out the trash. I hate to see things change.

When I got back home to my one room apartment, there was a message from Amy, Cheryl, Todd, and Janis. They were going to Judy's wake;

did I want to come? Sure. Sounds like a history-making event. A friend had been keeping my dog for me. I got him and had no idea what a life-changing moment was in store for me.

The next day, we made our way across to Fifth Ave and we walked up to 81st Street. I remember passing the Metropolitan Museum and thinking there must have been an exhibit there because the crowds were so big. The crowds weren't for the museum, they were for the funeral. The line stretched from 80th to 81st on Fifth Ave. *Wow,* I thought, *what a tribute.* We got in line. It took about an hour for us to travel the one block and make the turn onto 81st street. When I saw the scene, I could not believe my eyes: the line went up 81st, back down 81st, then up again, then back down, and then back up again. There must have been ten thousand people there. The line was moving at a snail's pace. I remember the rest of my group dropping off one by one as the hours stretched by, first Janis, then Cheryl and finally Todd. The hours ticked by, one, two, three, five, six as we snaked our way through 81st street. It was a hot, humid June day but no one seemed to complain. It was just Amy and I. The sun was beating down and Amy said, "I can't take it anymore." I wanted to stay. She left.

It was just me alone in a sea of people. I'm not good in a crowd—funny that's how I should make my living. I'm just not good in crowds of strangers, but I stayed. It must have been three hours after Amy left that I was about fifty feet from Campbell's entrance. My heart was pounding. I didn't know what to expect, and before I knew it, I was standing inside the chapel and walking down the aisle. It was small and dark and had wooden walls. Very somber. Then, there she was. This is my memory of that moment: *Look how small she is.* It was an open casket covered with glass. The grandness of the event made her appear tiny; her hands were clasped in front of her clutching a bible. I looked at her face and it just didn't look like her. I was out of there in exactly thirty seconds. Over nine hours waiting in NY summer heat and I was out before I even knew I was in.

I walked all the way home to 58th Street knowing that I had just participated in history. I had seen something I would remember for the rest of my life. Now, as I write this, the memories are growing faint, however, I absolutely remember her clutching that bible. I have never thought about or mentioned that moment to another human being to this day. I'm sharing something with you that I've told no one.

Years later, a friend opened for Liza Minelli at the Riviera in Las Vegas. I stood backstage and watched Liza getting ready to go on. It was amazing seeing how she pumped herself up before the show. It was then I learned to prepare before going onstage and do it myself when I'm working.

After the show, I was introduced to Liza. I didn't know what to say to her so I did the obligatory, "Wonderful show," and shook her hand. What I wanted to say was, "Sorry for your loss," but it had been so many years and the show had been so glorious, why bring up her mother's death?

I know this crap sounds like a fantasy, but it's not. Seriously, I always thought everyone had adventures like I have had, but after six months of writing this book, I can see it's really been a very special trip I've been on. Maybe the chemicals are back in balance and I'm feeling better about myself, but today, I'm happy.

Van Johnson

IT MUST HAVE BEEN AUGUST in New York. You know, when the air is so thick with humidity that you can cut it with a blowtorch. There is a smell New York has in the summer that is like no other place on earth. It's a bittersweet smell made from hustle and bustle. It's a mixture of bubble gum and dog shit. It's melted ice cream and cat pee. It's soda pop and vomit. It hangs in the air like a hooker's perfume. It's what makes New York the place I love and the place where my history remains crystal clear. That history is burnt into my memory banks like an acid-dipped computer chip.

Susan and I were looking for something to do on a Thursday night. We had no money. None. It was before her B'hai (no drugs or alcohol) period and so we went clubbing regularly. God, I miss being young. I could stay out until 4 a.m. and get up the next morning and go to work. Today if I'm not in bed by 11 p.m., my rectum shuts down. It's nature's way of telling me I'm about to die. I have learned my limitations, obeyed my body, and curtailed my wild days. Today, a wild day for me is a nice bowel movement with rough toilet paper.

When I was living in New York in the late 60s, there was a hot club called Hippopotamus. It was on like 61st street, very close to my one-room apartment, and Susan and I walked over there one night at about 1a.m. to check it out. It was a very hip club and very restricted in its clientele. Only New York's hipper-than-hip were allowed in, but we were willing to try. After all, we were hipper than hip, young, and good looking; the trifecta of hip.

We get to the club; not a single person in line. The club had a stoop, a flight of stairs to get to the entrance, and we climbed it to where there is this very well-dressed man at the door with hair on his knuckles. I walk up to him.

"Two please."

He looks me up and down like I was wearing a suit made from shit. "No," is all he said.

"No?" I repeat.

"No," he says, and with the back of his hand waves me off like he was dismissing a servant.

I looked at Susan. Susan was a native New Yorker, born on 65th street and raised in the city. She was a hustler and is to this day a wheeler and dealer, a finagler. She pushes me aside.

"We would like a table for two."

He just shakes his head no.

"What do you mean no? Do you know who my father is?"

The guy raises one eyebrow.

"We would like a table for two or tomorrow you'll find your building condemned," she was out-and-out bluffing.

All he said was, "I live in New Jersey."

At that very moment, Susan looks across the street and her eyes focus on a man walking. She was like one of those jet fighters with night vision. "Look," is all she said.

Huh?

"Look!!!" She left the gorilla from New Jersey and she crosses the street without looking both ways to approach a man in a white linen suit. I follow. "*Miracle in the Rain. Miracle in the Rain*," is all she said. The man stops and looks back and it's then I see she's actually following Van Johnson. He stops.

"My dear, you are much too young to know who I am."

To which Susan says, "Are you kidding? I've seen every movie you've ever made. I'm your biggest fan. I adore you."

"Aren't you sweet?"

I'm watching all this like it's on TV.

"What are you adorable children doing out this late?"

"We're trying to get into Hippopotamus but they won't let us in."

"Well we'll just see about that," and he crosses the street and yells to the guy at the top of the stairs, "You there at the door. Let my friends in, will ya?"

"Certainly, Mr. Johnson."

He turns to Susan, "There you go young lady. Have a wonderful evening," and he walks on down the street. A five-minute encounter, a lifetime of memories.

Susan takes my hand and climbs the stairs to the club. The guy drops the velvet rope and lets us in. He's suddenly warm and gracious. I cannot tell you the awe I was feeling. I'm this kid from a small town and I have just witnessed New York moxie and Hollywood pull. Susan is acting like this happens all the time. Maybe it does, but not to me. We get inside to find we are the only people in the club. It is completely empty. We sit at a table that we had to tip to get and I turn to Susan, "This place sucks. I'm not paying cover to sit here with *you*." She agrees. We get up before the waitress returns.

As we pass the guy at the door he says, "Come back, won't you?"

Then I, who has said almost nothing the whole time, say, "If you weren't so picky, you could get some people into this shithole," and we walk up 61st to Second Ave and disappear into the bowels of New York.

Three Years Later

I'm working a club in New York. This was before comedy clubs, so it wasn't a comedy club, but it was a real nightclub. I just can't remember where it was, but I had to take an elevator to get there. It was either the Rainbow Room or the Playboy Club, but it must have been an important gig because my manager sent in one of his flunkies to be with me for the opening. A Flunky is a manager in training.

The opening did not go well. It was right after the divorce and I was emotionally not stable. I was off my game and was really angry that my managers had allowed the press in for the first show. I had asked them to arrange one night grace so I could get my feet wet before the press came in. I was having a screaming fit in my dressing room when the flunky says,

"Do you want to go to Studio 54?" A sudden hush comes over the room.

"Can you get us in?"

"I can get us in anywhere."

He makes a few phone calls and next thing I know, there is a stretch limo waiting outside the club and we're heading downtown to Studio 54. Now this was at the height of Studio 54, when it was the hottest spot not only in New York, but also in the world. We are in the back of the limo doing drugs and smoking grass. It was the early 70s, what good would a limo be if we didn't do those things?

We arrive at the club and the door swings open. My manager steps out first and I follow. I remember hearing someone in the crowd saying, "Wow. A real linen suit." He was referring to me and my Zeidler and Zeidler $89 suit, which I got on sale. It's all done with mirrors and wizardry. We get to the door and we are let in with no problem. I had arrived. We are ushered into the main dance floor where I was to see the most magnificent disco I have ever seen in my life. It was easy to see why this place was so popular. The music was blasting and it was filled with clouds of mist, which made it look like you were dancing in heaven. Beautiful people were everywhere. *Everywhere.* It was a collection of beautiful people and freaks and I remember fitting right in. Don't ask me with which group.

You want to know what my clearest memory was of that night? The light poles that dropped down from the ceiling. There were three or four vertical poles that dropped down from a fly space above. They looked like light-covered totem poles with all kinds of theatrical lighting creating visual effects. At the top was a rotating light, which sent a beam of light traveling all over the room. I wondered why people weren't impaled as the poles dropped down but it seemed to miss everyone, every time. I sat there that night feeling a part of something very special, something that would remain with me forever. I thought how strange it was that if Van Johnson wanted to come in here tonight, I could get *him* in. I was feeling like I had actually succeeded. I had actually become somebody. It was one or two days later that my whole world came tumbling down.

I was waiting to go on stage and the phone rang in my dressing room. It was my manager in Los Angeles; the big one, not the flunky. The flunky reported back to Los Angeles about my behavior after the opening and the reports were not good. I was not easy to deal with, the show had not gone well, etc., etc. The fact that I was losing my mind because of the divorce and finding out I was not the father of my son made no matter to them. This was business, "We're letting you go for your own good."

Five minutes before I go on stage they call to let me go. I was in total shock. I had lost my family and now I was losing my career. It was a rollercoaster I was on that week, and it finally came off the track and came crashing to the ground. It was the beginning of a four-year self-destructive streak that would take almost fifteen years to repair, but in those fifteen years I learned so much about self-importance—or lack thereof.

Remember the story I told about the TV show that stiffed me for me with a bounced check but gave me a limo for the day? Well on that trip, I remember sitting in the back of the Limo at 57th Street and 3rd Avenue and seeing two women huddled over the heated exhaust pipe of a huge apartment building. They were trying to keep warm in the midst of a biting New York winter. I remember feeling very guilty that I was in a limo and they were in the street. It was the very first time I had considered others over my own hedonistic lifestyle, and it was the beginning of the new me, a me that tried to do for others and tried to care about the world more than myself. It was a great eye-opener that night and it all happened in New York, around the corner from my one-room apartment and just up the street from where Van Johnson had gotten me into the disco. There's a reason New York has a special place in my heart.

The Freezer

IT WAS MY FIRST HOME in the suburbs, my very first home. I had sold my Condo for a very nice profit and was moving on to my first single-family home ever. This one was a fixer-upper, as are all my homes, but it had a swimming pool and a huge garden with a gigantic covered patio. I was working on a sitcom at the time and proudly announced that I had bought a house, "Hey guys, I bought my first house." The head writer asked where it was. I told him and he said, "That neighborhood is so conservative, the Girl Scouts sell Nazi Bundt Cookies." Ha-ha, we all laughed. Little did I know, he was right. I had moved into redneck central. It would take me years to figure this out, and right then I was living under the delusion that I had finally bought my dream home in the 'burbs.

The only role models I had for 'burb living were my aunt and uncle on Long Island. They were the ideal family in the ideal home in the ideal location. This aunt was the happy homemaker. Her house was always spotless and there was always an apple pie baking or a brisket cooking. To me, this represented happiness, and since my childhood had made *Ripley's Believe It or Not*, I decided to copy everything "the perfect family" had done so I too would have the perfect home.

The one thing I did remember about my aunt's house was that they had a freezer in the garage for back-up food. Jews back up food. We don't just buy one steak; if it's on sale, we buy the cow. A red-letter day in my house was when tuna went on sale for 28¢ a can. I can remember the cases coming in like we were a receiving center for Star-Kist.

The image of my Aunt's freezer was solid in my mind, and so I set out to buy a freezer of my own for my own happy home. I scoured the newspapers and finally there it was at JC Penny. I drove almost forty-five minutes to the nearest Penny's and proudly announced, "I would like to purchase this freezer. Does it have a light inside?" Alas, it did not; it was the smallest, cheapest freezer Penny's made. However, the next size up, the sixteen-cubic-foot one, did have a light inside, "I'll take it."

The man goes to the register and says, "Ya know, the twenty-eight-cubic foot freezer is on sale. It's cheaper than the sixteen-cubic-foot." Did he say "cheaper?" It was to be delivered in two days.

Two days later I'm waiting for my freezer delivery, and I see this huge truck pull up in front of my house. I think, *who's getting airplane parts?* It had one of the little three-wheeled vehicles hanging off the back like a dingy. I'm watching the driver as he maneuvers the truck on the street and I'm appalled as he pulls up in front of my house and walks up the driveway. He doesn't even have to ring the bell because I'm standing there watching the circus come to town on my doorstep. Small children have started to gather around the truck like they do in African Villages when a strange jeep drives through. They're setting up lemonade stands; they're pulling out lawn chairs. It's like a Fourth of July celebration. The big truck is here! The big truck is here!

The driver says, "Your freezer is here. Do you own a restaurant?" This is the first indication that I have purchased the Spruce Goose of freezers. He starts looking at my front door and pulls out a measuring tape.

"This will have to come off."

"No! It's going in the garage."

"Oh. You'll have to move your car."

Move my car! What have I bought, a barge?

I pull my car into the street and look back as the driver is opening the truck. There, seated at the back of the truck, is this box. It's not so much a box as it is a small town in Indiana. This fucker had its own zip code. It had time zones and tidal patterns. The thing had two moons and was affecting the polarity of the earth. Jesus Christ. I bought a universe.

The little dingy truck gets lowered and it lifts the carton off the truck. It swings around and takes the top off my pepper tree. Peppercorns are flying everywhere and the neighbors are rushing to get them like pigeons after popcorn. The dingy goes up the driveway, and like a choreographed ballet, drops the box exactly where I told him to put it.

"Are you going to take it out of the box?"

"We don't do that," is all he said as he lifted the dingy back into its nest on the truck. He gives me the paperwork to sign and he's out of there like that bird who deposits its eggs in other birds' nests and then flees to let the host bird raise its young.

The crowd breaks up and it's me and my neighbor Vern and the box from hell. I start cutting and snipping. I'm chopping and hacking. I'm pulling and tugging. The plastic bands that keep the box together begin to give way. Styrofoam and reinforced cardboard sections begin to part; plastic sheeting and bubble wrap encase the sarcophagus. I'm ripping and pulling for twenty minutes. I've filled two recycling bins and there's still more to come. Then, there it is, my new freezer. I could put wheels on it and it could pass as a PT Cruiser. To this day, when I see a PT Cruiser, I see freezer frost. I plug in the freezer and the motor starts up like the Martian Space Ship in *War of the Worlds*. The lights dim in the garage for a second as the motor cranks up, something I learned would happen every time it turned itself on.

I lift the lid and look inside. As a joke I sing, "I'm wishing (I'm wishing)/ For the one I love/ To find me (To find me)/ Today (TO-DAYYYYYYYYYYYY!)." Vern laughs and asks me what I'm going to put in this thing. This is the first time anyone had asked me this. I respond "food?" I run inside and take all the food out of the inside freezer and bring it into the garage. I carefully lay it all out, two chickens and a half-eaten pizza. It was like trying to empty the Pacific Ocean with a thimble. The two chickens rolled around on the bottom of the freezer like it was bowling alley. I need more food.

I go to Vons and buy $278 worth of frozen food. That's six shopping bags of steaks, chops, and popsicles. One small corner of the freezer was almost full. This thing was like the plant in *Little Shop of Horrors*, "Feed me Seymour." I went back again and bought another $100 worth of food. I got it almost half full, however, I now had enough frozen food for an expedition to Antarctica.

I loved my new freezer and would visit it in the garage often to take out a steak or a chicken or a half a cow. It made me feel good knowing I had created a little bit of heaven for myself. Then summer came. As the garage heated up, the freezer would crank up. The hotter it got, the longer it cranked. It wheezed and puffed all hours of the day and night. Then, my electric bill came. I saw lots of zeros and all in the wrong places. The Little Freezer That Could had increased my electric bill by about $125. Who knew heaven was so expensive? I took everything out of the freezer and put it into the kitchen freezer. I unplugged the monster in the garage and threw a tarp over it. It looked like I was storing a coffin, and that's how it sat for two and a half years.

Oh, it didn't go to waste. I used it to saw on. I used it as a table. I groomed the dog on it. It was perfect height when you had a garage sale. If you laid it on its side the kids could use it as a clubhouse. A Mexican family hid there from immigration. They held the Israeli-Palestine Peace talks in it. I brought it to the marina and sailed around Cape Hope in it. I'm telling you, it did not go to waste.

Finally, it became apparent that I had totally fucked up and was not going to use this escapee from the Ice Age. I put an ad in the newspaper. All it said was, "Brand new twenty-eight-cubic foot freezer for sale." I expected families to call. Wrong. Institutions called. Colleges, hospitals, food chains, prisons! I finally sold it to the highest bidder—a catering company that told me they hoped they had enough food to fill it. That's my insane life, me trying to find happiness at any cost, only to get the cold shoulder once again.

Gary

WHEN I WAS FIRST STARTING OUT in show business, it was imperative I got an agent who believed in me and would fight to get me work. Sounds simple, but it's almost impossible. The business is tough, agents don't have time, and some just don't have the inclination to develop new talent; it's easier to work with established stars. The quest to find representation was endless but it all changed for me in the blink of an eye.

It was a smoky Saturday night at the Improv in Los Angeles. I was standing in the hallway and a figure approached me from out of the darkness. I didn't know this man, but he had a smile on his face and seemed pleasant. He extended his hand,

"Hi, I'm Gary Weinberg. I saw you at the Comedy Store a couple of days ago. It was the first time I laughed in two weeks."

I sort of shook my head in a humble kind of "stop you're embarrassing me" way.

"I'm with I.C.M. Do you have an agent?" I.C.M. was the biggest agency in town at the time and getting an agent there was considered a coup.

"No."

"Good. Would you come in to see me tomorrow? I'll have my secretary set up an appointment." He hands me his card and walks back into the shadows. It was as simple as that.

The very next day, Wanda calls to set up the appointment and I'm sitting in his office with all the pictures of stars on the wall, but I'm not hearing a word he's is saying. I'm in shock. I think I hear, "You could be a big star, I think you're talented." Within four days there is a contract in my mailbox and I'm signed to the agency. Three years of struggle working for Photomat, as a gardener, in an antique store, but never a waiter! I had some dignity. Now the doors were opening. It was a very exciting time.

Usually what happens after you sign with a big agency is the agent forgets about you and you get lost in the roster of huge stars, but that didn't happen with Gary. I was immediately sent out on interviews. I was working at the Comedy Store one week and flying to Lake Tahoe to open for Kenny Loggins the next. Gary was unstoppable. People would come up to me, "Man, does your agent love you," and they would tell me how he fought to get me in to see this producer or that casting director. It was unheard of. I was the envy of all my comedian friends.

You have to understand how worthless I felt at that time. Somehow, I managed to pull myself through that pile of muck and make a life for myself. Gary was making my career. I wasn't so much grateful to Gary as I was in awe. Most entertainers are selfish people who think only of themselves. I was different. When you feel so worthless and someone works so hard to make you a success, you can't take it for granted—you have to repay him. It's only right. I repaid Gary the only way I knew how—with unconditional friendship. I made sure he knew how much I appreciated what he was doing and made myself available if *he* ever needed *me*. I adored this man; he was my big brother, my muse, my mentor, my best friend. We spoke at least once a day. He was the friend I always wanted; the brother I never had.

Gary was a fantastic businessman. It was Gary who taught me how to buy real estate. I always knew that I could never achieve what Gary had or make as much money or… did it matter? I wasn't going to be a good as Gary. Gary was buying houses and flipping them. He was making millions—so much so it finally came to a point where he didn't need to work for I.C.M. and he quit. I knew it would be the end of my career. No one else really cared about me, only Gary. I remember making a conscious decision to remain his friend even after he left the agency. It was sort of my way of saying thank you. The last thing he did before he left the agency was make sure I got signed to a huge management firm. They picked up the ball where Gary had set it down and used their power to get me even more work. His parting gift to me was to ensure I would work even if he wasn't there to guide my career.

Once I started working, I was in and out of town regularly. Gary and I spoke but the conversations became shorter and were further between. He never left my mind though. He was still my brother. Then, one day, I realized that I hadn't spoken to him in several weeks. I called him. There was no answer. I called and called and finally left a message on his machine, "If I don't hear from you tomorrow, I'm calling the police".

The next day the call came, "I'm sick."

I ran to Cedars. He was so sick that day, he asked me to leave. "They don't know what's wrong with me. My immune system is shutting down. It's me and seventeen other guys at UCLA," is all he could say.

Over the next several weeks, I watched as he got better and worse and better and worse. The doctors didn't know what was wrong with him; the disease didn't even have a name back then. He was sent home and had twenty-four-hour care. One night he called me, "My nurse can't stay the night." I was there in five minutes. I slept on the sofa in the living room and checked on him during the night. In the morning, he was sitting up in bed, "God, I feel better. I'm going to be fine now."

About a week later I called Gary to see how he was doing. There was a message on his answering machine, "I've gone to Florida to be with my parents." I called immediately and was told Gary was in the hospital with cancer throughout 90% of his body. I knew the end was near and I started making deals with God, but none of them worked. He died on November 18, 1981, and a little bit of me died with him. I had lost my brother, my mentor, my muse, and my best friend. I didn't care about my career. I only cared about the loss of my dearest friend. I remember standing at the kitchen sink holding on to the counter as my knees buckled under me. I had never experienced such grief before or since. Later in therapy, I learned I was crying because I didn't believe in myself and had just lost the only person who I thought did.

The years passed. I had my ups and downs, a divorce, a nervous breakdown, another nervous breakdown, several failed relationships, but my friendship with Gary never faltered. I could not forget this friend, this champion of my talent, and when I did not become a superstar, I felt I had let Gary down.

Miami

My agent, Gary Weinberg, had been booking my little tush all over the country. I was green, but I was learning and doing well everywhere. He called me and said, "I just booked you at the Doral in Miami."

Cool, I thought.

"When you get there, give my parents a call," he says, and I do.

Here is the first thing his mother says to me: "Why did he book you there? You're gonna bomb."

I get to Florida and my aunt picks me up at the airport, first mistake. It begins, "Have you called your mother? Why haven't you? Do you want your mother to die of a broken heart?" I'm not in the city five minutes and the guilt has already started. There must be a guilt school these women go to. My aunt drops me off at the Doral; the car is three feet from the curb. A bellman takes my bag from the car to the curb and sticks out his hand. While he's doing that, a second bellman takes my bag from the curb to the front door, where a third bellman is waiting to take it inside.

"Wait a minute!" I scream, "Am I going to have to tip one of these guys every six feet?"

The show is that night. I have never worked Miami before. I arrive at the hall at the designated time. The MC approaches me and tells me I'll be going on in twenty minutes. I start my pacing and in twenty minutes the MC enters the stage, "Ladies and Gentleman, Steve Bluestein". That's all he said. A light smattering of applause can be heard. I begin. Nothing. Gary's mother's words come back to me, *you're gonna bomb*. I continue talking. Nothing. The sweat begins to pour. I try talking off the cuff. Nothing. I do my twenty minutes and get off. They never noticed I left the stage.

I'm thinking, *I wonder if there's a gun shop in the hotel.* I'm standing at the elevator when a man comes up to me.

"Hey, kid, nice show."

I just smile.

"I'm Joey Villa." I know the name; he's a Vegas comedian, "You can't fight the fork."

"Huh?"

"They were eating dinner when you started. You can't fight the fork."

This stranger, this comedian from another era, sits me down and talk to me, "First of all, they were sitting at round tables. Half the audience had their back to you. Bad. Second, they were serving dinner. You can't work when people have food in the mouths, they can't laugh. Third, comedy needs focus and their focus was on their food not you. And, your intro sucked. Your act is good. I know comedy and you're a funny kid, but they tied your hands.... Never let this happen to you again." He shakes my hand and goes back inside.

To this day, I will not work if there is food on the table. I won't work to round tables and I will *not* work in Miami. If it's a round table of food in Miami... forget about it. But not for the reasons you think. About twelve years later I get booked at the Comedy Club in Miami Beach. The manager of the Miami club is a lady who worked at a club in Newport Beach. She had been the manager of that club and the story goes that she had gone out after work with two of the waitresses to grab a bite to eat. There had been an auto accident and the two girls were killed; a horrible thing to experience. It's alleged the manager, who was sort of a tart looking woman, carried around the guilt of those deaths and began to self-destruct. She left California and opened a club in Miami. She called me, and I was booked. I had always liked this woman; she was over the top but fun to be with. Besides, I wasn't going to marry her, only work for her. It was a two-week gig.

Week One

The shows were going very well. We were sold out every night, the crowds were wonderful, the management seemed happy. Then the club manager tells me, "We're going to do a publicity show for your second week. All the TV and press will be there. Will you do it?"

"Sure, where?"

"At Children's Hospital."

"Wait. You want me to do comedy in a children's hospital?"

"Not in the hospital, in the auditorium for the doctors and the staff."

"Oh." That seemed strange, but I agreed.

The day of the show, she drives me to the hospital. As we're walking in she says, "There's been a change. We're not doing the show in the auditorium."

"Oh, where are we doing it?"

"Here."

She walks me into the children's ward, complete with oxygen tents, plaster casts, and dying children.

"You want me to do comedy in here??"

We get into a heated debate. I tell her all the reasons why I can't do the show here and she says, "If you don't do it, the boys at the club will be really pissed."

"What boys?" and she pushes her nose to the left.

I'm standing on a milk crate in the Leukemia ward of Miami Children's Hospital doing comedy. The audience is composed of doctors, nurses, parents, and sick children. You have no idea how I wish they had been eating dinner at round tables.

I know I cannot do my act under these conditions, so I pull out, from the dark reaches of my mind, a children's improv exercise I learned at Emerson and work with the kids that way, all the time making funny asides to the parents. Right in the middle of the set, a boy to my left begins to cough. He coughs and sputters, his screen goes blank, alarms go off and fifteen nurses start pounding on his chest. Suddenly there is a blip on the screen, they settle him down and all eyes go back to me.

"Thank you! Good night!"

I'm out of the room and into the car. I am really upset. That night is the end of the first week. I am to be paid as per my contract but there is no check. Despite repeated promises, there is no check the next night or the night after when I open the second week.

Week Two

I open the second week. I have not been paid for the first week, and I have been forced to do a comedy show for free in a children's ward in front of TV cameras. I am not happy; however, I have faith that they will come through and I open the second week. I'm doing the show and I'm talking to the audience. There is a guy on the ring and I start talking to him.

"What do you do?"

"I'm the chef here," he says.
"Did you get paid this week?"
"No."
This sets me off on a twenty-minute tirade about not getting paid. I said, "I think the hotel is in trouble. I asked for towels and the maid said I had to share mine with room next door."

The place went up for grabs. The more they screamed the funnier I got. I started talking about the hotel and the show at the hospital and not getting paid. The audience was laughing with the kind of energy that spurred me on. It's like throwing gasoline on a fire. Now I'm getting angry. The angrier I get, the funnier it gets, because I pull out all the stops. I have worked many years, and there are magical nights; this was one of those nights. Nothing I said was wrong. The audience was not laughing, they were convulsing. The more they convulsed, the funnier I got, I was a snowball going downhill and there was no stopping me.

I finished the show, and to my surprise, there was my roommate from freshman year in college, Mark Hurwitz; my roommate from senior year, Jon Stierwalt; and my cousin Susan, her husband, and kids. Susan was standing on her chair screaming, as the audience demanded an encore. I did a few more minutes and got off stage thinking, *this is one for the books*. The manager comes running up to me, I think, to congratulate me. Instead she takes me under the arm.

"Get out of here and get out now. The boys are furious about what you said about the hotel."

"Huh?"

"Honey, I'm telling you. Leave. Run. Get out." It's like a B movie. She pushes me out the door.

I go to Jon Stierwalt and tell him, "The Mafia is after me." We run up to my room and, like a Marx Brother's comedy, we are packing and throwing clothes in suitcases and bumping into each other and I'm shitting a brick. I check out surrounded by Jon and his wife Ronnie, who are protecting me like I'm the Pope. We get to the car and they take me to an "undisclosed location." I never hear from the club again, I never get paid, I never work Miami beach again. Ever.

Melissa Manchester

IN ONE OF MY PLAYS, I say, "When you're hot in this town [LA], you're hot; and when you're not, you're handled by an agency in the valley." By the end of the 70s and early 80s, I was hot. It was my fifteen minutes of fame. After closing with Donna Summer and Barry Manilow, I went on tour with Melissa Manchester. I thought being on tour with Seals and Crofts was fun. That was a work camp in comparison to working with Melissa. I never enjoyed anything so much in my life.

While other headliners like Seals and Crofts were familiar and fun to be with, Melissa and her group felt like family! The whole memory I carry with me to this day. It wasn't like being on tour with all this, "Don't do this and you can't say that," it was like being in someone's loving family. A nice family, one that just happened to be forty musicians and backup singers.

It started in Reno. My cousin Sheila from my mother's side came up to see the show. Now, you have to understand, this was the first and only time any member of that family had made an effort to see my show; no one before nor since. In any case, in Reno I met Steve and Claudia Cagan. Claudia is Melissa's sister and Steve, Claudia's husband, was Melissa's musical conductor. The three of us clicked at once. They weren't "show folk," they were friends who happened to be in show business. They included me in their plans; they invited me on their excursions. They made me feel like an equal when I always felt less-than. With these guys, I never felt like I was outside looking in, I always felt part-of and, for someone who never felt a part of anything, this was a wonderful experience—one that gave me hope. I drank it in like an alcoholic in a wine tasting room.

Reno went well. Uneventful. It was Reno. The crowds were sold out for Melissa, and rightly so. Unless you've heard her live, you haven't heard her. There is a warmth to her voice that just drips off the stage. She's an intelligent songwriter and her throaty, sultry voice caresses each song like it was nursing a newborn.

I think our first stop after Reno was Boston (Framingham, actually), and I was so looking forward to it. Coming back to my hometown, coming back to Boston doing what I had talked about doing all my life. I had goose bumps just thinking about it. Cut to opening night (note: In my hometown, my mother did not come to the show, nor did a single member of her family), and I step out on stage. I look out into the audience and I see a sea of young faces that look like their parents. They have no style or flair, eighty-five percent of them are overweight. They were the most unhip group of drips I have ever worked for. It was then I remembered why I moved to New York after college. While Bostonians are nice people, their roots are firmly planted in the Pilgrim heritage. They are very conservative, very unemotional, very plain people. While it may be different today, back then the crowd was old, plain, and fat. That's the name of that tune.

I begin my act, editing all the while. The material was too hip for the room. I would leave them behind if I had not done so, but I was having a good time and the show was going well. Then, all of a sudden, I get a heckler. I *love* hecklers! I love to drop my act and just toss it back and forth with someone in the audience. I have to have fun too, you know? That is exactly what I did. I started bantering with this guy in the audience and I was laughing as hard as the audience. He's getting in some pretty good lines and I love it because the audience likes to see the heckler get the edge over the comedian, but I have the mic and have to stay in control. I deliver some pretty funny lines myself. The audience loves that as well. He stays with me to almost the end of my set but I need to move on so I can close my set strongly and that's what I do. Solid applause.

Twenty-five years later I'm at John Laroquette's house for his Christmas party. Lenny Clarke, who is also on The John Laroquette Show, comes up to me, "Hey, Steve. How ah ya? Rememba me? I was the guy in Framingham givin' you a hahd ti-em. I wuz the heckla." I realized it had been a young Lenny Clarke who was breaking in his comedy chops at my show in Framingham. He remembered almost every joke we told that night. I said to myself, *welcome to my world. I do the show; the heckler gets the TV series.*

After Boston, we headed for the Catskills. I had only heard about the Catskills and the legends of comedians who got their start there. David Brenner used to tell me about what his beginning was like working there.

David Brenner was a very special person to me. When I first came to The Comedy Store, the comedians were not supportive and were extremely competitive, but David Brenner and Gabe Kaplan both took the time to not only be supportive, but also give me tips. David was booked on the first TV show I did in Canada. I can't tell you how happy it made me. I was able to show him what I had become with his advice. I was looking forward to getting on stage in The Catskills, a place where comedy had been created.

Randy Kirby was in New York City at the time and he drove up to "the mountains", as they are called, to the gig with me. We get to the Concord and I'm in shock. The hotel is a toilet. A toilet, and that's being nice. This place had blood on the pillow from where Lincoln had been shot. It was old and run-down and dirty. I really didn't care about that, what I cared about was the show room. I walk into this massive show room, maybe seating twenty-five hundred to three thousand people. It's row after row of long tables and white tablecloths. It's like the perfect comedy room. I was excited about working there. Then I noticed the waiters putting out wooden mallets at each place setting. I thought, *how strange is that?* and went on my way.

That night, the air was charged with energy. I was like a racehorse waiting to get on stage. I can tell how the crowd is going to be by listening to the murmur before the show. If it's high-pitched, it's a good show; if it's low-pitched, it's a dog of a show. This was a high-pitched murmur. I'm pacing backstage waiting to go on and I hear them start the show. The crowd is murmuring.

"Ladies and Gentlemen..."

The crowd murmurs.

"The Concord is proud to present..."

Louder murmuring.

"Melissa Manchester..."

Fast murmuring.

"With comedian Steve Bluestein"

Louder murmur.

"And now, please welcome, Steve Bluestein!"

I step out on stage to what appears to be a prison riot. The crowd had not heard a thing the announcer said. They were walking from table to table, kids were running, old people were talking and eating, and teenagers are throwing food. It was Jews gone wild! I start my act; the murmurs got louder. It's like I was interrupting their interrupting. I do the first joke and I hear this banging noise like a hundred wood peckers are knocking on the roof. I do the next joke, same thing. I look out into the audience and instead of laughing they are banging on the tables with the wooden mallets. Oh my god. They're too lazy to laugh! The entire audience was in revolt, like when the warden won't get better food. I'm talking, they're banging. Talking. Banging. Talking. Banging. Finally, I say, "Give me a break will ya, I'm a Jew." Three thousand wood mallets begin to bang in unison... *bang, bang, bang, bang...* it sounded like the troops were marching into Poland. I had to do twenty minutes with the Von Trapp Family Bangers and somehow, I did.

I get off stage and fall into Randy Kirby's arms. "Let's go to New York City," is all I said and we went from the stage to Manhattan. Our next date was in Philly. I had not spoken to Melissa or Claudia, mostly because I was so embarrassed at how the show had gone. In New York, I had a t-shirt made and I walked into the sound check in Philly backwards. All Melissa saw was my red t-shirt, which said, "Jewish Audiences are slightly irregular." This got a huge laugh from everyone, but I had a better one. I turned around and on the front of the shirt it said, "FUCK THE CATSKILLS," It brought the house down. Melissa, the musicians, Claudia, everyone was laughing.

That is why I loved working with this group. Another headliner would have had me fired for the bad show, but Melissa knew it was just that, a bad show. The rest of the tour went smoothly, and to show you how well it went, Claudia, Stephen, and I remain friends to this day. To me, that's what it's all about: putting quality people in your life. I will never forget the time I spent with Melissa and her group on the road; I can honestly say it was worth The Concord and the mallets to be part of that memory, and I never once cried out loud!

Kenny Loggins/ Frankie Valli

ONE OF GREAT THINGS about being on the road for so many years: I got to see a lot of this country. A lot. Many places I didn't want to see or think I'd ever see, like Missoula, Montana. They have a college there and I did a comedy tour sponsored by Schlitz Beer. It actually turned out to be a lot of fun, but the best place ever was Lake Tahoe. Magnificent scenery, clear air, and every morning you wake up with a bloody nose.

Kenny Loggins

Of all the headliners I worked with in Tahoe, my favorites were Kenny Loggins and Frankie Valli. I had been working at the Improv in Las Vegas when I got a call, "You're opening for Kenny Loggins tomorrow night. Get up to Tahoe." I grabbed the first plane back to LA, threw some stage clothes in a suitcase, and was back at the airport in twenty-four hours. On the plane going up to Tahoe, I notice Kenny sitting three seats ahead of me. I went up to him.

"Kenny, I'm Steve Bluestein. I'll be opening for you."

"Nice to have you on the show. What instrument do you play?"

"Glockenspiel" is all I said. He had no idea who I was or what I did.

Kenny was another one of those "nice people" to work for. He did not have the star mentality and was very nice to me during the week. One day he asked me if I wanted to go to the health club with him and a couple of the guys in the band. "It helps the throat" is all he said, and I thought, *why not?* I meet them in the hotel spa. I arrive a little late and walk into the dressing room and all the guys from Kenny's band and Kenny are there stark naked, "Come on. We're takin' a steam bath." Now you have to know this about me, I dress to get undressed. I don't get naked in front of a mirror. I am *that* self-conscious. The whole band is waiting for me to show my love handles. It took every ounce of strength I had to take off my clothes and go into the steam bath with them. I'm sitting in there, legs crossed with a towel around my shoulders and my eyes closed. In all the years on the road it was the strangest experience I ever had, naked with Kenny Loggins.

The week goes well. We're having great shows that are sold out every night. Kenny's music is incredible, and every single show, after my set, I'd run out into the audience to watch Kenny and listen to that incredible music. I'm told Sunday is going to be a special show. Sunday we're doing a show for the employees of the hotel. I had heard Liza Minelli did a show like that in Vegas and it was the hottest show in town. I was looking forward to it; I can't tell you how much I was looking forward to it. Just a bunch of hip people and me being able to say whatever I wanted.

Come Sunday night I'm pacing backstage and I hear the murmur from the other side of the curtain. It wasn't so much a murmur as it was a jet plane taking off. The crowd was at a fever pitch. The lights come down and the crowd starts to scream like at a football game, "Ladies and Gentlemen, The Sahara is proud to present, Kenny Loggins!" And people, the audience begins to roar like I have never heard, ever. The roof comes off the place. The announcer continues... "With the comedy of..." that's all he said and the booing started. It builds and builds and builds. Now they're stamping their feet and pounding on the tables. "Steve Bluestein" and the booing explodes. I want to die and die now!

I walk out on stage and they're still booing, only now it's orchestrated like a choir. I begin my set they are booing. Not so much booing as screaming their boos. I think, *make them stop, God, make them stop.* Be careful what you pray for. Now they are yelling things, things like, "You suck!" and, "Get off the stage! We want Kenny! We want Kenny! We want Kenny!"

I have to do nineteen minutes and I plod through. Things start flying up and hitting the curtain. I'm dodging napkins and olives, toothpicks, a baby blanket, six bottle caps and here comes the bottle. At one point, I look down and a girl has crawled onto the apron of the stage and is crawling towards me. She is on her hands and knees. I say to her, "You're not invisible ya know." This gets a huge laugh from the crowd. She looks up at me and says, "Get out of my way, asshole," and I have to move as she continues to crawl toward the wings. Two stagehands come on stage and physically lift her up and drop her back into the audience. I look at my watch and think, *I've done my nineteen,* and I get off. I head for my dressing room; the stage manager is waiting for me. "Congratulations. You just did seven minutes." Kenny is in his dressing room with one leg in his pants going, "He's what?"

Needless to say, I was devastated. The stage manager pulls me into his office and I am expecting to get a lecture. Instead, he says to me, "Those people were drunken animals and there was nothing you could have done to save that show. They were here to see Kenny and no one else. My report to the office on this show will be like all the others. 'Comedian did fine job. Nineteen minutes.'" My eyes filled up and I shook his hand. All he said was, "Come on, the stage hands and I are going to grab a bite to eat."

The second show that night went as planned. I felt a lot better about myself. You know, a comedian is only as good as his last show. Kenny asked me to grab a bite with him and Eva, his wife at the time. We're sitting in a booth talking about the show and Kenny is being very complimentary about my work that week when I hear the couple in the booth next to us say, "Did you hear that comedian? What a piece of shit. He was awful." Sitting next to Kenny Loggins, I wanted to thrust the butter knife through my heart. Kenny put down his fork, looked at me and said, "I'll mail you some of my early reviews. You'll feel a lot better." Nice guy, no?

Frankie Valli

Must have been two months later when I'm back in Tahoe, this time opening for Frankie Valli. The stage manager is there to welcome me and takes me backstage to show me my picture on the wall of stars. I can't tell you what that did for me. Frankie Valli is a singer I grew up with. I knew his music and could not wait to see his show. I was not let down. The music was wonderful, the crowds were great, and Frankie was very nice to me. Very. For the most part, with the exception of two headliners, my opening experience has been very positive. The headliners all treated me with respect. I have been very lucky.

The week marches on and we are having great shows. Frankie is a very easy-going guy backstage, no ego, and no problems. He comes into my dressing room one night after the second show smoking a joint, "Wanna hit?" And we're off. I start smoking and the more I smoke the funnier I get. Frankie stays in my dressing room till almost 1 a.m. and then says, "Let's get a bite in the coffee shop." We head down there and are seated at a table for two. The menus in the coffee shop are huge, maybe twenty-four inches tall. When you open them, you block out everything around you. All you can see is the menu and there was a lot to see. I'm looking over a thousand choices and I've got the munchies. Frankie is doing the same.

While we are buried in our menus, the waitress approaches. We don't see her, we just hear her, and she has the worst lateral lisp I have ever heard. Every time she gets to the letter "s" she sprays like Sylvester, "Would you like to see our Sunday Special?" I see Frankie's hand reach out and grab for a napkin. I start to laugh. I can't stop myself. I'm laughing, and the more she talks, the more I laugh. "A Sundae is always good on a Sunday, especially after the show." I look around my menu at Frankie's menu and all I can see is his hands holding the menu and the menu shaking. This sends me up for another round of laughter. I manage to get out "Can we have a minute?" She sprays "Sure," and exits.

Frankie and I let out a scream of laughter and scramble out of the coffee shop. It was one of the moments that would have been fun if you had experienced it with high school buddies, but having it with Frankie Valli just made it special.

I sorely miss those opening act days. Soon after, the opening spots in major nightclubs closed up. They began using two headliners to bring in the crowds. I was forced to switch from big clubs to Comedy Clubs, and that was the nail in the coffin for my career. I was on the road and out of sight of the industry for over ten years. I made a nice living, but was penny-wise and pound-foolish. Oh well, I guess everything happens for a reason. The doctor says it's time for my medication (The nurse slips on the straight jacket as the comedian shuffles off to the day room).

Nancy Walker

JEFFERY GLASSMAN WAS a childhood friend. His mother went to school with my mother and they were like two peas in a pod. Jeff and I grew close because our mothers were close. Jeff was worldly; I was shy. Jeff was curious; I was afraid. Jeff was dull; I was funny. It was the strangest friendship of my childhood. We were so different and yet so much alike. To give you an idea of what we were like together, Jeff and I went on a double date. We walked into the restaurant and the hostess said to Jeff, "Can I help you, sir?"

"Table for four," I said.

"OK dear," she replied.

That summed up going out in public with Jeff. He was sir; I was dear. He was mature; I was a baby-faced caca head.

Jeff did things I never even thought of doing or knew existed or thought I should know about doing. My world was encased in my parents' daily battles in their relationship. I was fighting to stay alive in that household and outside activities were nonexistent. One day Jeff called.

"Want to go to the theater?"

"You mean a movie?"

"No! The theater. Live plays, actors singing and dancing live on stage."

"What's that?"

I had never heard of the theater, had no idea what it was or why it existed. Jeff explained to me there was this place called Broadway in New York, and plays ended up on Broadway, but first they come to Boston to try them out. I thought the whole process was strange, but it interested me and so I agreed to go if Jeff would go with me. We bought two tickets to see *Bye Bye Birdie*, $3.50 each. That's not even the tax today.

I can remember walking through the Boston Commons heading for the theater, not knowing what I was about to experience, but I was curious and excited. We walked through the magnificent lobby of the Schubert. It was nothing like the Olympia Theater in my hometown of Chelsea; it was massive and ornate. It was gold and black; the Olympia was old and dirty and told of a day when movies were in their heyday. The Schubert was something else. It was alive and pulsing with energy. You could smell the magic in the air.

We sat in our seats, center of the first balcony, and I leaned over the railing to see the hundreds of people below us. My eyes went from detail to detail; the lighting fixtures that hung from an ornate ceiling; the plush velvet seats; the impressive red curtain; those boxes on the side where only four people could sit; and the ushers, those strange people in their red and gold uniforms and white gloves. This was definitely not the Olympia.

The house filled rather quickly and I sat there in anticipation. The lights dimmed and the conductor entered the orchestra pit. The spot hit his back. He lifted his baton and the overture started. I remember chills going down my spine. *What is this magical place?* My toe was tapping from the first note; they had me hook, line, and sinker. Then, the music came to an end, and the curtain parted. The audience applauded as Chita Rivera entered. Soon, Dick Van Dyke, Paul Lynde, and a cast of teenagers were dancing and singing and falling in love. I sat there like I was in a trance. I looked at Jeff and he could see the amazement in my eyes.

"Ssh. Watch the play," is all he said.

The actors transported me to their little town with their little problems, and then they changed my life. It was one of those defining moments. There was a musical number where all the kids were on this jungle-gym contraption and they sang a telephone medley, "Hi Margie. Hi Alice. What's the story, morning glory, what's the word, humming bird? Have you heard about Hugo and Kim?" Can't find my keys, but if you were in the room with me right now I could reenact the entire scene for you.

The number ended and I remember feeling this pain deep inside. It was a yearning, a longing, a need to be doing what those kids on stage were doing. I experienced my very first depression. I sank into a low that took me weeks to get out of. Why? I wanted to be on stage. Jeff had introduced me to the theater, and I was hooked. I think it's why I loved stand-up so much. It was live like theater, and it makes perfect sense to me that when I stopped doing stand-up I turned to the theater to vent my creative energy. The biggest excitement I've had in thirty-five years is getting my plays produced.

I got hooked on the theater. Jeff and I went to the Saturday matinee of several more plays. One in particular was *Do Re Mi* with Phil Silvers and Nancy Walker. Being a comedy buff, I adored Phil Silvers from his *Sgt. Bilko* days. I sat in the audience and drank in every minute of that show. From that moment on, my frame of reference became *Do Re Mi*. It was either before I saw *Do Re Mi* or after it, when Nancy Walker was Rhoda's mother, I thought, *there's the lady from Do Re Mi*. When I saw Nancy Walker in musicals from the 40s, *there's Phil Silver's wife from Do Re Mi*. *Do Re Mi* just struck a chord with me. Oh, oh, a pun, somebody slap me.

Flash Cut Thirty-Five Years Later

I'm sitting in Roddy McDowall's living room for an informal dinner with friends. Roddy was famous for his dinner parties and always played a movie afterwards in his screening room. I was sitting in his living room and in walks Nancy Walker. Roddy says, "Steve, do you know Nancy?"

"Hamma, hammma, hammmaa, ha" is all I can manage.

He shuffles her off quickly.

Must have been about a year later, I'm turning onto the Ventura Freeway from Coldwater Canyon. There is a big maroon Rolls Royce in front of me, and just as we pull onto the freeway a third car speeds up the ramp and forces the Rolls off the road. The Rolls crashes onto the embankment and the fender is crushed. The car that caused the accident jumps on the freeway and is gone. I get out of my car and run over to the Rolls. I find Nancy Walker screaming in hysterics. Her window is down, and I calmly say, "Nancy, remember me? I'm a friend of Roddy McDowall's and I will stay here with you until the tow truck comes."

She looked at me, with tears in her eyes, and said, "You have no idea what my week was like. Thank you. Thank you so much."

I remember thinking how fitting it was that I was able to repay this lady for so many years of enjoyment she had brought me.

Nancy and I talked while waiting for the tow truck. It finally came, and she asked for my phone number and address. I gave it to her and we parted. Soon a note arrived at my house with an invitation to lunch. I accepted, and in a week, I was sitting in Nancy Walker's living room chit-chatting with my childhood *Do Re Mi* memory. I asked her if she remembered me from Roddy's and she said, "The hamma-hamma guy." We laughed. Then I got to explain to her why I was so awe struck.

She paused for a moment as if to collect *her* memories. She began to tell me all about *Do Re Mi*, "Phil Silvers wouldn't do it without me. Every day we were on the road he would cling to me like a child. I didn't want to do the show, but Phil insisted." We chatted and chatted and chatted until lunch came. I learned every disgusting detail of *Do Re Mi*. I think it was the first time I was disenchanted with show business. The stories she told me were not pretty; stories about backbiting and feuds and horrific travel experiences on the road. The show had been the cornerstone of my memories; it had been a nightmare for her. We stayed together another hour or so and then we parted, never to have lunch again. I told Roddy about my time with Nancy and he just smiled. He was such a wonderful man.

How very strange my life is, so filled with contradictions and Forrest Gump moments, so exciting and mundane, so strange that a boy from a small town would have all these weird experiences and be able to retell them. I wonder if my friends in the business would sit down and write their memories as compulsively as I have; I wonder if they would also report a strange life. I think the answer is yes. I think we're all the same. You, the readers, and us in show biz. We all have memories that affect us and leave us in wonder. I think the difference is that I just know how to put them down in a book. The more we are different, folks, the more we are all the same. Don't you forget it.

Post Script

Must be about ten years ago, I got a call from my mother, "Jeffrey Glassman committed suicide." I remember thinking, *that could have been me*. You see, Jeff and his parents, while not divorced, were very much like my parents. They were overbearing, interested in money, clingy, unaware. Jeff had grown up missing something. He married our mutual friend Sandy, they had two or three children, but things were not going well in the marriage. Jeff, with no skills to cope, took the only way out he knew by jumping out of a window. I knew that if I had not left that small town with its oppressive atmosphere, I too would have had the same fate. I had to follow a dream, and I did. I may not have become the star I thought I would be, but I had a good run. Besides, I'm still here to complain about it.

Lauren Bacall

MY COUSIN HARVEY was the one driving when I found my dog Crosby on Cross Bay Blvd. Harvey, in his youth, was a lady-killer. He must have had sixteen girls going at the same time. My Aunt couldn't keep the phones clear because all the girls were calling him. One of Harvey's special girlfriends was Rhonda. I can remember sitting in my Aunt's kitchen hearing hours of conversations about Rhonda. My Aunt loved her; she was the only one of the harem she *did* love. My Aunt was all, "Rhonda said this" and "Rhonda said that". Rhonda was like a folk legend in my growing up years much like Paul Bunyan. Rhonda, Rhonda, Rhonda! I never met her.

Flash Cut: Thirty Years Later
I'm working the Improv in LA and I see this beautiful young woman sitting in the front row. After I get off stage she comes over to me, "I'm a casting director and I'd like you to come in for an interview," and she hands me her card. Rhonda Young. Okay, you're way ahead of me. I did not make the connection that this could be the Rhonda from my cousin's harem. I was totally focused on my career.

The next week I meet with Rhonda and she becomes my biggest fan. She tells me she's been watching me and she thinks I'm going to be big. Seriously, she and Gary Weinberg of I.C.M. were personally responsible for sending me out on every casting call they could get my little olive-skinned ass in on. She also told me I should write. I don't think of myself as a writer, I don't think of myself as anything. She's casting a show called *The Lohman and Barkley* and she gets me hired as a writer on the show; my first real job. All the while I'm on the show, she's the proud Momma.

While I'm telling her I'm no good, she's telling me how good I am and how much the show loves the material I'm submitting. She saved my ass on that job; I would have quit without her.

Rhonda and I become friends and soon she's casting a movie called *Perfect Gentlemen* with Lauren Bacall. She calls me in to read for a part; it's a small part, but still, it's a part in a movie with Lauren Bacall. I meet with the director Jackie Cooper. Jackie was a child star and had a TV series in the mid 50s. I recognize him immediately. I do the reading, it takes six minutes, and I get the job. Rhonda has done it again. I'm over the moon and thank Rhonda profusely. The movie shoots in six weeks. I have costume fittings and make up calls. I'm in the movies.

I get the Donna Summer and Barry Manilow gigs in Vegas and I have to fly into LA every day for meetings and do the shows at night. The movie shoots the day after I close with Donna Summer. I'm exhausted, but I drag myself out of bed for the 5 a.m. call. I drive myself to the location and crawl into my trailer. I'm sound asleep when there is a knock on the door.

"Wardrobe! Come get your costume," The woman sticks her head in my trailer. "Get up!"

"Could you do me a favor, please? I just closed in Vegas last night and I'm exhausted. Could you bring the costume here?"

"I don't know who you think you are but I don't have time to wait on you! Get off your ass and get the costume." Welcome to show business.

I get the costume and am told to report for make-up. I go to the make-up tent and Lauren Bacall is in the chair. "Good morning," I say to no reply. Bacall is holding make-up in her hand and throwing it on the table. She's telling the girl this color is wrong and that color is wrong. She's sweet yet bitter. She's oppressively overbearing and pushy. The make-up girl is applying make-up; Bacall is taking it off and applying make-up herself. She's running the make-up girl through the ringer, and after an hour of this, Bacall looks in the mirror and says, "That will have to do," and leaves. I have never seen this before and not since, but the make-up girl sat down and cried. She just sat there and bawled. She sees me, "What do you want?"

"I'm scheduled for make-up."

She checks her list and slaps some make-up on me and leaves. No conversation. No chitchat. Nothing. Slam, bam, thank you Ma'am. Welcome to show business.

When shooting a movie, it's hurry up and wait. I was in costume and make up at 7 a.m. I wasn't called until 3 p.m. I was told not to sleep in my costume or get it wrinkled. I stood in my trailer while I waited. I knew I didn't deserve to be here, and the make-up and costume department reassured me of that. I just wanted to do my lines and not make waves, so I stood.

I'm finally called to the set and Bacall is there. She is playing a gun-toting bank robber and I'm a bellman with a seriously bad attitude. I guess I'm a method actor, because I got into character and didn't break it the entire time I was on the set. I was a sarcastic twit and Bacall loved it. She talked to me in character and we made direct "fuck you" eye contact that was perfect for the characters. Inside, however, I'm a scared kid. I have never shot a movie in my life and I know I'm getting fired because I have no talent and I have no idea what I'm doing.

The camera starts to roll and we do one take. Bacall and I have locked eyes and we are not letting anyone or anything between us. We were deep into our characters. We do one take and Jackie asks me when I lift the empty bag to give it some weight. We do a second take, "Cut. Print. Let's move on."

I'm feeling pretty good, and I hear the cameraman say to Jackie, "His head was out of the shot."

Jackie answers, not thinking I could hear, "That putz."

Folks, that's all I needed to hear. I literally fell apart. I started to shake and got shooting pains in my back from my heart pounding so badly. I wanted to flee the set. I wanted to run and hide. My face became beet red; they needed to pat me down. The AD asked if I was okay. I nodded and they went on with the shot.

Jackie comes over to me, "Steve, when you enter the shot, move to here. Okay? You were out of the last shot." He couldn't have been nicer, but I know what he actually thinks of me and I'm petrified. I don't know where I pull it from, but I pull some strength from somewhere and when he shouts "Action!" I hit my mark and say my lines. "Cut. Print." He looks at the cameraman, he nods, "Let's move on." I'm done for the day.

One week later, Gary, my agent, calls me, "You need to go back and re-shoot your scene." I wanted to die. My worst nightmare: they saw the dailies and realized I was so bad I needed to do it again. Gary assures me it was not my fault. I don't believe him. I call Rhonda. She tells me it's not my fault; they had technical problems with the camera. I don't believe her. Jackie Cooper calls me to apologize for the redo. I don't believe him. The only one I believe is the little voice in my head that tells me I'm a piece of shit and this is my fault they are re-shooting.

The second day of shooting goes without a hitch. I'm in and out in five hours. I've earned a second day's salary so it's really a good thing. Now here's the best part: that little movie played on TV for years and stills plays to this day. I made a fortune on that shitty little part, and to this day I still get a residual check for those crappy few lines and my near fatal heart attack on the set.

Flash Cut: Twenty Years Later

Rhonda and I are meeting socially. She's no longer a casting director, and I'm now an established comedian on the road. We're chatting at a party and she happens to mention that she's from Boston. All the time I've known her I never knew this.

"What city in Boston?"

"Brookline."

"Really? My cousin lived in Brookline."

"What's his name?"

"Harvey (last name)."

She looks at me like I just killed her dog, "You're Harvey's cousin. I dated him in high school."

I finally put two and two together and say, "*You're* Rhonda!!!"

We are amazed at the smallness of the universe. How strange it is that people's lives touch. We are just amazed that there must be some cosmic plan for us all to meet. That's why I say to you, "Life is like a box of chocolates. You never know what you're going to get." In my case it was nervous diarrhea after working with Jackie Cooper.

Alan Thicke

IN THE 1980S, my agency would send comedians to Canada to get experience in front of the camera before they would send them out for American talk shows. I must tell you, I hate doing television, and it's one of the reasons why I'm not a big name today. I learned how to do stand-up in clubs and related directly to live audiences. In a TV studio, there is a hundred feet between you and the audience, there's also a stage crew and lots of distractions. I never learned how to relate to the camera, and so I worked clubs for years while comedians who were much less funny than I became famous. Why? They had mastered that six-minute spot and how to look right into the camera. I had not, and spent fifteen years on the road working shitholes and sleeping in scabies-infested comedy condos.

I'm doing *The Alan Thicke Show*; I had done this show when it was the *Alan Hamel Show* and I had done very well. This was a return booking for me. The trip up was uneventful as was the hotel and travel. As I remember, Lonnie Shorr, William Shatner, and Raymond Burr were taping the show that day. I was to follow William Shatner.

The show is going along well and then it starts to fall apart like a crystal vase in an Iraqi shopping mall. Shatner, who has an ego the size of a Mac Truck, shared a limo with me. He didn't talk to me. Do you know what it's like to be with someone in a six-foot space and have no contact with them? Creepy. I hated him immediately. He got out of the limo and closed the door before I could get out. I was shocked. When his Star Trek co-star George Takei said in an interview that Shatner had an ego problem, I said, "I know". Okay, the show starts and I have to follow Shatner's segment. Alan Thicke says to him, "I understand you have some footage you'd like to show us." I think its Star Trek outtakes. No. It's his latest cause, whales. He goes into this detailed description of how they are slaughtered. Now the footage starts of whaling. The audience gasps in horror. Three hundred and fifty pound stagehands are crying. The audience is crying. Thicke is crying as he looks into the camera and says, "We'll be right back with the comedy of Steve Bluestein."

I'm backstage going absolutely insane, "Whales! They want me to follow dead whales??" I'm furious, which means I'm scared. They move me to the studio; I'm complaining all the way. They could care less. I am set on the stage, the lights come up, the camera light goes on and the stage manager points to me. I smile and say, "I can't tell you what a thrill it is to be back on *The Alan Hamel Show.*" I realized I have just said the wrong host's name. My heart drops like Dolly Parton's breasts when she takes off her bra. We are live; I can't stop tape. I phumfa though the next joke. I phumfa through the following joke and finally said, "Could someone please harpoon *me*?" They laugh and I finish the set.

Alan asks me to the couch, the "You've made it" sign where Shatner and Raymond Burr are seated. Shatner has moved down to find someone else's act to fuck up and Burr is right next to me. Alan says, "So I understand you just got divorced." I start in a set of divorce material and for some unknown reason I switch in mid-set from the divorce material to material about fat people. The audience is laughing and I look over at Raymond Burr, who looks like a beached whale. He has this glazed look on his face. I suddenly realize I am doing fat jokes next to a man who is so big he has central heating in his thighs. I die inside and look at Thicke. My eyes are as big as saucers. Thicke says, "We'll be right back with the body of Steve Bluestein after this." I just cup my hands in my face and move down the couch so the next guest, a man talking about global cooling, can sit. Talk about getting it wrong.

I go back to the green room and Lonnie Shorr is there. He is wiping his eyes and runs up to me. Lonnie is a Vegas comedian who was a regular on *The Dean Martin Show*. He grabs me and says, "That was the funniest thing I have ever seen." He was talking as a comedian and seeing the irony in what had happened to me. He and I became friends immediately. We hang out in the hotel after the show and share a limo to the airport the next day.

Lonnie is a wonderful, down home, no ego, easy to talk to kind of guy and remains a friend to this day. We're at the airport standing in line going through Canadian Customs and he asks me what's my next gig. I don't have a next gig. In show business, you have to bullshit to look important and so I'm telling Lonnie about this deal and that deal that is pending for me. It's all bullshit. I know it's bullshit, and he knows its bullshit, but it's show biz, and it's bullshit. I was pumping out some grade-A bullshit this day. Just as I'm sharing my bullshit the customs officer opens my case. I had taken the towels from the hotel. Lonnie sees them and says, "Yah, I can see how well things are going for you. Did you happen to take the soap too?" I lift up the towels to reveal the soap underneath. Lonnie almost wets himself, even the customs guy laughed. Isn't it nice how I share my most embarrassing moments? Now, if you don't mind, I have to go clip coupons.

P.S. Just so you'll know, those white washcloths from the hotel are perfect for dusting. Steal them!

Chapter One

I CAN REMEMBER the first time I was able to remember. There was a void that lived in my head, and then, one morning I woke up and said, "Wait a minute. There was a yesterday." The next day there was a day-before-yesterday and so it went from then on right up to the present. Unfortunately, I have spent the remaining years trying to forget those accumulated memories, but I cannot. Those moments are hard-wired into the mainframe with code that only electric shock can release. God has gifted me with this incredible memory. It's a gift that I cannot return and I have struggled all my life trying to find the refund window of my psyche. I am fascinated with my ability to remember things, but more so with what my mind has chosen to remember. I have in my head literally hundreds of "photos", snap shots of an instant in time that my mind has chosen to categorize, put on a file card, and store away in the corners of what's left of my brain. These images come flashing back to me at the most inopportune times, like when I'm driving in my car or auditioning for a part or trying to have sex with a stranger in a hotel in Ohio. For the most part, these memories don't inspire me, they cripple. It's not a catalogue of "warm fuzzies," it's a litany of one nightmare after another. It's a series of bad memories followed by a catalogue of disasters. It's my childhood.

Let's get back to that "first time I could remember." The photo in my brain is as clear as if it were yesterday. There is no question in my mind what this scene looked like or what the colors were or who the people were or the smells or the tastes. It was my miserable life and here's how it started.

It was a hot August evening. I know it was August because the humidity hung in the air like a wet sponge. The sun was just setting and the sky was that dull grayish-blue that it gets in New England around sunset. I can remember feeling oppressed by the heat and sitting at the table in my t-shirt and damp training pants. I was so small I was seated on two telephone books to bring my chin up to the lip of the table. In front of me was the evening meal, a bowl of Cheerios. The morning paper was propped up and open against a half-full bottle of humidity-beaded milk. The moisture made wet spots on the newsprint and made them cling to each other like they were holding on for dear life. I created a little shelter for myself behind that paper, a place to hide from the world. I couldn't read, I could barely use the spoon. Milk and Cheerios were spilling down my shirt, only adding to my discomfort in the thick August twilight air.

We lived in Chelsea, Massachusetts, a town that had burned to the ground in 1908 and unfortunately had been rebuilt. The master planner of the time had built triple-decker homes. These masterpieces of modern architecture had no central heating. Their main source of warmth was the huge iron stove in the kitchen. Each home consisted of a large kitchen, which included a pantry housing the sink, and on the other wall, a screen door that led to a back porch where one could hang laundry. Oh, so convenient. Off the kitchen was the bedroom, to capture the heat from the stove, a long hallway, a front room followed by a dining-room, and somewhere in the mix was nestled a bathroom. This floor plan was replicated a thousand times all over the city and it was the floor plan of my childhood on Poplar Street. Sounds like a wonderful place to grow up, Poplar Street. It conjures up visions of tree-lined boulevards and broad sidewalks where flowers lined the paths. It was not so. My Poplar Street was and remains a dark, dirty alley hidden behind the back side—the ugly side—of an ancient school building. From our front room, we looked on to a foreboding brick wall. It was the sentry guarding our view; it was the symbol of my existence on that street. Trapped. The street, which was constructed for horse drawn carriages, was much too small for modern day automobiles and was always congested. The school building shut out the light; sunshine was never my companion. It was a forgotten enclave in the city, an oasis of despair, and my own personal hell.

As the years passed, central heating was added to these wonders of modern living. The front room became a bedroom, turning a one-bedroom unit into a two-bedroom apartment. Sometimes the front room remained as the living room and the dining room was converted to a bedroom. That was the configuration of my Poplar Street home. That was the memory that stays in the photo album of my mind: two bedrooms and long hall with a bathroom off it, a kitchen, a pantry, and a bedroom off the kitchen next to the porch where one could hang laundry.

That evening I sat on my phone books, with Cheerios running down my front, in front of my newspaper. Now add my mother screaming in the background and you'll complete the picture. All that was missing was the grim reaper and the cast of *Les Mis*. I can picture my mother as if it was yesterday, and, with her, it probably was. She was in a floral housecoat, over it, an apron. Her hair was wrapped in something and the apron was wet from washing dishes. No modern appliances for us, we were extremely poor at the time. My mother was screaming at my father, who was sheltered in the front room. Her voice was like nails on a blackboard, and I remember at that young age wanting to be someplace else, with someone else, anyone else. I remember the ill feelings that would follow me the rest of my life, the feelings of *why me?* I remember her turning her wrath to me, "Finish your dinner!" I dutifully scooped another spoonful of Cheerios into my mouth. I also remember wishing I wasn't there, a wish that would be repeated over and over again as I grew older.

I climbed down off the chair and walked over to the screen door. In the background, the soundtrack of my parent's battle raged. They were fighting about God knows what. It was always something with them; clothes not picked up, lights left on, bills not paid, work not found, his being a man. I had my face pressed into the screen as if to push myself through it and escape the insanity of the moment. It was growing darker. There was no breeze to evaporate the humidity collecting on my baby skin or dry the milk on my t-shirt. It was just little damp me in a world of screaming adults, feeling lost and alone at the age of two.

I remember being so small that the light switch was way above my head. It was a good foot from my reach. That's how small I was. It was growing darker as twilight turned to evening and I needed the light on. Children always need the light on. It's their source of protection from the boogieman. I couldn't reach the switch and there was no one there to turn it on to protect me. Welcome to the theme of my life. They weren't there to protect me. They weren't paying attention to me, they were fighting. The echoes of their battle bounced off the walls of the adjacent three-story house, which mirrored our building and formed our mutual back yard. A yard I could look out on and see the kitchens of happy homes, of families having real dinners, of mothers caring for children and turning on lights.

I had backed away from the backyard images and was going God knows where when suddenly, out of the darkness, a cat sprang onto the screen door and hung there for dear life. She was calling for help and I screamed to my mother, "Momma! Look!" Suddenly the house grew quiet as all eyes focused on the miracle of the back-door screen. My father ran to the door and opened it. The cat came flying in. It brushed up against me and was making this humming sound I would later learn was called a "purr." I remember my heart soaring. My dreams had been answered; I had something that loved me. That's where the memory ends. The photo album closes as if it were cut off by a huge paper cutter. I don't know what happened to that cat. It didn't stay with us. I never had a pet growing up, but I do remember that tabby and the happiness it brought me in the midst of my parent's fight. It would be the first of many fights I would witness, battles that would draw blood and would forever color the edges of my personality. For now, I will remember the cat that showed me love on the night my parents were unable to. I will remember the photo and put it in my album of memories. I'll see it with protective corners that hold it in place and I'll write in white ink on a black page, "How it all began…" The first of many memory photos that will form my life.

Rita Moreno

THERE HAVE ONLY BEEN a couple of stars I have worked with repeatedly. Makes you kind of wonder if I'm a pain in the ass on the road, doesn't it? I think it's more likely the nature of my business. When a star is available to work, I'm not, and vice versa. However, there was one lady that I worked with repeatedly. I remember her fondly, Miss Rita Moreno. Rita is one of the only actors in town who has won an Oscar, Tony, Emmy, Grammy, and shopper-of-the-month at Macy's. She is a true triple-threat dancer, actor, and singer, and her long career is a credit to her resiliency and talent.

In the late 1970s she had a nightclub act that was getting rave reviews. She was going into Vegas but needed to tour to make sure the material worked in the hinterlands, not just in hip LA and NY. They booked her into the Blue Max in Chicago, and since I was one of the approved comics there, I was paired with her and got to spend two weeks at the airport hotel, stranded alone with nothing to do. We got to see a lot of each other and I've got to tell you, there's no one finer.

Let me tell you about the first time we worked together. I was doing the *Merv Griffin Show*. Merv was out and Mel Tills, the stuttering country singer, was the host. Merv was either out sick or had to stay home and count his money. Mel and I had never worked together before. I knew from country like he knew from chicken soup. There was no chemistry there and we both felt it.

I did my stand-up set and walked to the panel where I'm supposed to sit and do more preplanned talk/jokes. Mel has the lead-in questions on 3x5 cards in front of him and he asks the first question. I answer and the audience laughs. Mel gets thrown like he didn't expect me to be funny and goes off on a tangent about his family and leaves me in the dust. He's asking me questions about stuff that was not on the cards. I'm looking at him like a deer in the headlights, *what are you doing?* Rita Moreno is seated to Mel's left and has a clear view of his cards. She interrupts, "Steve, I understand you just got married," and we're back on track and I'm doing the preplanned material. She saved my ass on national TV and I thanked her profusely backstage.

The next week I'm working the Sahara in Tahoe, and Rita's across the street working the other casino. I leave her a note and she calls me. I go to visit and we spend some time together. Right after that I learn that I'm opening for her in Chicago, and I know she's asked for me. It was a good feeling.

I guess we were working there Christmas week. I say that because I remember having a Christmas Party with her and her two back-up dancers. Like I've told you before, when you work with someone on the road, you become very tight for that week and then never see those people again. That's what happened with our little troop, Rita, her back up dancers, and me. Rita held a little party in her suite for all of us where we exchanged gifts. I had found this really wonderful costume jewelry necklace in the hotel gift shop that I gave to Rita as a gift. I will never forget the expression on her face when she opened it. You'd think I just gave her the crown jewels. As a joke, I gave her a second gift: a box filled with silverware, towels, soap, dishes, and glasses from the hotel. Rita laughed and said, "You joke. I'll use these," and put the entire collection in her road trunk. I also had the Marriott make up an official badge that said, "Rita, Front Desk." She loved it.

Rita gave me a travel bag that folded down into itself to the size of a pack of cigarettes. I carried that bag with me for twenty years until it finally gave up from exhaustion and fell apart at the airport in Rome. Talk about a good gift. There was one gift that was given to me that day that sits next to me as I write. The date on it is December 24, 1978, and it was given to me by one of Rita's back-up dancers. It is a leather-bound journal. I had just gotten divorced and everyone knew about the baby. This wonderful man, whose name was Cordell, gave me this journal and said, "You need to write about what you are going through." From that day on, I have written in that book when I was profoundly sad or wildly happy or depressed or angry or needed to vent. The pages in the book have turned brown, but I will not part with it for a million dollars. As a matter of fact, when the mudslide destroyed my office, the first thing I grabbed was that book of memories. It was my record of my emotions over the years. Although I have never seen Cordell again and do not know where he is, I thank him daily for the most wonderful gift I was ever given. A place to remember.

Working with Rita was a piece of cake. She had a wonderful act and we attracted the same kind of audience: Middle America. The only time it got a little tense was once after I had a really good show. Rita came into my dressing room.

"I want you to follow me. You close the show."

"Huh? What? What's going on?"

Turns out that my style of talking to the audience made it difficult for her to work because the audience then wanted to then talk to her. She had a different kind of act; it was mapped out and scripted. There was no room for improv, and so when the audience interrupted her, it threw her. Knowing that if I closed the show it would be the kiss of death for me I said, "Rita, this is your show. I am here as window dressing for *you!* I will stop talking to the audience," and that's exactly what I did. We never had the problem again and the rest of the gig went smoothly.

No matter how big the star, the insecurities are still there. One night I had just gotten offstage, and Rita came in the wings ready to go on. She looked magnificent. She turned to the mirror and said to me, "Not bad for fifty, huh?" and waited for assurance. Her comments didn't make an impact on me for years. Then I turned fifty. You see, to me, Rita was ageless. It didn't matter when she was born, it only mattered that she looked beautiful then!

Rita continued to be a joy to work with and was a giving person. She was invited to the Playboy Mansion for a Christmas Party; she invited me along. When we were at the Mansion, the booker of the Playboy Clubs came over to meet her. Rita, without any coaxing from me, said, "This is Steve Bluestein. We're working at the Blue Max this week. He's wonderful and you should really have him booked in your club." Three months later, I had a four-gig contract with Playboy. It was all because of the generosity of Rita Moreno.

Rita and I also talked about a show idea I had. She helped me develop it. It was a reality show where we would go from city to city and tape the street performers in the street as they did their act. It was a variety/reality show and it was way ahead of its time. I wrote the treatment in my room at the hotel and put Rita's name on it. When I showed it to her she said, "Steve, this is your idea. I was only the catalyst," and told me to take her name off the treatment. I never did and it sits in my book of projects I never pursued.

When we got back to LA, I crossed paths with Rita several times. Rita was always warm and sweet to me. She invited me up to her home on Capri Drive in Pacific Palisades. We would bump into each other at TV tapings and award dinners, and it was always like seeing an old friend. I later learned that she had sold her house in California and was buying an apartment in NY. That was the last time I saw her, right before she moved to The Big Apple.

I miss seeing her, miss talking with her, and miss working with her. I just miss her. But that is what show business is like; you are close for a while and then your friendship never existed. You get used to it, but it is never a comfortable place for me. I love my friends and want them around because there are a lot of bad eggs in the biz and I collect only the good ones. Show biz, screw-everybody-that-you-know biz. It's not just a song lyric.

Barry Manilow

DURING MY FIFTEEN MINUTES OF FAME, I was getting offers left and right. I had just opened for Dolly Patron at the Roxy in LA when I heard that Barry was in need of an opening act for The Riviera in Las Vegas. One of his writers was Roberta Kent. Roberta and I had been writers on a syndicated TV show called *The Lohman and Barkley*. I called Roberta and literally begged her to put in a good word for me. She said she would. She had Barry's ear at that time, and within two days I had the gig. I firmly believe that it was Roberta who was responsible for getting me that job, along with the pushing of another Manilow assistant, Paul Brownstein.

Then I got the call from Roberta, "Okay, you got the job, but there are a few things I need to tell you about Barry."

"Like?"

"Like he's not friendly."

"I can deal with that."

"Like he's really not friendly."

"I got it. There will be no chitty-chat backstage."

"Don't talk to him, don't mention him in your act, don't look at him."

"Don't look at him?"

"Don't look at him."

"Why? Will I turn into a pillar of salt?"

I remember I had to clear my material with Manilow's office. I could understand that. He didn't know me; he didn't know my material. He couldn't afford to have someone open for him with blue material. However, I did not—nor did I ever—do that kind of material. I was wearing saddle shoes and tennis sweaters. It was my All-American period. My material was squeaky clean. The contracts came and I was about to sign them when I noticed there was no provision for billing. I called my agent.

"What's the billing on this gig."

"There is no billing. All the marquee will say is 'BARRY.'"

"Oh?"

When I get to the Riviera, all the marquee says, in letters fifteen feet high, is "BARRY" and "Roast Beef Dinner $3.50." The roast beef had billing. I did not.

I check into the hotel and in my room is a bottle of Dom Perignon with a note, "Have a great show. Barry" (Remember this champagne it's important). I thought, *what a nice guy* (Remember the champagne).

It's tech rehearsal and I go down to the showroom. Barry is on stage. I walk in and Roberta yells, "Hey, Steve!"

Barry says, "Is that the comedian?" He puts his hand over his eyes like he's scouting with the Indians to search for me in the darkness. He flips me a "hello" wave.

So much for the introduction. Barry finishes his rehearsal, which was like watching paint dry; long and tedious. Then I go up on stage to hear the sound. It's fine. The whole thing takes ten minutes and we're done.

I go down to the dressing room. At the Riviera, the entertainer's dressing rooms consisted of a large sitting room and a bathroom. The opening act and the headliner had side-by-side dressing rooms. Barry had a curtain installed in the hallway between his dressing room and mine. There was also a guard to keep out unwanted guests like myself from coming in. Okay, I get it. Not friendly.

I go into my dressing room and discover Manilow has taken over the sitting area for his band and given me the bathroom to prepare in. I'm supposed to get dressed in the toilet. I don't say a word. You know me, I'm just happy to get hit with a stick, especially if you take out the nail.

I'm a nervous wreck for the opening. I've been told the reviewers from all over the country will be there that night. TV and radio were there. International reviewers were there. This was a huge opening and I was part of it. I begin my pacing to concentrate before the show but stagehands are pushing me and walking by me and yelling in my ear and shoving me out of the way. It's impossible to concentrate, but I'm focused and somehow muddle through the distraction. The lights dim and the orchestra begins the overture.

"Ladies and Gentlemen, The Riviera is proud to present Barry Manilow with comedian Steve Bluestein!"

I enter to a nice round of applause. The place is packed. The faces are smiling. The murmur was high-pitched. I start my act and they are laughing right away. The show is going gangbusters. I start my piece on natural childbirth and out of my left ear I hear, "Get a doctor." I think, *oh shit. A heckler. Not tonight. Please, not tonight.* Then urgently, "Steve, get a doctor."

I look down and a girl is having an epileptic fit two seats in front of me. I look out into the audience and say, "Is there a doctor in the house? We need a doctor up front." The house lights come up and suddenly there is a stretcher coming down the aisle. I'm saying things like, "Let's stay calm, she'll be alright." In my mind I'm thinking, *why doesn't she die so I can go on with the show?* Flash bulbs are going off as they load her onto the stretcher and take her out of the room. She exits, the house lights go to black, and the spotlight comes back up on me. In one tenth of a second, I'm thinking, *oh shit, what do I do now?* I say to the crowd, "I don't think comedy is appropriate right now. Why don't we all take a break before we welcome Mr. Manilow?" I leave the stage to thunderous applause.

I got down to my dressing room—I mean my bathroom—and I closed the door and cried. I had just blown the opportunity of a lifetime. Then there is a knock on the door. Paul Brownstein and Roberta Kent come in laughing, "Well that was certainly something." I'm drying my eyes. "Barry wants to see you," and they take me into the inner sanctum, past the shower curtain and the guard, and there is Barry sitting at a dressing table in front of more make-up than The Playboy Mansion on bare tush night. I don't mean twenty products, I'm talking five hundred powders and bases and combs and eyeliners. It looked like a hooker exploded. I thought, *he has such a small face. Where could he put all that shit?* Barry assures me I did the right thing and not to worry. Friendly. Nice. Made me feel better.

Barry does his show and, I must tell you, there isn't a better showman working the Strip. His show is high-powered, funny, touching, and eye candy. It's a standing ovation every night. He's truly magic on stage. It's offstage you want to kill yourself. I heard there is a clause in his contract that the stagehands have to turn to the wall when he exits. No one can look at him or talk to him (Play *Twilight Zone* theme song here).

The reviews come out and they are raves. One of them says Manilow and Bluestein share the stage like corned beef and cabbage. Folks, Barry shares the stage with no one. It was the kiss of death review for me. However, my quick exit after the medical emergency turned out to be the right one. It's all the press is talking about. *The Mike Douglas Show* flies me out to do the show and brings a columnist who was at The Riviera that night. She gushes over me and praises me on camera. Talk about turning lemons into lemonade. All I could think was, *if they only knew it was fear that got me off stage, not good judgment.*

The week goes on. The shows are getting better and better. Manilow has legions of fans that come to every show; for a comedian that's not good. They've heard the jokes but these girls were either morons or very supportive because they laughed every night. On the other hand, Barry's mood was getting darker. He kept complaining about the sound. He said it dropped out and he couldn't hear himself. One night I'm waiting to go on, Manilow comes out and yells at the sound guy, "Listen. If you can't do the job I'll get someone who can. This is your warning, either get it right or you're fired." I wish you could have seen the expression on the guy's face. He was devastated. Barry leaves. I know the best way to get someone to work better is to support him, not rip him down before he's supposed to do his job.

I say to the guy, "Take a deep breath and calm yourself. We have a show to do. The sound has been perfect all week for me. So, you're doing fine." The guy smiles and shakes my hand.

"Thanks," is all he said.

Barry does his show and he's in full swing. The sound isn't right, the lighting isn't right. He's bitching about this and that and the musicians. The entire band and crew are a nervous wreck. Saturday night's show is an explosion of energy and excitement. I get a standing ovation. Me! Barry's show is through the roof. The audience screamed and pounded the floor. After the show, Barry gets all the crew together and says, "You guys are the most wonderful bunch I have ever worked with. Thank for you for a wonderful show." Twenty-four hours later it would be a different story.

Some crowds are good, and some, for some unknown reason, are not. The very next night the crowd was not good. Flat. They were flat for me and, sadly for all of us, they were flat for Barry. He came off stage screaming. The sound was wrong, the lights were wrong, the musicians were wrong. He got the same people he had praised the night before into the same room and read them the riot act. He was livid and I sat there in amazement watching this screaming temper tantrum thinking, *nope, not friendly at all.*

He's been very kind to me but he's just not fun to be around. I start making jokes like, "With all his money, you would think he could buy himself a tush." Barry has been gifted by God with the strangest body known to man; he's high-waisted, barrel-chested, and has no ass at all. I never saw him nude—thank God—but I would suspect on stage he's padded and trussed in like a Thanksgiving Turkey.

That's how the week went, eggshell-stepping and stagehands facing the wall. We close and I get my hotel bill. On the bill is one charge: "One bottle Dom Perignon, $65." I hit the roof. I was not paying for that and demanded to see the room service charge. It was my name, but not my signature. Some gift. They deducted the charge from my bill. I left the Riviera to never work with him again.

Four Post Scripts

1. After the rave reviews, one of my agents, Jim Murray of ICM, comes to Vegas to see the show. He takes me out to lunch and says, "Kid, you're incredible. I can do great things for you. Why don't you come up to my office? I would like to sign you." I say to him, "Schmuck. I'm with ICM. You booked me here." He finishes his pasta without saying a word.

2. About thirty years later, I'm in an elevator going to visit John Bowab, the director. Into the elevator walks Jim Murray. John says, "Steve, do you know Jim Murray?"
"Know him? He was my agent."
Jim says, "Really? I don't remember."
I couldn't help myself. I said, "You didn't remember thirty years ago, you don't remember now."

3. I'm at a party at Bruce Vilanch's house. I'm standing in the kitchen, and who should walk in but Barry Manilow. Bruce says, "Headliner, meet opening act." Barry looks at me and smiles. He had no idea who I was. The corned beef had forgotten the cabbage.

4. Twenty years after opening for Barry, I'm running through an airport when I hear "Steve". I turn around and a long- haired guy is standing there. I have no idea who he is. "I'm (name). I was the sound guy for Barry Manilow."
"Oh, my deepest regrets."

He laughs, "I just wanted to thank you. You saved my ass."

I shrug and say, "Hey, I always help fellow prisoners."

We laugh, shake hands, and head in different directions for our planes. In Barry's defense, I understand he's mellowed—that's what I've been told!

Donna Summer

MY YEARS ON THE ROAD included the Disco Era. I worked with Donna Summer at the MGM Grand in Las Vegas. That gig was the beginning and the end of a chapter in my life. During this time, I was burning up Las Vegas with great reviews for a newcomer, and lots of high-profile gigs.

When I got to Vegas, my name was on the marquee in letters ten feet high. There was a billboard on the Sunset Strip in Los Angeles with Donna Summer's name and my name for the world to see. I was on lobby cards and menus and my face and name were everywhere. Each time I'd see it, I'd think, *it doesn't look like it belongs there.* No matter how much success I had, I still didn't feel I deserved it. I was doing TV shows in Vegas to promote my show, radio interviews, and was the darling of the press. I still didn't feel I deserved it. Why? Not a single acknowledgment from my family. Nothing. Not a single word!

It's opening night and I'm in my dressing room. The MGM gave the opening act a huge dressing room, and unlike Manilow, Donna did not take it away from me. I sat in this huge living room with a basket of fresh fruit every night and wondered how I got there and what they would do when they found out that I was a sham. Unlike other entertainers, I always kept my door open so that the guard outside my door wouldn't feel I was too good to talk to him. I always invited him in and told him to sit and have some fruit. One of my friends from LA flew in for the opening, actress Janet Wood. She's a member of my family of friends, and having her there meant the world to me. Later in the week others came, Stephen Michael Schwartz, Wendy Shaal, and there were others, but who can remember?

The opening show was gangbusters and the audience responded to me like they had been following my career for years. It was huge laughs and wild applause when I finished. I was walking on clouds. Donna was at the height of her disco fame and the audiences were throbbing to love her. Her show was short on production value, but the power of her voice overshadowed any visual you could ever want. When she sang, you didn't care if she was standing in a cardboard box in quicksand, all you wanted to do was bathe in the glory of that voice.

After the second show, the well-wishers came backstage. I opened my door and Robert De Niro was standing there. He was going in to visit Donna. Oh my God! This is the big time. I was in my dressing room when an agent from William Morris came in to greet me. At the same time, my agent from ICM came in. Now, Janet was sitting there and can testify to this.

The William Morris agent said, "I think you are wonderful. I'd like to represent you."

"He's mine," the ICM agent says, and grabbed me by the arm and pulled me away from the William Morris agent.

The William Morris agent grabbed my other arm and pulled me toward him, "No, he's mine!"

"No, I signed him first."

"No, I want him."

The two of them played tug-of-war, pulling me back and forth between them. I looked over at Janet and we both laughed. This is what we had wanted all our lives, to have agents fighting over us. Six months after the MGM gig, neither agent would return my call. Why? That was six months ago, they were only interested in today.

After everyone left the room, I was getting my stuff together when there was a knock on my door. I opened it and Donna Summer was standing there.

"Can I come in?"

"Sure!" I said with glee.

She took both my hands and said, "I just wanted to tell you how happy we are that you are on the show with us."

In that space and time, my dreams had come true. This was a star of the hugest magnitude telling me, Mr. I-Don't-Belong, that she was happy she was working with me. It is twenty-five years later and I can still feel the love that she shared with me that night. She wasn't a star; she was a kid from Roxbury, Mass. telling a kid from Chelsea, Mass., "Hey, we made it," and I thanked her with all my heart. It's many years later; I still thank her.

Donna's group and I grew tight. Her sister was a back-up singer and we would have lunch together or sit by the pool. It was the dream gig of a lifetime. Then I got a call from my manager, "Donna is canceling the rest of her gig. She's pregnant." My ten-day gig was cut to about four days. Donna saw me in the hall that night and apologized. I didn't know what to say. It was hard to hide my disappointment. This cut the momentum of my career short and put a pall over any forward movement. However, the hotel was very interested in me and there was talk of a long-term contract, so some good was going to come of it.

The last show will remain with me forever. It was Donna's "Hot Love" medley—truly the high point of the show. Every night the audience jumped to their feet and danced in the aisle. I was in the back of the room watching. It was like Donna was pulling out all the stops for this last show. It's a fever pitch; the last note is sung and held. The crowd goes wild and the huge apron curtain starts to come down. At that very instant, a mother sitting on the ring picks up her eight-year-old daughter and pushes her on the stage toward Donna and right in the path of the falling curtain. Donna, who is now singing her encore refrain, walks over to the child, takes her hand and pulls the child close to her as the curtain slams to the ground missing them both by three feet. The crowd explodes and I remember thinking I had just seen the ultimate professional; a woman who could keep her cool and still hold a high note. No one really knows how profoundly special Donna Summer was!

The next day, our names came off the marquee. They were gone from the lobby and were declared missing from the coffee shop. It's like we never played there. Welcome to show biz! I fly back to LA and am living in the glow of my four days of excellence.

Must have been about three months later when my friend Irwin Shamah came out to visit from New York. I was still in the town house I had rented when I was married. Irwin was in the guest room when he shouted, "Hey, Steve, turn on the TV!" I turned it on in my room and my jaw dropped as I saw pictures of smoke billowing out of the entrance of the MGM Grand in Las Vegas. Irwin ran down to my room and found me in bed frozen, my eyes transfixed on the television, "What's the matter?"

I turned to him in the calmest, most distant voice I could muster and said, "We're watching my career go up in flames." In actuality, it wasn't just my career that was lost that day. I know that. The loss of life was far more important, but I was right. The long-term effect was devastating. The contract with the hotel never materialized and I went on the road working shitty little Comedy Clubs.

I spoke to my comedian friends trying to find some solace in their condolences. That's like asking the fox to feel sorry he ate the chicken. If I fail, they succeed. That is, everyone but Tom Dreesen, who told me that everything happens for a reason. Maybe the timing was wrong, maybe if I had too much success now I wouldn't be able to handle it. I listened to those words and tried to rationalize the destruction of what I had built in Vegas, but it was very hard. I had just lost my wife, my child, my money, my agent, and now I was losing my career. Little did I know, it would get a lot worse before it got better. And I went through it alone.

Linda

IT WAS A COLD, BRISK winter day in Boston when I was walking home from school with a group of friends. I guess I was in the tenth grade. I remember this like it happened yesterday. MK was walking with me, and ahead of us, about fifteen feet, was a girl walking alone. She was overweight and carried her head slung low.

"Who is that?" I said with curious mock.

"Oh, that's Linda," and MK got very serious, "She has had the worst life that anyone could ever imagine."

She's got my attention.

"Her mother died when she was six and her father remarried a bitch who has a son. She hates Linda and only loves her son. The stepmother beats Linda and neglects her and..."

I didn't need to hear another word. I knew that I would have to be Linda's friend.

A few days later, I was at the community center and there was Linda at a table with two other people, another Steve B and another Linda. This was my chance to meet her. I knew the Steve B, so I sat down pointing to the four of us said, "Hey look... Steve, Steve, Linda, Linda."

Without a beat my Linda said, "Yeah, we are Berman-Blue-Pop-Ney" (taking a portion of each of our last names and making it one), and Berman-Blue-Pop-Ney we became. From that moment on, whenever we would see one another, we chanted "Hello Berman-Blue-Pop-Ney." It made us laugh and it connected us. It's what teenagers do.

This was the first time I had ever really met Linda, and I found her to be funny and smart and warm and loving. I could relate to her. I could relate to her pain. Even though she was two years older than me, I adopted her. Linda and I did everything together. We went to the beach, we hung out in Bellingham Square, we drove to Marblehead, and we did all the things kids do in the summer in Boston. I remember one day Linda and I were in Nahant and we had to walk to Punks Corner in Revere (a hang-out by the beach). It was quite a distance, but Linda and I began walking and talking. We talked about everything; family, friends, life, our future. One thing we talked about will mean nothing to anyone but Linda and me. I won't even try to explain it. I'll just say it, "Peanuts, Popcorn, Cracker Jacks and beer, in Coke cans." It's one of those silly things you say as kids, which has meaning at the moment but loses something in the translation. Just trust me, it's important to us. Linda and I shared a bond, and on that day the bond was sealed for life. That walk joined two souls as one and we both knew it.

I went off to college, Linda stayed in Boston. When I got my apartment with my two roommates from Emerson, Jon and Bob, Linda would come by and hang out. She was funny. She had this weird sense of humor that just made me howl and I wondered if her sense of humor came from the same pain as mine. One night she came over to our combat-zone apartment with a group of friends from high school. It was very strange having my high school friends and college friends in the same room. It was fire and water. One group knew me as one person while the other group knew me as another. Both were struggling to fit me into a mold that I no longer fit. Linda and her group left early and I didn't see much of her after that. I suspect she thought I changed. However, the next morning when I got up to go to class, I found a little gift Linda had left me. I opened my closet door and Linda had tied all my clothes in knots. My shirts were tied to my pants, my pants to my jackets. I screamed with laughter. I fell on the floor laughing. Jon ran in; he laughed. It was a great moment. It was Linda saying, "Don't get too big for your britches, we know who you are."

I graduated college and went to NY. Linda moved to LA, where she got married. Three years later I moved to LA as well. I called Linda almost the first day I arrived. She was living in Thousand Oaks, about one hour outside LA. It might as well have been Phoenix. We never saw each other. She had married an older man and seemed happy, until one night when I got a phone call from her. He had beaten her and she needed to come over. Linda told me her husband was an alcoholic and had beaten her regularly. All I could think was she was repeating a pattern of abuse she learned as a child. I told her to leave him, she could move in with me. Soon after, she got her divorce but stayed on her own.

Time passed and I got married and Linda was part of my extended LA Family. When the baby came, she was Aunty Linda, and when I found out I was not the father of the baby, Linda was the first person I called. She ran to my side. I can remember her holding me in her arms as I cried my heart out; she stayed with me the entire night. After all, we were now closer than soul mates, we were the best kind of family, the kind you can pick for yourself.

All through the divorce, it was Linda who was by my side. When I had to travel to do comedy, it was Linda who came with me. She made sure I kept my sanity. When I went to court, it was Linda whose name came up in an alienation of affection action. How ridiculous!

We got through my divorce and it appeared that it was one crisis after another. Linda was always chubby but was now extremely overweight. She was diabetic and was one of the first to have intestinal bypass, but it had not been perfected and the complications were severe and many. More than once I rushed her to the hospital at 3 a.m. because her potassium was low or her blood sugar was out of control.

I guess God thought she had not been through enough, because soon after that she was diagnosed with cancer. I remember the phone call. Her voice was distant and resigned. She was going to die. I wouldn't hear of it but Linda was ready to do nothing. No radiation, no surgery, nothing.

"Linda, you just can't give up!" I screamed

"Why?"

I was not letting her go that easily. I insisted she see a shrink, and she did. Finally, after months of counseling, she agreed to have the surgery and radiation. We just prayed it had not been too late. Thank God it wasn't, and one year later Linda was given a clean bill of health. But there was more to come.

The dates are all mixed up in my mind. Maybe the cancer came before the bypass; maybe the divorce was sometime later. I simply can't remember. I do remember that Linda had a complete nervous breakdown and I was sitting by her bed in a hospital, looking at this childhood friend who was lost in her own world. I remember thinking, *I hope her father and step-mother rot in hell for what they have done to this girl.* They are both dead now, and I *still* hope they are rotting in hell.

Like the Trojan warrior she is, Linda pulled through that episode and soon met someone and married again. Soon after that, she was pregnant and over the moon with joy. However, her second husband was—shall we say—not a catch. He didn't work, he had no motivation, and he had low self-esteem. I couldn't effing stand him. They divorced soon after, and Linda was a single mother with a child. For some strange reason, she planned to move back to Boston, but not before she came to my rescue one more time. I had just had a relationship break-up. It wasn't so much the break-up as the way it happened. After a fight, I woke up the next morning to find my house empty. I had been wiped out again, and I fell apart. I called Linda and remember not being able to control my emotions. I was screaming and babbling and crying.

Linda said, "Honey, you're having a nervous breakdown. Go outside and count the cars driving by your house. I'll be right over," and that's what I did. I sat on the steps counting cars until Linda sat by my side and held me. It wasn't lost on us that I had been there for her and now she was there for me. As she sat there holding me, she whispered in my ear, "Peanuts, popcorn, Cracker Jacks and beer, in Coke cans," and I knew I would be all right.

Sometime soon after, she moved back to Boston and left me on my own. I think she wanted her son to have some sense of family. I think my words to her were, "Are you out of your mind? Your family is here with me," but I couldn't stop her and she moved back to where it snows in January.

At first, Linda seemed to flourish back east. When I heard her stepmother had dropped dead I sent her a card I made on my computer. On the outside it said, "At this sorrowful time of passing, I would just like to tell you how I feel about your loss," and on the inside, it said in huge letters, "YIPPIE!!" (with confetti all around it).

She called me laughing hysterically, "Thank you…. Best card I ever got." She seemed to be doing well back east, but then the health issues surfaced again. Her weight ballooned, her diabetes returned, and she had one, two, three strokes. Her kidneys failed and she was moved into a nursing home.

I call her from time to time and this elderly woman answers with slurred speech and a weak voice. It's a shadow of the funny, warm girl I knew as a teenager, and each time I hang up from our talks, I sit down and cry at what life has done to her. Like the little engine that could, Linda keeps chugging along. I get reports on her health and her progress—or lack thereof—but my love for her will never falter. We are connected deeply to each other by a bond that blood could never ever try to match. I love that woman more than any sister or cousin or aunt could ever hope to be loved. I would swim rivers, climb mountains, and walk through fire to be next to my Linda. Sometimes family is not about genes and blood, sometimes it's about heart and soul and friendship. Linda, I love you!

Post Script
One year after I wrote that entry, we lost Linda after she had emergency surgery for a blocked intestine. Truth be told, we lost Linda when that bitch of a step-mother beat her daily and never once showed her love.

A Year At the Top

PAUL SCHAFFER AND GREG EVIGAN had a sitcom together in the late 1970s before Paul was on *Letterman* or Greg was *B.J. and the Bear*. It was called *A Year at the Top*. We, who wrote it, called it "A Year at the Flop". The show was produced by Norman Lear, who was so hot at the time, the networks gave him whatever he wanted. He produced *All in the Family*, *Maude*, *The Jeffersons*, *Good Times*, and on and on and on. No matter what he put on the air it was an immediate hit, with the exception of *A Year at the Top*, which I wrote with my writing partner, Mary Willard.

Here's the premise of the show: two musicians sell their soul to the devil to become rock stars. *You've got to be kidding!* That's what I thought too, but Lear was producing and the networks bought it. Lear could have pitched a show about Nazi Youth camp counselors and they would have bought it. As a matter of fact, I think there was a show *Oh You Adolf You*. Am I wrong?

The original cast of *A Year at the Top* included Mickey Rooney. Now, this was a trip for me because he was a legend. He was also a monumental pain in the ass. The man did not shut up. He had a mouth like a whippoorwill's asshole, it was always moving. The director would shout "Action", Rooney would say his lines, then "Cut", and Rooney would go on like a babbling brook. He was doing jokes, he was telling stories, he was doing bits with props; it was annoying, time consuming, and was costing the production company beaucoup bucks. He was wonderful in the part, and while I never worked directly with him, I could see it being a major problem when the show went into production.

Gabe Dell replaced Rooney. Gabe was a wonderful comedy actor whose claim to fame was he was an original Bowery Boy. Now, Gabe was a gentleman to work with, but there was just one tiny little thing wrong. He could not remember a single line of dialogue. Years later we would learn that it was a medical condition. Back then, no one understood it and just thought he was learning impaired. When the cameras rolled, he was wonderful and could pull it off, but he did it by hiding lines all over the set. He would walk from point to point where he had written his lines like on lampshades, on tabletops, chair backs, and door frames; anywhere he could put a note to keep him going. If you watch the show today (I don't know why anyone would), you can see him reading the furniture. He was a joke writer's dream. We used to tease him mercilessly and he was a good sport about it.

Paul Shaffer was new to the business, but had come off *SNL* as musical director and there was a lot of buzz about him. He was and is a brilliant musician. As an actor, he was a brilliant musician. There would be no Macbeth from Paul.

Greg Evigan was different. He could act, he had sex appeal, and he was also a great musician. Greg's life crosses mine every fifteen minutes. When I lived in that apartment building in Hollywood, with the kidney shaped pool, there were two sisters who lived there. They were magnificent beauties, working actresses. They moved out long before I did and long before the building became a comedy haven, but I kept bumping into them all over Hollywood, at parties, at openings, at plays. They were always there.

I am signed to do the show with Greg and discover he has married one of the sisters from my building. After we worked together on the show I start bumping into Greg everywhere, at The Emmys, at The Comedy Awards, parties, opening, etc, etc. and he's always with his wife, who was my neighbor. Then Greg signs with my agent at ICM and so I see him at the office. It didn't end after we stopped writing the show. This bumping into each other thing still happens to this day. I have a play reading, in walks Greg and his wife. I go to a party, there is Greg and his wife. I seriously believe that there is a master plan that certain people are meant to be in your life. Greg and his wife are two of those people.

Basically, that was the cast of the show. Julie Cobb (daughter of Lee Jay Cobb and Nedra Voltz) and an eighty-plus actress who was in vaudeville rounded out the ensemble. The cast that finally made it to the screen was not the problem; the problem was in the office. The staff was, um, unfunny egomaniacs that guided the show much like the Captain of the Titanic guided his ship. These were people who wouldn't know a funny line if it stood on its hind legs and spit in their face, and boy, were they concerned about story lines. The stories had to be real and Mary and I would say, "It's a show about the devil. How real can it be??" We would pitch story ideas or jokes and we would hear, "The devil wouldn't say that," or, "The devil wouldn't do that."

Writing sessions were torture. It was hours of sitting around a table pitching story ideas to people you hated, on a show you hated, about characters that were preposterous. To give you an idea how political the show was, Mary and I had written an episode. The other writers had read it and hated it. Every script had to be approved by Norman. He came in and threw our script on the table, "Good job. This one's ready to go," and walked out.

No one said a word and then a choir of, "Fine. Great. I liked it too," erupted.

The only thing that kept me going was working with Mary. She and I could have a good time in solitary confinement, on fire, in hell, with my entire family singing Sandy Duncan show tunes from Peter Pan. Here's an example: we were under a lot of pressure and the deadlines were coming up fast and furious. I was a nervous wreck and asked my secretary if she had something to calm me down.

"I have a Seconal," she said.

"What'll that do?"

"Oh, it will mellow you out."

I took it. About an hour later, Mary and I are in a meeting with Norman Lear. I'm seated across from Norman and the pill hits me. Mary is seated to my left. As Norman is talking, I'm deflating like a balloon with a slow leak. I'm falling forward and every time Norman looks away, Mary pulls me up by the back of my hair. She pulls me up, I fall over, Norman looks away and she pulls me up. I fall over, Norman looks away, she pulls me up, and this goes on the entire meeting. She drags me to my office where I spend the rest of the day unconscious on my sofa. I was mellow all right; so mellow I was almost in a coma.

The show is filled with these kinds of memories for me. We were all sitting around a table in the conference room and someone came in and said, "Elvis just died." The room just went hush. It's like someone said, "Kennedy has been shot." I was never an Elvis fan, but the reaction in the room was monumental. The man had a profound impact on the world and his death slowed up production that day; everyone was in mourning. It's a moment in time that sticks out like someone put a bookmark there.

Of all the memories I have of that show, I think the best one is of my ex-wife. She had just had the baby and, shall we say, was challenged to find happiness in her role as a new mother. She would call me at the office crying about something important like a lost phone bill or a broken fingernail. These calls came at least six times a day. It became a standing joke at the office. One of the writers, Terry Hart, would burst out laughing every time he would walk by my office and hear me say, "There's no need to cry over that." Our secretary would write me phone messages, instead of "Your wife called" they would say, "Your wife cried." We were under a lot of stress and it was getting to Mary. She came into my office one day and just sat down and cried. While she was crying my ex called and she started to cry. I had bawling women in stereo. Just for the record, Mary is one of the strongest women I know. If she cried, you can imagine what working on that show was like.

The show did have perks financially. I bought myself a new Lancia Scorpion. On my first day out with it, I was rear ended by an eighty-five-year-old driver. When I came into the office and told the other writers, the laugh was ten minutes. You see, even back then, I had a dark cloud over me.

I can honestly say that the show was a living hell to write but was filled with wonderful memories. Mary and I still laugh over them. *A Year at the Top* was the reason I told my agents not to get me any more sitcom gigs (a directive I would regret for fifteen years as I sat in shithole after shithole comedy condo on the road). Three wonderful things came out of *A Year at the Top*: Mary Willard, Greg Evigan, and Yolanda Tisdale (our secretary, who has become a very successful businesswoman in Beverly Hills), so it ain't all bad!!

Fox News

I'M SITTING ON MY SOFA, ASLEEP. I have the magic sofa. If you sit on it, you immediately fall asleep. I have had guests drop off in mid-sentence, "So any way I was about to fight off the shark when... zzzzzzz." I have seen celebrities with their heads rolled back and snoring with their mouths wide open, "Will someone please wake Lorette Switt?" It's the magic sofa. I sat down there to find some comfort from my depression and was out like a light in two minutes. The phone rang and I snap to attention.

"Hello."

"Steve, this is (name) from Fox News. Cathy Ladman gave us your number. Would you be interested in doing an interview with Judy Tenuta about who is smarter, men or women?"

I am foggy but I say, "Sure."

The Fox person says, "You will?" like she's asked a hundred comedians and no one has said yes. "That's great. We shoot tomorrow at 7:30 p.m.; we'll send a car for you. I'll call you for the pre-interview at eleven and I'll email you the article the interview is based on." It's all set and I hang up.

My depression immediately ends. I am viable. I have meaning. I am going to work. I now switch into work mode. I get the Fox email and read it. My heart sinks. It's bullshit. It's about how men are smarter than women because men's brains are larger and how women seek smarter men because they need to be protected. Now I see why she said, "You will?" There is no way I can go on camera and defend this anti-woman position. I call Judy, "What are we going to do?" We discuss options, one of which is my suggestion that we take opposite sides. I take the women's side and she defends the men. I thought it would be funnier. She agrees.

I email Fox and tell them I've gotten the article and here's a switch we think would be interesting. I tell them the idea with the caveat, "This is your interview. I'll do it any way you wish. I just thought it might be funnier if we did it this way." Ten seconds later I get an email back, "We are having problems with the segment. I'll call you tomorrow." I have been in the business long enough to know what that means: "We need a bigger name."

The next morning I've traded depression for anxiety. How can I go on TV and defend this inane article? What will my friends think? At 11:30 a.m. the phone had not rung. I knew what this meant. I'm not doing the interview. At 12:30 p.m. I'm on the phone with Fox.

"Hi, Steve, well we're going forward with the interview. We shoot at 7:30, however... "

That was the word I was waiting for!! I said, "OH THANK GOD! Who did you get to do the interview?"

"David Brenner," she said.

"Thank you so much. I didn't want to do this interview in the worst way."

"Really?"

"Oh yes! I couldn't say men are smarter than women. Look at Madame Curie and the woman who found the double helix and..."

"Well thank you for making it so easy for me." She hangs up and I immediately crash dive like a Japanese warplane over Pearl Harbor.

About an hour later Judy calls. She's upset that they have replaced me, but she needs jokes, so we work on her jokes for about an hour. Here are some of the jokes I wrote for her:

"Obviously this article was written by a man who wasn't breast fed."

"Men have all the power but it's only because women let them think they are running things."

"There was always a woman behind every successful man. It was MRS. Edison who said to Thomas.... What are you sitting in the dark for?"

Judy is very happy and I set my TiVo to tape her interview. About this time, I get a phone call from a new friend, Elaine Good, someone who is a friend of a friend who has been reading the book and calls herself MNBF (my new best friend). She called and I said, "Come over. I could use the company." Two hours later, there she is and we're laughing and talking and decide to go out to dinner. She's a corporate chef and she talks to me about a TV show she wants to do. I, in turn, take her to my favorite Lebanese Restaurant, where the waitress blows herself up if she doesn't like the tip. We had a great time.

After dinner, I came home and turn on the DVR. No interview. I'm thinking it didn't air and go to sleep. The next morning at 7 a.m. I get an email from Judy, "DAVID BRENNER HAD NO JOKES. HIS MIC WAS OFF FOR THE FIRST HALF OF THE INTERVIEW. I GOT A FEW GOOD JOKES IN." Then I learned it aired at 7 p.m., not 10 p.m., and that's why it didn't record. Freudian DVR. I really didn't want to see the interview anyway.

Judy and I started talking about other stuff and I told her about my play being optioned. She has a play she wants me to look at to re-write. Out of all this shit came something good. I have a project for next week.

This weekend was the perfect example of the highs and lows of show business. I'm on TV; I'm not on TV. I'm doing the interview; I'm not doing the interview. When it's all done, it's never good enough, something goes wrong, or you are treated like shit. If I wanted this kind of abuse, all I would have to do is go home for Thanksgiving. Do you see the insanity of the whole thing? They called me. They got my phone number and dialed. I didn't call them. *They* called *me*! Then after I say I'll do it, they reject me. If I had said, "No!" they would have chased me down until I agreed to do the effing thing. It is total and complete insanity. You can attach the electrodes now!

Tina Turner

RIGHT AFTER MY AGENT GARY DIED, my new agent, whose name happened to be Steve, called me about a series that was being done. There was no pilot, it was going right to air, and was called *Woofer's Supersonic City*. It took place in a music store and was sort of a sitcom within a variety show. My agent had booked me an audition for the next day and told me to dress "Rock n' Roll".

After Gary died, I had taken all his clothes and would wear them. One of Gary's things was a tour jacket from K.C. and The Sunshine Band, one of his clients. As a matter of fact, K.C., Gary, and I went skiing one year. When I saw the jacket, it immediately brought back fond memories of my brother/agent, Gary. I decided to wear the jacket to the audition, knowing that if I did, Gary would be with me.

The next day I went to one of the Studios, I think it was Gower, and met with three guys from New York who had come out west to cast the show. I walked into the office and kicked ass at the audition. I was funny. I looked hip. I read the lines well. This audition I felt good about. The producers were extremely interested in the fact that I was a writer and asked me if I would consider writing on the show if I got the job. This meant double money and my little brain went *ka-ching*, "Sure, I'd love to write on the show."

Two days later, Steve called, "You got the gig." I couldn't believe my ears. I had been cast in the title role of Woofer on a national TV show, starring Tina Turner, with me as co-star. There was a fifty-show guarantee at $3500 a week. Ka-ching a ding ding.

The producers met with me and told me how happy they were that they found me. There was a lot of ass-kissing being done, and I thought it was strange. They sent me the script. I read it and my heart sank, it was abysmal. It was drivel. It was unhip. I was sick to my stomach. I had a really good relationship with the producers and I called them.

"Hey guys, nice script. I'm using it to line my bird cage."

"Yeah, it's a little weak," they admitted.

"A little weak, this thing couldn't fly with a stick of dynamite up its ass. Let me try a re-write."

They agreed, and I spent the entire day rewriting the script. I dropped it off and within two hours they were calling my agent. They wanted to make me head writer, fly me to New York, give me $100 per diem and an apartment close to the studio in Manhattan. That's $5000 a week plus perks. If this is a dream and I wake up in a pool of my own body fluid, I'm going to kill myself. It wasn't a dream, it was for real. I was co-star and head writer. Somebody slap me now!

I thought I had died and gone to heaven. This whole thing happened right around the time *Saturday Night Live* went on the air. New York was the center of hip because NBC has made it that way; the whole project had an air of hit surrounding it. New York, Tina Turner, Rock n' Roll; what else could a comedian ask for?

We make the deal for $5000 a week for fifty weeks. They fly me to New York two weeks early and I'm set up in an office with a staff to write the shows. No matter what I turned out, they loved. This had never happened before, and I couldn't understand why they were being so nice to me. I asked them what was up. Turns out Tina Turner had seen me open for Donna Summer. She asked them to find me and cast me in the role opposite her. They were keeping her happy by signing me, and my humor was a bonus. If she loved the script, they loved it; and she loved the script. This doesn't happen to me, this happens to Jay Leno, Jim Carey, and David Letterman. I get shows like *Good Morning San Diego*. I don't get cutting-edge shows in which major stars are singing my praises. Nope, this doesn't happen to *me*.

The day of shooting for the first episode arrives and I finally get to work with Tina Turner. We are introduced and I make a deep bow of thanks. She laughs. She was absolutely a dream to work with; no temperament and no ego, just professional and sweet. The days were long but I didn't care, I was finally living my dream.

We're on the set and Tina has to do a musical number. She stops and says, "I think it would be good if Woofer joined me here." I turn around to see whom she's talking to. She's talking to the network people and they're nodding, and so this kid from Chelsea, Mass. gets to sing with Tina Turner. After the take, people are coming up to me, "I didn't know you could sing like that." Evidently, they hadn't been to the Golden Anchor on Cape Cod, where I was a singing waiter right after college. The truth of the matter is, I can't sing like that, but if you think I was going to *not* sing like that next to Tina Turner, you are crazy. Mick Jagger suddenly possessed me. I rocked!

The shoot is over and Tina and I kiss and say good-bye. She has to go to Europe for a tour date and will come back in ten days to continue shooting the rest of the series. The production company sends me back to LA and gives me a round trip ticket so I can come back to New York. In the meantime, I'm writing new shows.

My contract had an option that had to be picked up by 5 p.m. on May 16th. On May 15th, I remembered I had not heard from them, and so I called my agent and asked what was up. He was going to look into it. On May 16th, I still hadn't heard and started to get worried. Steve called again. They didn't return his call. This is not good, and this went on all day. At 4:45 p.m. LA time, they called. Tina had signed with a new manager, the one she is presently with and who made her an international superstar. He had seen the episode we shot and, "It wasn't the direction I want to take her," so Tina pulled out of the series. No Tina; no sponsor. No sponsor; no show. The whole thing was cancelled. Two hundred and fifty thousand dollars gone!

I sat at my desk in my house and just stared at the walls. I had just gotten divorced, I had just lost my son, I had just lost my best friend, and now *this*. I went into shock. My hands were numb and my eyes glazed over. I was frozen in anxiety and could not move from my desk. The sun went down and I was still sitting there. Suddenly the phone rang; it shook me out of my trance. It was a good, dear friend, Lynn Turner, who just happens to be a Beverly Hills shrink (God does put into your life what you need when you need it). I told her what had happened fully expecting to hear, "Oh, Steve, I'm so sorry," but what I heard was, "Well, at least you came close."

Something clicked in my head and I said, "Yeah! I almost came close." The anxiety stopped, my muscles freed up, and the vise that was holding my neck in a ridged position disappeared. Lynn said exactly the right thing. She saw the glass half full, and I know in my heart if she said, "Aw, gee, poor Steve," I would have fallen apart. She would have validated my feelings of being a failure. That's not what she said, though. Instead, she made me feel good about my experience and myself, and it's why she is one of the top shrinks in Beverly Hills today and remains my dear friend.

I have slides of Tina standing in front of a neon sign that said, *Woofer's Supersonic City*, and when I see her on tour or interviewed in her mansion in the south of France, I know that she deserves it all, because she truly is one of the good ones. Her manager was right, the show would have been wrong for her. It was right for me, but wrong for her. I know I may not be a star and I may not be a household name, but at least once, just for about a week, I was all of those things, and I got to sing with Tina Turner on my own TV show. Now that's not bad.

Maggie Vomit

IN LA, I HAD TWO DOGS: Maggie, the English springer spaniel, and Tori Spelling, the mutt. They got along famously in my Northridge—soon to be destroyed by an earthquake—house. One day I came home and I saw a box of ant traps opened and chewed to bits on the garage floor. I look on the box and see "POISON" in big letters. My heart drops. I look at the dogs and say, "Who did this?" Like I expect them to answer, "Well, that's not an easy question, Steve, she chewed it but I got the box down." Tori, however, sinks her head and runs to her bed, just like the real Tori Spelling. I scoop Tori up and call the vet, who tells me to bring her in immediately and to bring the poison boxes as well. I'm in the car in two minutes and half way to the vet's when I look at the box. The puncture marks are huge; it couldn't have been Tori. It must have been Maggie. I slam on the brakes and head back home. I open the garage door and Maggie is on her hind legs trying to get a box of soap powder off the shelf, "Shit. Caught red-handed." She runs out the doggie door and hides in the back yard.

I throw Tori in the house and track Maggie down. I put her in the car (this is my brand new Lexus coupe) and take off for the vet. Maggie is in the back seat and I hear her start to gag. She's coughing, and suddenly she projectile vomits on the back of my head. You know that moment when you think, *that didn't just happen.* That's what it was like inside my car. I'm gagging myself, and I hear Maggie start to throw up again. I scream, "Look Maggie! Squirrels" and she looks to the right and vomits on the back seats. Now she jumps in the front seat and looks at me. It's like that moment when Sigourney Weaver sees the Alien in her cabin. She knows it's going to strike, but when? Then Maggie starts to gag again. It's like the moment before Mount St. Helen exploded. "She's gonna blow," I throw a breath mint on the floor and Maggie goes for it as she heaves another stomach full of Alpo between the center console and bucket seats. At this point I'm thinking, *well, I think we've established it was Maggie who ate the poison.*

Have you ever smelled dog vomit inside a closed car? It's so vile I threw up all over myself. Maggie jumps in the back seat and she throws up again. It's like she wants it to all be balanced. She jumps in the front seat and heaves some big chunks on the dashboard. I instinctively turn on the windshield wipers. She jumps in the back and takes a huge shit. Why not? It was coming out of every hole. My car smelled like a sewage treatment plant on wheels. I can't roll down the windows because Maggie jumps out when the car is running. At this point it's not such a bad idea. I'm stuck in my own private vomitorium.

Finally, I arrive at the vet. I open the door and the vomit drips off the door panel. I look in the backseat of my car and, I swear to God to you, the seat wells were filled with vomit, two shimmering pools of it. I leave the car and run into the vet's office. The nurse takes one look at me and screams! They rush Maggie into the emergency room and make me take off my clothes and take a shower. They give me scrubs to wear.

Then an assistant says, "You better go out to your car." I go out there and ten million flies are having a meet and greet. It looked like they were trying to lift the car up and take it to wherever flies go to eat dog shit. The vet gives me towels and hot soapy water and a shovel. I'm serious, a shovel. I start scooping out dog vomit. I won't eat a soft tomato, and I've got dog vomit up to my elbows. Now here's the curious thing: good is good and the interior of that Lexus cleaned up like it had never been used as a toilet. The carpet repelled the moisture, the leather cleaned up beautifully, and the seats moved all the way forward so I could get to all the vomit between the bucket seats. The smell was something else.

When my preliminary clean-up was done, I ran back inside. Maggie was still in the emergency room. The doctor comes out and takes both my hands. This is not good. She said, "She ate poison. We've stabilized her. The next twenty-four hours will be very telling." I finally break down and cry. "We'll do everything we can to save her," but I know I'm about to lose my best friend.

I didn't sleep much that night. The next morning at 9 a.m., the doctor calls, "You have to come over here right now, you won't believe it." I speed to her office, and Maggie is running around the yard jumping and barking, and when she sees me she runs to me and pulls me to the door. She's ready to go home. She made a complete recovery. The vet was astonished.

Something like $1,500 later, I'm driving home. Maggie's head is out the window. The world is good. The next week I take my car in to be detailed. The guy wants to know if someone had been killed in it. I explain about Maggie and that he'll need an industrial strength deodorant. He nods but I'm sure he thought I was a mass murderer.

One year to the day later, that car was stolen. The last vestige of my success was taken right off Ventura Blvd. I was a basket case, but I hoped whoever stole it was forced to sit in it on a nice hot summer day. Oh, by the way, after the whole Maggie poison thing I doggie proofed my garage and nothing like that ever happened again. Maggie lived to a ripe old age of fifteen.

Surprise Gardener

ONE OF MY GOOD FRIENDS is TV Producer Gary Bernstein. He and Larry Hovis, from *Hogan's Heroes*, had a production company, and they used me a lot on shows they produced. I mean, a lot! I must have done ten pilots for them, all game shows. I would do the pilot, then David Brenner would do the series. Welcome to my world. Gary—whom I call my second Gary—and I became good buddies. No one laughs harder at my jokes than Gary Bernstein. I was playing a club in San Jose; Gary, Larry, and Susan Simons (then a CBS exec and presently an agent) were in San Francisco for a broadcasters' convention, and they drove to San Jose to see my show. That night the room was packed and I absolutely destroyed the place, but I honestly feel that having Gary in the audience and hearing him laugh spurred me on to say and do things I never would.

The years go on, and my road gigs are fewer and fewer. I'm starting to write, but it's like starting a whole new career; work was very sparse. I called Gary one day to see what he was up to.

"My production coordinator just quit," then there was a long pause, "Why don't you take the job?"

My immediate reaction, "I don't know how to be a production coordinator."

"Listen. I've known you for fifteen years. There is no one more organized than you. If anyone can do this job, you can."

I accepted and became production coordinator on *Surprise Gardener* for HGTV. What does that mean? I didn't have the slightest idea.

My first day at work was interesting. My immediate boss, let's call her Bitch, was a new experience. Bitch had all the warmth of a black widow and the tact of a charging pit bull. I'm sitting at my desk and she throws a set of keys in front of me, "Get us some coffee cups and paper towels." Huh? She wanted me to go to the 99-cent store and pick up some coffee cups and paper towels. You have to understand, as much as I say I don't have an ego, I've got one. For twenty years I was picked up in limos and now I'm going to the 99-cent store. I'm a messenger?? I get into my Mercedes and I head to the 99-cent store. I feel like a complete failure.

By the time I get back, I'm ready for a straitjacket. I put the paper towels down by the sink and I head back to my desk. About twenty minutes later Bitch yells across the room.

"Don't you *ever* put paper towels on the counter again!!!"

I don't turn around because I know she can't be talking to me.

"HEY!"

I swing around in my chair, "Are you talking to me?"

"Yes."

From deep in my soul I got this surge of energy, "You can't talk to me that way! Don't you ever talk to me that way again!"

Her face goes beet red, "Into my office!"

I go in ready to get fired. She reads me the riot act telling me what I will and will not do. I say to her, "I was hired to be production coordinator, not messenger. It does not make sense to send someone with an IQ of 128 to the 99-cent store in a Mercedes. That's what production assistants are for." The line had been drawn in the sand.

I walk back to my desk and get a round of applause from everyone in the office. It appears Bitch has been treating them like shit for years, and no one ever spoke up to her. You see, I didn't care if I got fired, big deal. I never wanted to be a production coordinator; I didn't even know what they were.

The next day, I learned what my job really was. I was to hire the designers, hire the help, get all the materials, do all the financial planning, order the food, deal with the home owner, organize the shoot etc., etc., etc. Oh! That's what a production coordinator does. I can do that. Piece o' cake.

The show had been on the air seven years. The premise was to go to someone's house and redo the garden in one day. This entailed new plants, new furniture, new pots, new everything. I asked them for the list of vendors who donated materials to the show. There was none.

"You mean to tell me you've been paying for this shit?"

Bitch says, "If you can get it for free, be my guest."

Within five days, I had over $100,000 in donated materials. OSH was giving us $500 a show. Vendors were lined up to donate materials in exchange for airtime, much like *Extreme Makeover* did. Suddenly Bitch was warming up to me. She was becoming *my* Bitch.

We do our first show, and it was the hardest day I had ever spent in show business. The day started at 5 a.m. and didn't end until almost 10 p.m. The next day we had to be in the office to plan for the next week's shoot. It was a grind like I had never had before in my life. Once I got the first couple of shows under my belt, however, it was a snap. I got restaurants to give us food at a discounted price. Bitch was in seventh heaven. We were saving money by the truckload and she was actually starting to like me.

However, the show was a living hell. A lot of the staff had been there a few years and were burned out. One in particular was not only burned out, but also bitter. This person did everything in their power to undermine my efforts to better the show. This person and I butted heads daily. For example, I had hired an artist to do a mural. As I am handing him his money, this person comes up to the artist and says, "Just so you'll know, they paid the artist $200 more last year." It made me look like a thief, and I didn't appreciate it. My enemies were changing on the show. Bitch and I were getting along, but this new Bitch was driving me insane.

On one weekend, we were scheduled to do two gardens in two days. This was almost impossible and took a monumental amount of work. I had in place a network of suppliers who would take my call day or night and would deliver whatever I needed. Finally, I had been given an assistant, Justin Lillge, who was a gift from God. This kid would do whatever I asked him to do.

"Justin, climb that tree and spit at birds."

"Yes, sir, Steve."

Being the kind of person I am, the more he worked, the more I wanted to protect him. After all, he was protecting me. We do the first show of the double-header, and while we're shooting, I get a call from the owner of tomorrow's garden, "Hello. Yes, we decided we don't want you to shoot here." Click. I have spent a week ordering materials, my budget is shot, and now I have no garden to work on. I remained very calm; I started walking up the street knocking on doors. After about three tries, I found the perfect backyard, one in which we could use all the materials we already had. I ran to the director and dragged him over there. I literally sold him on the yard, "We are here already. We don't have to move the trucks. The materials are here!" He smiled and we used the garden. It was a savings of about $100,000.

At the end of the second days' shoot, Bitch calls and tells me to send Justin and the other production runner back to the office to do some work. These kids had worked forty-eight hours straight and were dead. I told Bitch that.

"They're young, they can take it," she said.

"I'm not sending them back, it's inhumane," I said, and told the boys to go home. The next day all hell broke loose. I just didn't care; let them fire me.

Conditions on the show grew worse. Morale was low. Nerves were shot. We were coming to the end of the season, and there were just four more shows. We all knew this would be the last season. Word had come down from the network that they were not happy with the product. The writing was on the wall. My new pain in the ass drops a materials list off on my desk. It was six pages long. I couldn't understand, and so I questioned. The answer I got was, "We have a balance left on donated materials so we should get it all." I was incensed. I had given my word to these vendors that their materials would be used on the show. What was happening here was, the materials would come in, the show would be cancelled, and then the *staff* would take the materials home. This is not what I signed on for. I refused to do it. The two Bitches got together and the list was reduced to four pages. I refused to send it in and my vendors knew not to accept orders from anyone but me. It finally came to a head one day in the office when New Bitch ridiculed me in front of everyone. Something clicked in my head and I quit right there on the spot. Bitch One, who was now my best friend and biggest supporter on the show, ran after me into the parking lot.

"Don't do this to me. I need you."

"Do something about (name)."

She refused, and I rolled up my window and drove out of the parking lot never to return.

In the car going home, I broke down. I felt like a huge failure. If I had handled it differently, if I had been calmer... if I... if I... I crawled into bed and stayed there for almost three weeks. Not a single soul called me from the show, with the exception of Dee Dee, who was a production secretary (Justin had left the show three weeks prior). The staff was like a herd of Impala grazing. Suddenly a lion kills one of the herd, but the rest of the herd just continue to graze. Their thought, *thank God it wasn't me.*

Amy Heckerling

WHEN I FIRST STARTED doing stand-up at The Comedy Store, there were all kinds of people hanging out there. The most memorable were Craig T. Nelson, Barry Levinson, Ted Lange, Lou Rawls, Flip Wilson, Redd Foxx, Jack Reilly, Pat McCormick and so many, many more. There were also many people who you never heard of; people like Steve Lubetkin, who threw himself off the Hyatt Hotel because he wasn't getting the exposure he thought he needed at The Comedy Store. Sasimo Hernandez, who brought a cardboard tube on stage, and while he did his act he would squeeze himself through the tube until he was all the way inside. It was the weirdest place on earth, those early years at The Comedy Store. The comedy club market had not been developed yet; it was being developed right before my eyes, and I witnessed it all.

One day I was at The Store, as we called it, and was approached by a young filmmaker. Would I be interested in being in his student film? "Sure," I answered with glee, but I answered too quickly. The script was about a man in his late twenties who was getting circumcised. I was the shyest man on the face of the earth back then, and the thought of shooting something of personal natural such as this made my blood run cold, but I said I would do it, and I did it. I made sure there were no nude scenes. I wasn't going to show off my love handles for a student film.

I remember very little about the shoot, except being consistently embarrassed and not getting any direction from the director. He was to direction what I am to piano concertos. The shoot was long and tedious, if not humiliating. I felt nothing in front of the camera and gave nothing back. The director also gave nothing. It was a nothing shoot and a waste of time. In my closet right now is a copy of that film, which I have not looked at in thirty-five years. I'm too embarrassed. There is a saying in show biz: no work is bad work as long as you're working. This held true for this little piece-of-shit film.

About a month later, I got a call from a young girl at American Film Institute (AFI). She had seen the film I had done for her classmate and she wanted to know if I would do *her* film. She was shooting a scene from *Carnal Knowledge,* and she wanted me to play the Jack Nicholson part. I agreed and we were to meet the very next day.

From our first meeting, I knew this girl was special. We had long deep discussions about the characters. We talked about mood and tempo and timing of the piece. We discussed character background and make-up style and costume choices.

She had thoroughly thought out this shoot and what she wanted of me. She mapped out how the shots would be done. I felt there was guidance there, something I had not had on the first film, and I looked forward to shooting this piece.

The film was going to be shot at AFI. I arrived there early and got into make-up. The directors thought we should shoot the simple scenes first and end the day with the hardest scene, the most emotional. The first scene was a two-shot of me and another character talking over breakfast. We did a take and I wanted to die inside. I knew it was crap. The director came in and talked with me. She gave me insight and direction, a sub-text to work with. We shot it again and it was like night and day, I became that character. She yelled, "Cut!" and came running over to me, "You got it." Then she told me that one of her professors had come in and watched on the monitor. He asked her if I was a soap opera actor because he thought he recognized me (I had just been fired from The May Company six months prior). The director put her arm around my shoulder and said, "Congratulations, you're an actor!"

Those of you who know me know how insecure I am. Those words of kindness from the director did something to me; they filled me with confidence. I was not afraid to emote, I was not afraid to look silly. All I wanted to do was become that character and make it believable on film.

We got to the last scene and I was totally prepared. My heart was pounding but my head was screwed on straight and ready to go. I hit my marks, I remembered my lines, but most importantly, I found the emotions to portray the character. We did it in two takes. The director yelled, "It's a wrap!" and I gathered my stuff and left.

The director called me about a week or so later. The scene was looking good, and she would tell me what the professor thought. Being who I am, I waited for that validating call. I never heard from her again, never knew what my acting debut looked like, never got a copy of the film. I never gave it another thought. I just accepted it as, *that's how show biz is*, and moved on.

It must have been ten or twelve years later when *Fast Times at Ridgemont High* came out. The film was a hit, and everyone was talking about the new female director, my director, and the person who guided me through her class project. Amy Heckerling. To give you an idea who Amy Heckerling is and what's she's done, here's a list of her films: *The Office, Hot Girl, Loser, A Night at the Roxbury, Clueless, Clueless* the TV series, *Look Who's Talking Too, Look Who's Talking* the TV series, *Fast Times, European Vacation, Johnny Dangerously, Fast Times at Ridgemont High, Getting It Over With*.

When you work in the business for a while, you can tell the ones that are going to cross over. I knew that day when Amy was directing me that this woman had something special, that she was going to cross over into the big time. There was intelligence to her work, thoughtfulness to her craft. She was a real director, not just a kid doing an assignment for AFI.

Most actors would have called Amy and said, "Hey remember me, I did your student film?" but not me. I sat back thinking, "If she really liked my work, she would have called me." I watched as she became famous, never once thinking of intruding on her success. Somehow in my soul, I think success is for others, not for me. How wrong is that?

Mills Brothers

TURN OF THE CENTURY nightclub, Denver, Colorado. I'm pulling into the parking lot of the club and see the marquee: "THE MILLS BROTHERS with comedian Steve Bluestein."

This was a special gig for me on so many levels. It was one of first times at The Turn of the Century. It was going to be exciting and wonderful and everything I had hoped it would be.

I went into the rehearsal to find three very old men on stage. One of the brothers had passed on, but their sound was still there. The one thing that amazed me so was how much one the brothers looked like my Uncle Nate. He was African American, we were Russian Jews, but we had this connection that went long and deep.

We opened that night and my show was good, as it always was. I watched the guys do their set. They were magnificent that night and there were only three of them—yet the harmonies were still there. After the show, we hung out in the dressing room and got to talking; they were warm, gentle men. They were gentlemen. They asked where I was staying. I was staying at their hotel, and they asked if they could give me a ride. For the entire week, they would drive me to the show and back in their limo.

I was in awe of them and would hold the door for them or get them water. I'd do anything I could to thank them because they were so nice to me. I was being as respectful and reverent as I could be. After all, this was show business history I was working with. On the night before I closed with them, we were driving from the hotel to the club. I was sitting up front with one of the brothers when I said to him, "This week has been very special to me." The reaction I got was a surprise, all he said was "hum." Like, isn't that interesting. He turned and looked out the window.

We arrived at the club and the brothers piled out of the car, but one of them waited and grabbed me by the arm.

"Son, I've been watchin' you all week. You need to get a little more attitude. You're too nice. Don't be beholden to anyone in this business."

"Yeah but it's just because it's you guys."

He stopped me, "Don't be beholden to anyone in this business." He got out of the car and walked to catch up to his brothers.

I watched the three of them entering the club and I thought, *that man could not have had it easy coming up, and still he took the time to give me advice.* All I could think of was how wonderful that man was and what a loving, giving gesture he had just made to me.

I never worked with The Mills Brothers again, but their music and message stays with me to this day. Actually, their message may have sunk in too deeply. You see, for years after my divorce, I had attitude for days. I took no crap from anyone, I allowed no one to step on my toes. It was a dog-eat-dog world, and I was fighting to be top dog; but if you ever come over to my house and hear music playing, eventually the iPod will get around to "Paper Doll" and you'll see me smile.

Vegas First Time

IT WAS NEW YEAR'S EVE, and my ex-wife and I had been invited to The Roxy to see *Women Behind Bars*. Gary had gotten tickets, and so we all were going to bring in the New Year together. If I had known then what I know now, I would have put the ex behind bars and gone by myself. I had never been to the Roxy, although in six months I would be opening for Dolly Parton there. That was all in the future; tonight was about New Years and having fun. Gary met us outside the Roxy and we all went in together. The place was packed. There were some celebrities and some minor names—one being Pat Carroll, former Broadway star and frequently seen on TV in the late 50s/early 60s.

I have radar for faces. I should have radar for car keys, shoes, and important papers, which I can never find, but I have face radar. Since I cannot remember names, my brain has developed a scanning device, like at the airport, which sees a face and recognizes it immediately. I noticed Pat coming and the radar bell went off. She was seated in a tier above us. I watched as she and her group sat. Suddenly, everyone in her party put on construction hats and, in unison, turned on rotating red beacons that sat on the top of each hat. The entire Roxy audience burst into applause and I remember making a mental note, *way to enter a crowded room. Red lights and sirens.* Maybe twenty-five or thirty years later, I met Pat Carroll in Palm Springs at the Palms Springs Playwright Festival, where my play was an entrant. I recalled that story to her and she said, "My mother had just died and I was so depressed I needed to do something to cheer myself up. So, I bought those hats and went to the Roxy." That was when I learned it's not always about making an entrance, sometimes it's about making yourself happy.

In any case, as we sat there, Gary was acting like the cat that ate the canary.

"What's up?" I said.

"You open at Caesar's Palace in three days," he said with glee.

I could not believe it. This was the big time: Caesar's Palace, on the strip, in Las Vegas. They were doing an all-comedy bill, a cavalcade of comedy: Phyllis Diller, Pat Cooper, and me. The ex and I were over the moon. We really had something to celebrate. It was Gary's Christmas present to me. He had given me something I had wanted all my life, and it's why I loved him like a brother and grieved so deeply when he passed.

Three days later, I was on a plane to Vegas with my manager Billy Sammeth. I'll never forget getting into a cab and driving from the airport to the strip. We pulled into Caesar's Palace driveway, and there on the marquee, in letters twenty-five feet tall, it said "PHYLLIS DILLER, PAT COOPER, STEVE BLUESTEIN." 100% billing, *me*! First time in Vegas, Gary had made the deal of my career. My heart filled with pride as I looked at Billy. I'm just about to say something about finally making it when the cabbie says, "Who the hell is Steve Bluestein?" So much for my touching moment.

I had never met Phyllis, but Pat I had met in 1968, although we had not actually met. I was in an elevator at the United Artists building. There were two other people plus myself in that elevator. We were going down and it stopped at a lower floor. The doors opened, and Pat Cooper was standing there. Pat, in a thick, put-on Italian accent, said, "Lem-me com-a in." He pushed his way into the elevator like it was packed with people, "Sukza-me, Sukza-me. Comin-a tru!" He made a huge scene. It was funny, but seemed so out of place at the time. I remember thinking, *how can anyone be that uninhibited?* Now I was working with him in Vegas equal billing.

Phyllis was another story. I had heard that she was this elegant, warm, loving person, but I had no idea how the rumors had been understated. I met Phyllis Diller, and she immediately made me feel accepted. It wasn't the new kid and the star; it was two comedians, equals and pals. She was this icon, and yet she was the lady next-door, the nice lady who baked cookies. Phyllis and I clicked immediately. She took me under her wing and gave me tips on how to work the "big room". She watched my act and told me which jokes she loved and which ones she hated. She hung out with me. She made the first time in Vegas easier and more enjoyable. She was what they call a "mench".

Pat Cooper was a surprise to me. On stage he is the loudest, most obnoxious person I've ever met, and in person the warmest, most caring person I've ever met. I remember watching him on stage and thinking, *look at him. Caesar's Palace is his Comedy Store.* He was as comfortable on that stage as I was at The Store. He would improvise; he would walk back and forth with ease, and he'd talk to the audience. He is truly one of the most underrated comedians of his time, but that attitude of anger is hard to take on stage, and I guess that's what kept him back. As for heart, there is no one better. Years later when I opened in New York City, it was Pat Cooper who was in the audience opening night. It was Pat Cooper who would send me cards from the road and make me feel included. While others may have made more money and gone farther, it's Pat Cooper that I remember with fondness.

As fondly as I remember Pat, Phyllis surpasses the memory with years of friendship. Phyllis adopted me on that gig; she took me under her wing. I remember one night she invited me up to her room. She had a limo and she was going to take me out to dinner. I knocked on the door and heard, "Come in!" I entered and said to the person standing there, "Is Phyllis here?" The person said, "I'm Phyllis!" She had on no wig or make-up. She was unrecognizable until she opened her mouth, then Phyllis Diller's voice came out of some strange being's body. It was like a real life *Invasion of the Body Snatchers*. She told me it was the only way she could go out in public and have some peace and quiet. It worked like a charm. I did all the talking when we got to the restaurant; I ordered and she never said a word to anyone. We were left alone and had a great time. "See, it works," she told me with a smirk.

The Caesar's gig went well. When it was all over, I remember thinking that fame wasn't like in the movies. You don't go out there a Nobody and come back a Star. It's years of hard work and an accumulation of credits that brought you fame. Although I had done well at Caesar's, nothing monumental happened. I didn't get a contract or a movie deal. It was just something to add to my resume. However, today on the strip, Caesar's has a billboard that heralds the "Headliners who have worked Caesar's," and if you stand there long enough, my name will scroll by. For me, it's one of the thrills of my career.

Now let me tell you how wonderful Phyllis Diller is. She's kept in contact with me for thirty years. Every Christmas a card came, or a note, or a letter. When she told me she loved getting funny postcards, I started sending them to her from all over the world. When I did my show in

Sydney, I sent her a card a week for three months. The one that stands out in my mind was a picture of three Koalas in a tree looking right into the camera. My caption on the back was, "Okay, who farted?" She screamed. When Phyllis and I did an infomercial for "The Complete Collection of Norm Crosby's Comedy Shop." she was still as funny and charming as ever. I just loved this woman!

Oh! Here's a little bit of interest. If you Google "Steve Bluestein memorabilia", you will come across a site selling personal letters. They are selling a letter I wrote to Phyllis in 1978, and after being for sale for two weeks it sold for $200. Go figure. Want to know the truth? I remember writing that letter like it was yesterday. Can you imagine my surprise when I saw it for sale? It's like finding a long lost relative you thought was dead.

Polio

I WAS ABOUT EIGHT YEARS OLD and going to summer camp. It was mid 1950s and the height of the Polio scare. The camp I was going to was a day camp very close to my home. I actually enjoyed going there and have friends from that period to this day. We had a daily routine at camp: sleep time, lunch, arts and crafts, and play period. It all started when I was on the swings. Instead of holding on to the sides of the swing—the chain that goes from the horizontal pipe to the seat—I held on to the seat, and when I pushed off I went flying backwards and smacked my head on the concrete. I had a huge lump on my head the size of an orange. I remember them taking me to the office and trying to get the bump down with ice and a knife. They put the blade across the lump with the flat side down and tried to push it out.

One counselor said, "Are you going to cut it off?"

"No, I'm trying to push it down," said the other.

I'm just lucky they didn't decide to throw a rattlesnake at the moon. Nothing worked; I had a huge lump on my head.

The camp called my mother, she told them I would be all right and to keep me at camp, and so they did. Later that day, they took us to a public swimming pool. At the pool, I began to get a headache. It was a horrible headache, one like I have never had before. I sat by myself as the other kids played. I got very tired, so tired they had to carry me back to the bus. When we were back at camp, I took matters into my own hands and walked to my parents' store (They owned a "Ma and Pa" grocery store at the time). My mother was working there and was shocked to see me. She put me in the car and brought me back to camp, "You're fine."

That afternoon, the camp took us to a local Boston kids TV show, *Big Brother Bob Emery* and there I was on camera, my very first appearance. I threw up all over Big Brother. I remember his comforting words off camera, "Get the little shit away from me." They brought me home and called my mother, she came to get me this time.

At home, I grew progressively worse. I was running a fever. My parents called the doctor and he wanted to see me at Children's Hospital in Boston. I remember lying on the sofa when my father came in with a family friend, Choc Glazer. They called him "Choc" because in the summer he got so tanned he was like Chocolate. "We're going to see the doctor now," is all he said and I started screaming. I didn't want to go. They tried to pick me up, but I wrapped my arms around the sofa cushions and they had a hell of a time separating me from the sofa as I kicked and screamed. The two men were much stronger, and soon we were in the car on the way to the hospital.

By this time, I was lapsing in and out of a coma. I would be wide awake and then just drop off. The doctors were not sure what it was, but they thought it was a mild case of Polio. In the summer, during that time period, I would tan extremely dark, so dark they couldn't find a blood vein in my arm. They stuck me repeatedly with the needle looking for that elusive vein. I screamed bloody hell. To this day I am petrified of needles. The test results were inconclusive, but they were going to do a spinal tap to see if that showed anything. They did the spinal tap, and that is why I have a bad back—one that goes out with crippling pain from time to time.

I was becoming a very sick kid. They didn't keep me in the hospital but were going to watch me. That night at home, I got even sicker. My parents were beside themselves. The next morning, my mother piled me into the backseat of the car and drove me into Boston to Children's Hospital. On the way there I got violently ill. She stopped the car and went into a bar to get me water. Funny, but that's one of my fondest childhood memories, she stopped the car and got me water. Sad, huh?

The illness stayed for about a month. I was paralyzed from the neck down, very stiff. I could move my arms and legs, but not my back or neck. During this whole period, I was in and out of comas. I remember one time waking up on an examining table with my mother and a doctor over me.

The doctor said, "Is he doing any coughing?"

"No, none at all," my mother said.

For some unknown reason, I thought it would be a good idea to start coughing, which I did. The doctor looked at my mother like, "You idiot," and my mother said something like, "This is the first time!"

For some reason, even at that early age, I got a great deal of satisfaction from that moment. I can't tell you why I did it or what I thought it would do, all I know is I thought it would be funny.

As the month progressed, the illness seemed to just disappear, and I was left with no side effects—unless you call a worthless back no side effects. Now here's the best—or worst—part of the story. I was scheduled for one more check-up with the doctor. They told my parents that if all the tests were good, this would be the last time they would see me, but if there was a problem, I'd need to come back. My father couldn't go with us, so my mother took me to that last appointment. The doctor gave me a clean bill of health and I would not be seeing him again. Happy? I was ecstatic.

Instead of going home after the appointment, we went to my parents' store. We pulled up in front of the store and my father came out to greet us. I can see this picture in my mind like it happened five minutes ago instead of years ago. He was broadly grinning as he walked over to the car.

As he approached, my mother said to me, "When he asks what the doctor said, tell him we have to go back again."

Like a little puppet, I said, "I have to go back."

My father's broad grin turned into panic, "Why??"

"I don't know, Ma told me to say that."

My father looked at my mother and said something like, "You bitch," and they had a nice fight as I sat there celebrating my clean bill of health.

I never thought about moments like that growing up, but as an adult I know it takes a great deal of cruelty to use a child as a tool to hurt your spouse. God, I wish there were some happy, funny memories I could share with you but seriously, this is all I've got!

Sha Na Na

I HAD SIGNED WITH NEW MANAGERS. They had connections with Sha Na Na, and so the very first gig I had with this new management team was at The Sands Hotel in Las Vegas opening for Sha Na Na. The Sands was real Vegas history. This was the room that Totie Fields, Frank Sinatra, Dean Martin, Sammy Davis, Jr., Don Rickles, and many more had worked. To stand on that very stage was a dream come true.

Only we weren't standing on that very stage. Sha Na Na had four-walled the room. Four-walling means they paid the hotel for use of the room. Sha Na Na would get the admissions and the hotel would get the money generated from drinks and food. The real money for the hotel is made when the crowd breaks after the show and they walk through the Casino to gamble. That is why there is a clock in the floor of the stage so entertainers know when their nineteen minutes are up. You do nineteen minutes; not eighteen or twenty, nineteen, or else the stage manager writes you up. Too many write-ups and you don't come back. It's strictly a business. We weren't in the main room, we were in the convention center that was set up with large round dining tables. I was overjoyed. Not!

I arrive at the hotel and check in. The girl checking me in seems a bit nervous. I sense this as she stalls while getting my key.

"Hon, what's seems to be the matter?" I ask.

"Um… ah…" Not a good answer, "Well, sir…"

Uh oh, she's using the "sir" thing. I'm in deep shit.

"It appears Mr. Brown has not vacated your suite," James Brown closed the night before and they were giving me his room.

"Oh, that's okay" I say, "I'll just wait until he's out."

"That's the problem. He won't leave and he won't answer the phone."

James Brown had my room and the only room available was some little crappy room facing a brick wall. I took it with the promise that they would move me when The King of Soul moved. Ha! Evidently Papa had a brand-new bag and he didn't want to pack it.

As I remember, it was a two-week gig. I had driven myself to Vegas so I would have my car there. It's horrible to be trapped in a hotel with nothing to do; a car is a great asset. James Brown remained in the room and the hotel gave me another suite. It was a lovely room at the back of the hotel, very private, very large, very nice. I was in heaven.

We opened and the shows were going well. I got along with Sha Na Na, the reviews were good, we had packed houses every night and they were receptive to the music and my comedy. My friends Mike and Wendy Churukian came up to see the show, some friends from college showed up, some friends from high school. It was a great week. Then I got a call from Wendy. Mike can't come to the show tonight, he's too sick. Sick? He picked up some bug in Vegas and it had him laid up in bed the rest of the trip. I felt horrible for him. Two days later I felt horrible for me.

I woke up a couple of days later with what appeared to be a cold. I was stuffed up and had body aches. I had chronic bronchitis as a child, so I knew the routine. I got the O.J., I got the pills, I started drinking lots of water, but nothing helped. I got sicker and sicker. I drove myself to the pharmacy and as I took a left turn, right in the middle of the intersection, my brand-new car died. The computer lights came on and that fucker was dead as nails. I was sick as a dog as I pushed my car out of the intersection.

I sat in my car waiting for a miracle. About twenty minutes, later it came. For some unknown reason, the car simply started again. I drove back to the hotel and immediately found a dealership. They couldn't take me for six days. I was beside myself and asked to speak to the service manager.

"This is Steve Bluestein. I'm working the Sands. My car died and I'm coming down with the flu. I've got one dark night before we open for our second week. I can't bring my car in! Please. Can you help me?"

"No problem. I'll send someone out to get your car," he said.

That's exactly what they did. If the man had sent fifty thousand dollars in gold bullion to my room I couldn't have been more appreciative. They fixed my car, took my credit card over the phone, and delivered it back to me. This is why I love working Vegas; they understand entertainers and they take care of us. When the gig was over, I sent the service manager a thank you gift and comps to The Sands.

However, my condition was to get a lot worse before it got better.

I did the two shows on Saturday night. Sunday, we were dark, no show. I went back to my room to sleep it off, and sometime during the night I woke up so sick I thought I was going to die. Whatever had gotten Mike had now gotten me. I was in agony. I ached. I was running a fever. I was throwing up. I was so congested I could barely breathe and I was coughing up small throw pillows—which this room really needed, I might add.

Around 6 p.m. I called room service and begged them to bring me soup and Jell-O. It's not on the menu; they weren't going to do it. I explained how sick I was, and when they realized I was in the show, they not only got me the food, but they also brought it to the room and all but fed it to me. The rest of the night was a living hell. Coughing, aching, fever, chills, and I was all alone. Then the next day, almost twenty-four hours to the minute that it began, the symptoms lessened. I was better, but weak as a kitten. I had a show Monday night, but I figured if I stayed in bed all day, I'd be fine. I was not. Come show time, I can barely speak. The flu symptoms were gone but the hacking cold and congestion were still here. The stage manager calls my room.

"You're doing the show, right?" He wasn't asking, he was telling me.

"Sure, but I can't walk to the showroom. Can you send someone to get me?"

They sent a golf cart to my room. I got dressed in my room, got on the golf cart with a blanket wrapped around me. They drove the golf cart to the stage and I got off at the mic, behind the curtain. I stood there as they announced the show (rather than entering from the wings) and when the curtain parted, there I was, the nasal congested comedian. I did my show and it was obvious that I was sick. I told the audience and they laughed when I said, "It's Vegas. I didn't want to miss a show. They break legs." Little did they know I wasn't joking. Halfway through the show I started coughing and I couldn't stop. I look out into the audience and say, "Does anyone have Vicks?" Another big laugh, and while they're laughing, a woman comes up to the stage and hands me a box of Vicks cough drops. "Oh, God bless you," I screamed to a huge laugh as I go to kiss her and she runs from me.

The show ended to huge applause. The curtain closes and the golf cart came on stage to take me back to the room. Second show, same routine. The following night I was well enough to walk to the showroom myself. We closed a few nights later. As I drove home to LA, I remember saying to myself, *this is what I wanted all my life, to be deathly sick in a hotel room in Vegas with no one to take care of me? This is my show business dream?* The rose was dying on the vine. The writing was on the wall. The ship had left the dock and other clichés that describe my life.

Many years later when I watched them implode the Sands, my mind was flooded with memories of that gig and I was saddened that another piece of Vegas history was disappearing. I knew that life is change, and for Vegas to survive, the old had to give way to the new. It grieved me, but I knew it had to be. As I watched the tower fall onto its side and a cloud of dust rise into the Vegas air, I wondered when they blew up the hotel if James Brown was still in his room.

Morristown, TN

IN MY SENIOR YEAR OF COLLEGE, after I studied in Europe for the first half of the summer, I did summer stock. That's right. I did summer stock in the tradition of all the great actors of my time. I trod the boards of a summer theater in Morristown, Tennessee, cultural capital of the South. I had a professor named Bob Ankrom, and he and his wife Ellie had this theatre. He asked certain students to join him that summer. I was over the moon because I had been asked to join the ensemble. Bob said to me once, "I expect big things from you in the theatre, Steve." When I told my mother this, she screamed at me, "They're paid to say those things," so I went to summer stock knowing that I didn't belong there and I wasn't really as good as the rest of the cast.

I get to Morristown, and how shall I describe it—Hootersville without the flash. Victorville was a metropolis in comparison. There was one main drag. They called it the main drag because that's where they would tie Yankees to the back of their pickup truck and drag them down the street. There was no supermarket, no major store, no drive-in. There was Fred's Grain Silo and an IHOP. However, Morristown had gotten a grant from the federal government for urban renewal. They built a "sky walk", a second-tier sidewalk that gave access to the second story of all the buildings downtown. The only problem: there were only two buildings with second stories. You'd go up there and be looking at the roofs of the businesses in town. An unfortunate side effect of the project: a spike in second story break-ins. It appears the walkway had given thieves direct access to the roofs and skylights of all the businesses; so much for urban renewal.

When we arrived in town, it was big news; real actors from real big cities. Real actors. The only *real* actor in the group was Robin St. Elizabeth

Rose Hunter. Her mother, Ruth Hunter, had appeared on Broadway in *Tobacco Road* and held the record for most continuous appearances by an actress on Broadway. Robbie was the closest thing to real show business. She had experience and a powerful singing voice a la Carol Burnett. Robbie and I were like the united duo. We did everything together; there was a connection that we held that was more than friends or lovers. It was two people who could feel each other's souls. We loved to laugh, and laugh we did.

That summer in 1967 was the last time I saw her (except briefly in 1984 when she came to LA with her family), and she and I have sent each other Christmas cards and Easter cards every year since. With the Internet, we contact each other more frequently, but we never miss a holiday to renew our friendship and our love. It's so weird. We have followed each other's lives through the mail. The birth of her children, my nervous breakdown, building her house in Florida, my other nervous breakdown, her move to Pennsylvania, the marriage of her children, my nervous breakdown, the birth of her grandchildren, and all done through the mail. Why? Because when I find a friend like Robbie, I don't let go. Neither does she, thank God.

Our productions were met with open arms. We were the cultural center of the South to those people. Every show was sold out and every show was met with rave reviews. We were also becoming the "people to invite" when having a social occasion. There was one lady, Mimi Schnitman, who lived in Morristown and appeared to be the only Jew in a six-hundred-mile radius. She would have us over to her house and feed us. There were others, but I just can't remember their names. I do remember the dieting that went on that summer, however.

Before I left for Europe, I sent the costume department—Ha! Costume department; the lady with the sewing machine—my measurements. While studying in Europe, it appears I had put on quite a bit of weight; so much weight that none of the costumes fit. I went on a crash diet of Metrical and cottage cheese. By the end of the summer, I had lost about twenty pounds. I came back to Boston looking quite handsome, if I had to say so myself. That lasted about six minutes when I got home, "You're too thin. You look sick." There was no chance for me to feel good about myself, none.

It was a summer that I would remember for the rest of my life. It was that summer that I started my scrapbook, which now is in two volumes and covered in mud from a mudslide that attempted to take it all from me. Wait. Something just came to me. You want to hear something? I'm sharing this with you for the first time because it's the first time I realized it. I kept everything pertaining to my childhood: books, pictures, articles, awards. You want to see my honorable mention medal for the ninth grade science fair? I've got it. I put it all in scrapbooks. I never knew why I did it, but as I wrote this paragraph it finally came to me. My parents were too involved in their own insanity, so I had to parent myself. I had to save this stuff because they wouldn't or couldn't or were too busy fighting with each other to put my needs first. I'm sitting here with my mouth open because I have just made that realization as I type. Wow! Talk about seeing the light.

You want to hear a funny story that happened to me that summer in Morristown? We had just finished our show that week and had struck the set (took it down). We were tired, so tired we couldn't go to sleep, so we went to IHOP. We took a table in the back and were laughing and carrying on. It was a Saturday night and all the farm hands were in town for a "good time." I noticed a guy who looked like a fat Lil Abner sitting at the counter. Whenever we would laugh he would act as if it bothered him. I didn't think anything of it, and we kept on talking, laughing, acting the fool.

We finished our midnight snack and headed out to our car. As we were walking in the parking lot, a strong hand spun me around. It was Lil Abner, and he was rip-snorting drunk.

"You all dem actors from up north??"

"Yes, we are."

"Well we don't want you around these parts. You are chicken shit! Ya hear me?? You are chicken shit! You are chicken shit!"

I was about to get an ass-whipping and I needed to think fast, so I said, without missing a beat, "You are absolutely right," and walked past him and got into my car.

The guy was standing there like, *Huh? Where's my fight?* I turned on the motor and sped out the parking lot as I opened the window and screamed, "And you're a rednecked fat fuck!" We laughed all the way back to the room, where we shut the lights, boarded the windows, and pushed furniture against the door.

Celebrity Sighting Fest

I WENT OUT TO DINNER with friends to Hamburger Hamlet on Sunset Blvd in Beverly Hills. This is a restaurant that has been around forever, and its clientele is a mix of young Hollywood and where old Hollywood goes to die—I mean dine. It starts with the hostess, who just happens to be Miles Davis's wife and she lets you know it, "Can I show you to your seat? As my husband Miles Davis used to say…" The only other place you ever see this is in Palm Springs, where everyone was someone once. You walk into Denny's and the hostess used to be a Ziegfeld Girl or the busboy was head of development at Paramount. It's just weird; anyway, back to Hamburger Hamlet. When you walk through the dining room, it's like being at the MGM Cafeteria in 1943 with Myrna Loy and Clark Gable, only these diners have bibs on and don't know where they are. At any given table is an eighty-nine-year-old woman with bleach blonde hair wearing enough jewelry to sink the Queen Mary. It's very loud in there; everyone is shouting things like, "The Brussel sprouts are good tonight!"

I get seated in a booth. I look up and Nicholas Cage is sitting across the aisle from me, two feet away. Cage has neck-length hair dyed jet black and is sporting two major tattoos. He's got a script on the table from CAA and I hear him pitching a movie to an actress that no one in our party knew. It was so Hollywood and so strange because you want to stare, but you can't. Every so often you give a little look-see. Twice I did that, and Cage was look-seeing me. I wonder who he thought I was?

Sunday night I went to Brentwood and had dinner at A Votre Sante, a very nice, organic, down to earth, Birkenstock and iPod kind of place. I had the falafel wrap, looked up to see Cheech Marin was sitting across the table from me.

Eating out in LA is like going on a safari in Africa. You don't know what you're going to see, but you're bound to see something interesting.

Monday was a rather somber day. Monica Johnson is a top Hollywood writer. She wrote all the Albert Brooks films, *Mother*, *The Muse*, *Lost in America*, and lots, lots more. She is one of the funniest writers in town, a sweetheart of a person, and a friend for over thirty years. Her brother was Jerry Belson. Jerry was the creative force behind some of television's funniest and finest shows. He wrote on *The Dick Van Dyke Show*, *The Odd Couple*, *Mary Tyler Moore*, and on and on and on. He wrote the films *Smile* and *The End*. His memorial was yesterday, and the stars of comedy writers came out to pay tribute to him. It was the warmest, most sincere expression of love that I have seen in this town in a long time. Gary Marshall hosted it at his Falcon Theater in Burbank. Rob Reiner, Carl Reiner, Tracy Ullman, Albert Brooks, Penny Marshall, and many, many more spoke glowing tributes of their dear departed friend. As I looked around the room I could see just how much Jerry was loved. I don't think a single person in comedy was not there. Because of that, we laughed and we laughed, long and hard. It's the most fitting way for a comedy writer, a comedian, or comedy actor to leave this life; giving them the laughter back that they have given to the world. Side note: In my will it is instructed to have my tombstone read: "Willing to sublet." I want people to laugh when they come to my grave, not cry.

The one thing I noticed at the service was how different comedy writers are from comedians. At the service, they showed a series of pictures taken of Jerry and his writer friends. They would meet every five years and take the same picture. It was an expression of kinsmanship that you don't see amongst comedians. Writers, although they can be neurotic, are basically givers. They give their words to actors, so they are basically, under all the bullshit, people with the capacity to let others take the spotlight. Comedians are takers; look-at-me people, validate-me people. For the most part, they are not givers. I cannot imagine a group of comedians meeting every five years to take a picture without it ending with the arrival of the SWAT team. It just doesn't happen. Seeing those pictures of Jerry and his friends it just reminded me how much I love writing and giving my words to the world. For me, writing really is an act of love. Jerry mastered that art.

After the service, I got to talk to several people I haven't seen in years. It was so good to see so many of those people again; one in particular was Carl Kleinschmidt. Carl was the head writer on *The Brady Bunch Variety*

Hour, my first big writing job. He taught me everything I ever knew about writing. He was at the memorial service and was as warm and friendly as if it had been thirty minutes instead of thirty years. I saw many other people there as well. This was the core of the Hollywood comedy community, and they had come together to say good-bye to one of their own. If a good thing can come out of a memorial service, it's to see that even comedy people have real heart. When Gary Marshall summed up the event and was saying good-bye to his dear friend and first writing partner, he cried openly. It was an expression of love that you don't see too often in Hollywood, and I felt honored to be present and to be part of it. Rest in peace, Jerry. God is in for some really incredible laughs.

Actor's Studio

I HAD THE HONOR of having my play *Gary's Gold* read by the Actor's Studio here in Los Angeles. It was truly a life-changing event.

For those of you who don't know what the Actor's Studio is, Elia Kazan, Cheryl Crawford, and Robert Lewis started it in 1947. It is a theater workshop for professional actors, directors, and writers, and it is a very prestigious space for anyone to have their works performed or asked to be included. I was asked to join the Playwrights unit, and I had not asked to have any of my works read until this reading. Why? I wasn't good enough. I didn't deserve to be in the unit. I couldn't be as well-read as these people, and on and on and on.

I got a time spot for the reading and was assigned a director. Not only did I get a director, I got one of the star directors at the Actor's Studio, Bob Burgos. On our first meeting, Bob sat down with me and we talked for almost two hours. He came to my home and discussed character motivations, comedy, plot, etc., etc., etc. He ran his list of actors by me and came up with two well-known actors here in LA. We held our first rehearsal last Friday. Before we read a single word, the actors spoke with me for forty minutes trying to find out who these characters were, who Gary was, why I wrote it, and what I wanted them to bring to the part.

I guess it's like a composer hearing his symphony for the first time, because when I heard these actors speaking my words, it was as if they were in my head when I wrote it. These are true professionals. These are people who take ink on the page and turn it into real people, people you care about and want to see more. They were a joy to listen to. Monday night was the reading at Actor's Studio; the theatre was filled with every playwright and director in town. This is the crème de la crème. These are not TV directors, although some have directed TV and film. These are the theatre directors, the creative backbone of this city. The lights came down and my heart started pounding. My head was resting on my left shoulder as the first words were spoken. Here comes the first laugh line. Big laugh. My head slowly moves to the upright position. Okay, here's the second laugh. Big one. The pounding in my chest slows down as the play progresses. I'm watching the audience, no one is sleeping, no one is rustling in their chairs, no one is looking at the ceiling or talking or picking their nose; they are all transfixed on the stage.

The last line is read, and there's thunderous applause. A director approaches me, "I loved it. I have some notes, but man, can you write."

Another comes up to me, "Very good work. Who are you again?"

The leader takes a break and we come back for discussion. This is where I sit on the stage and the entire unit throws questions at me. Martin Landau is one of the moderators. He's been in the Actor's Studio since day one; he's seen it all. Everyone is talking, throwing out ideas, giving their opinion, then Landau butts in, "I just need to tell you, I loved it. I was entertained, I laughed, I cried…" I'm sort of looking at him in a coma. I can't believe this is happening to me.

The consensus of the discussion was this: ninety-five percent of them liked the piece. Every single one of them had comments, suggestions, and changes. In show business, this is normal. Opinions are like assholes, everyone's got one. I listened intently to their comments. Some of them are valid, some are just plain stupid. I make notes. I'll make changes at my discretion. Landau wants to read other things I've written. I'm sending him the optioned play.

Bottom line is, in a setting where ninety percent of the plays are ripped apart and torn to pieces, my play was accepted with open arms, and I was accepted as an equal. Folks, this is the first time you will ever hear me say this, I felt like an equal. I felt like I belonged with these people. I felt like this was my home, not HA-HA's Comedy Club in Ohio.

I left that place with my feet ten feet off the ground. I'm a playwright.

John Ritter

WHEN I FIRST STARTED OUT in the business, I would do anything I could to get noticed. Being a regular at The Comedy Store was a major coup for me. You have to remember, at that time there was no comedy club circuit. There was only The Improv and a few clubs around Los Angeles. The Comedy Store was a new concept in showcasing entertainment, and I was there from day one.

Two people that I was close with during that period were Pat Proft and another guy, let's just call him Bob. I've written about Pat but never mentioned Bob. Why? My mother always told me if I couldn't say anything nice about someone, I should just keep my mouth shut. What can I say about Bob that won't get me sued? He had nice eyebrows? Suffice it to say, we had a love/hate relationship. Bob fulfilled my need to be put down, to be degraded and embarrassed and made to feel less-than. He fulfilled a need started by my family and continued by my subconscious. I allowed it. I encouraged it. It was my fault, not Bob's. Mine. I should have stood up for myself, but I didn't and Bob went in for the kill.

Let me give you an example of the kind of thing Bob would do to me. I can say without a doubt it was the cruelest thing ever done to me in all the years I've been in the business. When I first started doing stand-up, I was not very good. I was tentative on stage, scared, and had no point of view. I worked like a champion to get better. I took classes and workshops, read up on comedy, and I studied. Eventually I got better, and the laughs did come. I worked with a tape recorder, taping every show. One night, I had placed my tape recorder on a table in the middle of The Comedy Store. I said to Bob, "My recorder is here. Keep an eye on it for me. Will ya?" Then I went on stage to do a set.

When I got home to listen to my set, what I heard all but destroyed me. I heard myself doing my act, but suddenly there was a break in the recording and something closer to the mic was being picked up. Bob was seated at the table where my recorder was and began talking while I was on stage. I heard Bob's voice over mine. I heard Bob calling Stuart Cohen over to the table, "Stuart, come here…sit over here!" Stuart, who has since passed, was a very powerful comedy manager. He could make or break any act at The Comedy Store, and several of us tried very hard to get Stuart to sign us. His opinion mattered a lot, and I was constantly trying to get his approval—approval that never came. In any case, I hear Bob calling Stuart over to the table and I hear Bob asking, "Stuart, so what do you think of Steve's act?" Now, Bob knows my recorder is running, but Stuart doesn't, so he answers honestly, "He's awful. He'll never work." Bob laughed, and the noise of the tape recorder being moved follows.

When I got home that night and listened to my set, those words cut me like a knife. It was like someone had taken my heart and stepped on it. My eyes filled up, I slumped into a chair, and replayed the tape over and over and over. I remember playing it several times. Then, in a manic state, I played it quickly in succession so all I heard was, "he'll never work, he'll never work, he'll never work, he'll never work, he'll never work, he'll never work, he'll never work, he'll never work, he'll never work," until I broke down and cried.

I found myself in a deep depression. I was seeing a shrink at the time, and he told me I had to use those words to make a change in my life, to be my challenge. Those words became my cause. I would prove Stuart wrong. I *would* work, yet there was always a portion of my brain that said, *he's right. I'll never work.* I fight those words to this day, that feeling of not being enough to be a success.

When I say I have nothing nice to say about Bob, there are reasons. The curious thing about him is he did have a nice side, a generous side, a giving side. Bob had been cast in a play with John Ritter. They were casting a very small part. Bob told me about it and got me the part. I think he liked doing things like that because it made him feel more important.

John Ritter was the star of the play. At the time, he was living in a one-room apartment on the edges of Hollywood. John was a very kind, sweet, sincere man. He had a terrific sense of humor and was generous and fun to be around. Bob had a sixth sense about who was going to be big and he latched onto them. Rob Reiner was another one Bob had latched onto, but for now it was John.

I can't remember what the play was or anything about it. I do remember that I played a thief and had one line. I had one line, and then I created some business that got laughs. I took a little nothing part and made it funny. John noticed this and was very complimentary to me. Bob never said a word.

John, Bob, and I hung out for a bit, maybe five minutes in my life, and then John was gone. Like I've said before, it's how it is in show business. You make close, intense friends and then you go your separate ways.

Here's something you'll never read about anyplace else: John Ritter had the strangest eye I have ever seen. I think it was his left one. The pupil was off center. I don't know if he was blind in that eye or not, but I do know that one eye's pupil was dead center and one was slightly left of the iris. I've never seen it before or since in any other person, and it didn't seem to bother John at all.

When John got *Three's Company*, I knew instantly he would be a huge star. I never saw him through all those years, but then I was doing a TV show in Canada and in walked John, "Steve! Hey, how are you?" and the man who I had not seen in years sat down and talked to me to find out how I was and what I was up to. It was nice to see that he had not changed. Nice. Really, really nice.

When I had learned that John died, it saddened me to no end. He was really one of the good guys in the business and it's so unfair that he was taken from us at such an early age. Bob is still with us, but not in LA. He moved back to Minneapolis where he became a successful producer. I can't tell you how strange I find it to be that Bob left LA and I'm still here. It was Bob that we all thought was going to be the big star. I remember being in a swimming pool with Bob, just floating on two rafts. Bob was planning his future, telling me about his series and his big house and all the money he was going to have. Then he turned to me and said, "Steve, you'll never be a comedian. You'll work in the business behind the scenes, like a writer or a producer."

As I stood on the stage in Las Vegas opening for Donna Summer, I remember thinking to myself, *I won't be a comedian, Bob? How wrong you are. How wrong you are.*

Alan Landsburg

RIGHT AFTER I LOST MY JOB at The May Company and had started hanging out at The Comedy Store, I collected unemployment. That only lasted for a year, and I was in desperate need of a job. I would work at anything to support myself as I tried to break into the wonderful world of comedy. I worked in a Photomat booth. I worked as a gardener. I was the assistant to a manager. I did anything. Then one day I got a call from Carol Ita White. Her good friend Sybil Edelman heard of a job with Alan Landsburg Productions. They needed a runner (a go-for). I ran to the interview dressed in a sports jacket and tie.

The offices were in the strangest set up I had ever seen. They were a series of houses in a compound around a swimming pool. Each house was used for a different purpose: the main house was Alan's office, the back house was the editing bay, the farthest house was storage, and so on. It wasn't like any office set up I had ever seen, and I loved the casual air the place had. I really wanted this job, and somehow, I got it.

Many, many times I think of myself as being blessed despite how much I whine. This was one of those times. While I didn't know it then, I was about to be launched on a nonstop educational tour that would open doors for me and help me eventually get to my goal.

Alan Landsburg was a documentary producer who had worked for David Wolper. He was rather famous within the industry. As a matter of fact, in the movie *Bob & Carol & Ted & Alice*, there is a line, "Oh look, there's Alan Landsburg." It comes out of nowhere, but it's poignant because I later learned one of the characters in the movie was based on Alan. You see, he had been involved in some of the best documentaries aired on TV at that time, but he wanted to do more. He set up his own production company to produce movies of the week, specials, and TV series. Alan's assistant was Marilyn Lassen. I just don't know how to describe her so you'll get the full impact of how wonderful this woman was. She was a very smart, sincere, handsome woman who had all the qualities of Aunt Bea on *Mayberry R.F.D.*, but the savvy of a businesswoman and the smarts of an educator. She was wildly protective of Alan and devoted to her job like a pit bull. She was simply a wonderful person who was the glue that kept that place not only together, but running.

My initial job was doing exactly what I was told. Take this here. Pick this up there. Run this over to this place or that. In case you haven't guessed by now, I'm anal-retentive. If I am given a task, not only do I do it, but I also find ways to do it better. For instance, we would be Xeroxing scripts up the yin-yang on regular Xerox paper. Then we would have to three-hole-punch them. This took hours. One day I said to Marilyn, "I wonder if there is three-hole paper sold? We could save a lot of time." The next day, a box of three-hole paper was delivered to my desk with a love note from Marilyn. Now this was a simple change in the way things were done, but no one had thought of it except Uncle Steve. Marilyn was very impressed.

When a production company is in production, there is no 9-to-5, it's whatever the production needs. Since I have no trouble getting up in the morning, I was the first one there and the last to leave. You have to remember, I think I was earning $70 a week, but Marilyn kept her eye on me and would tell the higher-ups what I was up to. She never had any children of her own although she was married, and I think she had sort of a motherly interest in me. I may be wrong. It's my perception, or maybe how I'd like to remember it. Yes, it's definitely how I would like to remember it. The truth is, she was just doing her job, which was to make that place the best it could be for Alan.

The longer I worked there, the more responsibility I got. There was a producer named Stan Chase who also worked there developing projects. He and I struck up a friendship. He asked me to start reading scripts for him and write a synopsis of what I had read. This was the first indication I had that I had a talent for writing. As I read these scripts, I could tell immediately which were crap and which were gold. There are two scripts that stick out in my mind. One was written by Steve Gordon, who was a Broadway playwright, and his script was so funny it made me laugh out loud. After I finished reading it, I ran to Stan and said, "Don't even bother having me write a review. Just see this guy, he's hysterical." This is after I had written maybe fifty reviews for Stan all basically saying, "This sucks."

Steve was brought in and was given a deal based on my recommendation. Who was Steve Gordon? Only the writer who later went on to write *Arthur* and a slew of other films. Sadly, he died in 1982 at the age of forty-four, but I always felt responsible for being one of the first ones to see his talent and get him started. Me, the go-for at Alan Landsburg Productions. The other script that I remember getting all excited about was *The Land That Time Forgot*. I ran in the day after reading it and said to Stan, "This is classic creature movie. Do something with it," and he did. He optioned it.

There were other neat things that happened to me while working there. I got to meet Lee Radziwill, sister of Jackie Kennedy Onassis. On several occasions, I was asked to deliver scripts to stars' homes. Three stick out in my mind. Walter Matthau, who lived in a powder blue Spanish stucco house that was so ugly I could not believe my eyes. Henry Fonda, who lived in a classic mansion in Bel Air; and Vincente Minnelli. When I was given the script to bring to him, I had no idea who he was. All I knew was I had to deliver a script to a director who lived off Wilshire Blvd near Westwood. When I got there, he invited me in. I was standing in his living room, and on the fireplace mantel was a framed picture of Judy Garland. Not a publicity shot, a shot like you and I take of relatives at Thanksgiving. Next to that was Liza's picture. It was then it dawned on me that I was standing in the living room of a legend. When he returned, I extended my hand and didn't say anything. He thought I wanted a tip and reached into his pocket, "No, no. I want to shake your hand." He smiled and shook it. Trust me, that was worth the $70 a week I was earning to have met Vincente Minnelli.

I guess I must have been working there a year or so and Christmas rolled around. Marilyn asked me if there was anything I really wanted for Christmas. I told her, "I'd really like to be able to join SAG" (The actor's union). She just smiled and said, "Wouldn't we all." Eventually Christmas rolled around, and everyone got his or her envelopes with a little bonus money in it, everyone but me. I just thought my position didn't warrant a bonus, and while I was a little upset, I didn't give it any thought. Then Alan called me into his office, "Steve, you've really done a great job for us. We've got a little special gift for you. We're going to use you on camera in a small part and get you into the union." I could not believe my ears. It was impossible to get into the unions, and still is. Alan Landsburg got me in as a Christmas gift, and I'm still a member to this day. Every time I get a residual, I thank Alan and Marilyn.

Alan had two kids, Valerie Landsburg and a son, Michael. Valerie must have been about nine when I worked for Alan. I used to pick her up from school for him or drop her off at his house. She was an adorable child who grew up to be a regular on the series *Fame* and later went on to be a well-respected director here in LA. Valerie and I remain friends to this day. While we don't see as much of each other as we used to, we still have a strong bond. It's nice, these friendships I established over the years.

I continued to work for Alan for another year. I got married and had a child and needed more money. They had given me a raise, but at that time I wasn't interested in production. I wanted to be a *star*! When Gary signed me to ICM and my career took off, I eventually left Alan Landsburg Productions to pursue my comedy career. If I had to say I made one mistake in my career, it was leaving that job. In just a few years, Alan was producing *In Search Of* and tons of other series. I would have had a very lucrative job there if I stayed. Oh well. Just one of many bad choices I made over the years. However, I can say without any fear of being called a liar, those years at Alan Landsburg Productions were some of my happiest, most productive, most rewarding, and certainly most educational I can remember. I look back on them with love and respect.

Post Script

I called Val and we got all caught up. It's always good to hear her voice and know she is doing well. I asked, "How is Marilyn?" All she said was, "Gone." For an instant, my eyes welled up as I remembered this wonderful woman who had meant so much to me in the very, very beginning of my career. I so wish I had been told at the time of her death. I would have been there. I guess I'm there now. Thank you, Marilyn Lassen! Thank you for everything.

Ella Fitzgerald

IT WAS A HOT, HUMID NIGHT in New York City. I was sitting in my one-room apartment, the A/C was pumping out at maximum capacity, and I was dying of the heat. I filled the bathtub with cold water and just soaked in it for forty-five minutes. When I got out of the tub, I was drenched in sweat within three minutes. That's how humid it was that night. I had to get out of my apartment, so at about 8 p.m. I headed out to nowhere in particular. I just needed to get out into the air. You can't call New York City air "fresh", it's just air, and I was out in it.

I headed for Central Park thinking there might be some relief from the heat there. When I got to 58th and 5th, I could see crowds of people heading into the park, so I followed. As we got closer to the theater past the zoo, I could hear music. It was jazz, and I quickened my pace. Soon I could hear the voice of a singer. It was a mellow, soft, clear-as-a-bell voice. It was Ella Fitzgerald. I had happened upon a free concert in the park sponsored by Schlitz Beer.

The arena was packed and I wasn't able to get in, but outside the arena was a grassy area where people were just sitting and listening. With Ella, just being in the presence of that voice was enough, so I sat there just basking in the glory of a legend, that magnificent legend. I heard all the Ella classics that night; she sang them all. Unless you've actually heard Ella Fitzgerald sing live, you haven't heard her sing. Live, there is a connection with her and the audience that only comes with years of practice and with generations of audience idolatry.

The concert ended close to 11 p.m., and the crowd erupted into thunderous applause. She did encore after encore, and then the lights came up and the crowd was forced to go home. There were literally thousands of people heading in all directions. I'm not good in crowds. I get claustrophobia, so I just stood in one spot as the crowd moved around me. Like standing up to your waist in a moving stream, the crowd gently moved me along with them. I knew I was headed in the right direction, but I wasn't making any effort to fight the crowd or set a course. I was just trying to hold on to my sanity in this sea of humanity.

Suddenly, and without warning, the crowd lunged forward. There was an excitement in the air that hadn't been there before, and I found myself moving at a faster pace. Then as suddenly as it surged forward, it came to a dead stop and parted. From the darkness, this frail, little African American woman entered into the sea of faces. Her head was down, her eyes looking only at the ground. I remember this picture like it happened yesterday. It was Ella Fitzgerald, and she was three feet in front of me. She didn't have her wig on and she was wearing thick glasses. She was tiny. I'm 5'9", she must have been five feet. That's how I remember her, frail, tiny, short. Perhaps she was bent over from the pressure of the crowd, but all I can remember is thinking, *look how little and frail she is. Her voice had been so powerful on stage!*

She moved past me, her eyes darting from person to person. She was like a deer caught in the middle of the highway. She tentatively smiled and nodded her head; then our eyes met. I didn't say anything, but she looked at me and said, "Thank you," and was whisked on by her caregivers. The crowd followed her, and I was left alone standing on the sidewalk in Central Park. I kept asking myself, *why did she thank me? What had she seen in me that prompted that response?* I started the debate between my ears, *I'm special. No, that's not right. How could I be special? Yes, I'm special she saw it and thanked me.* I decided she felt my love for her and was thanking me for loving her but not coming too close. Truth is, she was just saying "Thank You" to anyone who happened to be in front of her.

This chance meeting started my obsession with Ella Fitzgerald and her music. I have loved that voice ever since that night, and when I finally got into the business I tried like hell to get her on every show I ever worked on. It never happened, and it saddened me. I wanted to sit with her and hear her stories and laugh at her jokes and just be around greatness.

Many years after she passed, I was at a dinner party with a British filmmaker. He was going on about how he had this project and could not get anyone interested in it. How he had some of the finest recordings ever made, and not a studio in town would touch his project. What was it?

The Ella Fitzgerald Story. It was that night I truly learned how cruel show business is. Without a doubt, this woman was the finest vocalist who ever lived; better than Garland, better than Streisand. She was the example the rest should have been held up to.

Show business is not about art; it's about making money. The almighty dollar rules the decisions on what gets made. I guess that's why there is such crap to be seen. The demographic is eighteen to thirty-five, and that group has never heard of Ella Fitzgerald, so the studios turned up their noses at a magnificent story. It will never happen, not until someone with enough money and enough passion comes along to produce a film about her. Someone with enough money they won't care if it's a financial success, they just want to tell the story for history to document. Oprah, I'm talkin' to *you*!

Celebrity Sightings

IT'S 1969, and I'm walking down 58th street one fine summer day in New York. I can actually tell you it was 58th and Madison, that's how good my memory is. I was walking over to my shrink appointment. He was on Central Park West at about 63rd. I would walk up 58th, around the park, and then down Central Park West to his office.

I'm rushing to my appointment, standing on the corner waiting for the light to change, and I happen to look to my left. Standing next to me, in a floral printed shirtwaist dress, white background with dark flowers, is Ethel Merman. She didn't say a word, nor did I. The entire exchange was ten seconds, but it stayed with me to this day and has become part of my celebrity sightings memories.

Bruce Vilanch told me the funniest Ethel Merman story ever. A friend of his is walking through Central Park and sees Ethel Merman with her granddaughter. The kid is sitting on a park bench screaming at the top of her lungs. As the friend walks by, he hears Merman say to the child, "Well, what the fuck do ya want?"

On that same walk to my shrink, different day, I saw Jessie White, character-actor extraordinaire and father of Carol Ita White, who was soon to be one of my dearest friends. I also saw Charlotte Rae, who I had fallen in love with on *Car 54, Where Are You?* and who we would cast when I wrote for Norman Lear, and would later star in *The Facts of Life* with Kim Fields (who I babysat for when she lived in my building).

Another day, I was walking down Broadway heading to my office at United Artists. The light was about to change, and like a good New Yorker, I darted out into the street to beat it before it changed. Running in my direction, doing the same thing I was doing, only heading west while I headed east, was Vivian Vance—Ethel Mertz on *I Love Lucy*. I think our passing was less than two seconds, but old eagle-eyes was able to give her the once over. I could not believe how pretty she was! This was the Ethel that was married to Fred and she had gotten a complete makeover and a nose job. I remember thinking I had just seen history and told everyone in the office. Turns out they had all seen her. She was doing a play in the neighborhood and was there every day. So much for being special.

In LA, celebrity sightings are so common you don't even make mental notes of them. I live in a very artsy-fartsy area in LA. It's Bel Air, but it's the slums of Bel Air, and it attracts a very artistic group of people. For instance, I have seen Brian Wilson of the Beach Boys about six hundred times. Vanna White owns a store in the mall at the top of the hill. I see her there all the time. Clint Black and his wife Lisa Hartman eat at the same deli I do. I mean, it's like you go to take out the trash, and there is Barbra Streisand. There was one time in LA when even I stopped and took notice.

I was going on the road and had just been dropped off at LAX. I was standing on the curb collecting my baggage when a Rolls Royce pulled up. Out of the back comes Diana Ross. A pregnant Diana Ross. She was in 70s platform shoes wearing bib overalls and looking like shit, however, that's not the sighting that excited me. When I went inside and checked my bags, I had a long walk to the gate. LAX has these long corridors that go underground to the gates. You've seen them in a thousand movies; they're covered with aqua and blue one-inch mosaic tiles. In any case, I'm making my way to my gate when who should come face to face with me but Fred Astaire. We sort of bumped into each other and I recognize him instantly. He was older here and wearing one of the worst toupees made in America. I remember thinking I had just bumped into greatness, into film history. It was one of the most exciting sightings I ever had and filled me with happiness for quite a long time.

One of the most recent sightings, and the strangest, happened about four years ago. I was at the school graduation of one of the Churukian kids; they all went to a private school in Pasadena. I'm late and arrive as everyone is leaving, so I'm pushing against the exiting crowd. I'm working my way in, when five feet from me, Kevin Costner is coming out. Now you have to remember we are packed as tightly as sardines. His eyes met mine and I recognized him instantly, but the strangest thing happened that has ever happened at a celebrity sighting. In my mind I heard him say, "Please don't say anything." In other words, he did not want anyone to know he was there, and so I diverted my eyes and he passed by in secrecy.

The all-time mother of celebrity sightings has to belong to Carol Burnett. When I was a senior at Emerson College, she gave the school a scholarship. She had come to the campus to do an interview and it was a big deal. Huge! The press was there and the entire student body was buzzing. I had gone to the student union for something and found myself in the middle of the fracas. Carol was sequestered in a room on the third floor, and since I had been giving tours of the campus, I knew all the secret passages. I took one that led me right to the room where Carol was doing her interview. I didn't enter, I just cracked the door open and listened as she talked. I had to be twenty at the time.

When the interview was over, I dashed out front and joined the rest of the kids waiting for her to exit. I was just a face in the crowd, but as she passed me, she reached out and caressed my face with her hand. I can't even begin to tell you how special that made me feel. I, who never felt enough, was just picked out of the crowd by Carol Burnett.

There's a burning image of that day that remains with me. It's a picture of Carol heading down the massive, hand-carved staircase, and Henry Winkler running up to her and descending the staircase with her as he actively chatted and asked for advice. It was fitting that Henry did this. He was the star at Emerson, and it was destined that he became famous. Here's where it gets good.

Flash Cut: 2004

I'm standing at the cash register at Armani in Beverly Hills. Standing next to me is an old lady in a hat and glasses. She hasn't said a word. The clerk gives her the credit card receipt and says, "Would you like that sent?"

The lady says, "No that's ok, I'll take it."

I recognize the voice immediately. It's Carol Burnett. Do I say something? Yes? No? I do. "Miss Burnett?" She snaps to attention and becomes not the old lady, but the Carol Burnett we all know and love. "I was at Emerson College the year you gave the scholarship."

"Well, dear, you must have been a child."

"Did you know that the boy who grabbed you going down the staircase and asked for advice was Henry Winkler?"

"Yes. I met Henry and he told me that," she said.

We chatted a few minutes more, and she was off, but for me it was like the circle had been completed. I had been witness to one of those strange moments in show business, a young Henry Winkler asking Carol for advice and then an old Carol realizing that the kid had become a star equal to hers.

Twenty-Five Years

TWENTY-FIVE YEARS AGO TODAY, my life changed forever when my friend and agent Gary Weinberg died.

He passed away twenty-five years ago. That means that twenty-five years ago, I stood in my kitchen holding on to the edge of the sink trying to keep myself from falling to the ground. It means that twenty-five years ago, I began drinking to dull the pain. It means that twenty-five years ago, I lost someone who cared about me and protected me and loved me like a brother.

There has not been a day in those twenty-five years that I have not thought about Gary. His briefcase sits next to my desk and the sign from his office hangs in my own office. There hasn't been a day since he died that I have not felt him with me. On the day of the mudslide, I felt his hand guide me to safety. It was his idea, put into *my* head, that I should have flood insurance. It was his guidance that helped me renovate this house. I have never told a single person this story because I thought I might be considered insane, but I'm sharing with you all today.

One night, soon after Gary died, I was crying so desperately that I thought I was having yet another nervous breakdown. It was the kind of crying that leaves you weak, the kind you can't catch your breath. I wanted Gary to be alive that night so desperately I would have sold my soul to the devil to bring him back. I walked around the house just pouring out my heart in uncontrollable tears. At one point, I was on the floor too weak to move. I opened my eyes and said, "Please, just let me know you are with me." I swear to God to you I swear it on my father's grave, the faucet in the bathtub opened and water came pouring out. It was like a slap in the face. It brought me around and made me stop crying. I got up off the floor and shut the water tap. From that moment on, I knew that Gary was with me and protected me and surrounded my life. That little bit of mystery was pointed out to me time and time again.

A few years ago, I wrote a play about Gary called *Gary's Gold*. I wanted an audience to fall in love with a character without ever seeing him on stage. In my play, other people talk about Gary and they tell how he affected their lives. While many of the characters are compilations of people, the effect is stunning. A production company in Boston mounted the play and I detested it. The cast was horrific, had no comedy timing, and had no acting experience. In my eyes, it was just bad. It was so bad, I refused to go to Boston to see it.

Soon after, the producers sent me the first review, on the twenty-fifth anniversary of Gary's death. Here's the review:

Reviewed by Larry Stark: Steve Bluestein's *Gary's Gold* is really a love-letter to a departed friend. It is a little over an hour long, yet its three scenes are packed with such fond nostalgia that it feels like a full evening. The play takes the form of cleaning out Gary's apartment and passing it on to strangers, but in each scene a family-member or friend who knew the man tries to explain to someone who didn't what was so special about him. This could be cloyingly sweet, but Bluestein's people bubble with glib, self- aware humor enough to maintain balance. *Gary's Gold* hasn't a mean bone in its body; it's a feel-good play; but is that such a bad thing these days?

It's not lost on me that this review came today, on the twenty-fifth anniversary of Gary's death. It's Gary telling me he's still with me. It's Gary telling me not to be so hard on myself.

I wanted to do something special on the anniversary of his death and he trumped me in spades. I wish for each and every one of you that you would have someone in your life as special as Gary. I wish for each of you a friendship that nurtures and cares for you. I wish you all had known him and how special he was. I wish he had never died, but if he hadn't, I wouldn't be who I am today: stronger, wiser, better.

I want to share with you a poem I wrote the day after he died. It's a poem I included in the script of *Gary's Gold*. I think it sums it all up:

> I lost a friend today.
> I've looked everywhere.
> Under the jokes we used to laugh over.
> Between the pages of our memories.

I couldn't find him.
He's hiding.
I know he is.
He can't be gone.
Where could he be?
It's not like him to run off and leave me.
I lost a friend today.
He brought me into the sunshine.
He stood in front of me when they threw rocks.
He stood behind me when I needed a push.
I've got to find him.
I lost a friend today.
He's gone.
I'm sure of that now.
There's nothing I can do.
It's out of my hands.
I lost a friend today.
A good friend.
And he lost me.

More Celebrity Sightings

I WAS WORKING AT ALEXANDER'S on the main floor. We were having one of our insane days where sweaters were $1.99 or something like that. On those days, the crowds of women are numbered in the thousands, and the intensity of their shopping was insane. Pushing, shoving, hitting, screaming was a daily occurrence. You'd go out on the floor with a box of sweaters, throw them onto the table, and women would come out of the woodwork to dig through what was just put up for sale.

On one day in particular, I was crossing the floor and happened to see a woman standing at the service counter. She was African American, and with her was a very light-skinned, blonde child. I took one look at her and instantly recognized her as Eartha Kitt. She was standing there in the midst of this melee of women, very calmly waiting her turn as some loud mouth bimbo from Queens was screaming about a return not being handled fast enough. I quietly watched as this legend stood motionless in the crowd, not demanding attention, just waiting for her turn in line. I had a great deal of admiration for this woman. She alone had stood up at the White House and denounced the Vietnam War. Her career had been gutted because of it. She was box-office poison and no one would hire her, yet she held her dignity and continued on with her life, despite the injustice of the retribution.

I was very shy back then, but I needed to thank her for speaking out. I needed to tell her that her pain meant something to someone. I wanted her spirit to be acknowledged and encouraged. I said, "Can I help you?"

In her most Eartha Kitt purr, she said, "Do you work in this establishment?"

I showed her my badge and she smiled, then asked some inane question that I have long since forgotten. I helped her and she was on her way. All these years later I wonder if she knew that I was saying, "Thank You. Thank you for trying to help." I can't imagine she did, but I did and it felt good.

I was working in the sweater department on the main floor of Alexander's. We had just gotten in a shipment of cable knit-knit pantsuit sets, top and bottom: $5.99. I couldn't keep them in stock. I would put out six hundred of them, and three hours later, there would be six left.

One day, I am standing at the counter and a woman approaches me. I recognize her immediately. It's Hermione Gingold. She was a regular on the talk shows of the 1960s and had starred in the film *Gigi*. She comes up to me like the cat that swallowed the canary and says, "Young man, can you reassure me that the price I am seeing on this charming little ticket is what I shall be paying in this fine emporium?"

Emporium? It was a bargain basement. I take the ticket from her and say, "It's $5.99."

"For the total ensemble?" she asks with smirking glee on her face, but you had to hear how she said "ensemble". It was coming right through her nose and she held the "amble" for four beats. She made the word sound like she was reading from Shakespeare.

Taking her comedy challenge I said to her, in a put-on Brooklyn accent, "That's the price, honey, don't wear it out in rain unless ya need a hankie."

She burst out laughing, "Touché dahling...Touché." She bought three suits.

Sharon Tate's House Party

MANY YEARS AGO, when I was just starting out in the business, I got a phone call from Liz Torres, "Do you want to go to a party at Rudy Altabelli's house?" Rudy was a very famous manager in Los Angeles and he was courting Liz as a client. Not being one to miss a good party, I said, "Sure, I'd love to come!" It was all arranged, Liz would pick me up and I'd be rubbing elbows with Rudy and all his powerful friends.

The day of the party was all about excitement and preparation. This was a big deal, this party, and I wanted everything to be right. Liz picked me up, took one look at me, and told me I looked like an accountant. I had to go back upstairs and change into something more casual, more cool, less nerd. I change and we drive up into the hills. We approach Rudy's house, the gate is closed, but I notice there is a ton of security cameras, lights, and an iron fence. It's very strange. Liz buzzes in and gives the code. As the gates swing open she smiles at me, also very strange, but I think nothing of it. The valet takes our car and Liz and I head for the front door. She pushes the buzzer and turns to me.

"Whatever you do, don't say a word about the murders."
"What murders?"
"This is the Tate house!" Liz tells me.

The doors swing open as Rudy greets us! "Liz! Darling. How are you?"

I'm in a coma; she's brought me to Sharon Tate's house twelve months after the murders. Now I'm shaking hands with Rudy and my blood is running cold.

Rudy says, "Steve, are you okay? Your hands are like ice." Liz's eyes are the size of footballs as she stares at me.

"Nope! My whole family has cold hands, my mother's are like a corpse." Open mouth, insert foot.

The backstory is the murders were about a year prior. It appears that Rudy had rented the house to Roman Polanski and Sharon Tate, and after the murders no one would rent it again, so he moved into it. Once inside, Liz and I were never alone and I could not press her for answers to my questions like, "A murder scene! You bring me to a murder scene? What's the matter, the Prom at Auschwitz was cancelled?"

We are ushered into the living room and my eyes gaze upward to the rafters where one of the bodies was reportedly hung. I have never been so creeped out in my life. This was the most notorious crime scene of the time, and I was standing right in the middle of it, but I wasn't alone. Sally Kellerman was sitting in the kitchen in her bathing suit. Valerie Harper was by the pool. Robert Blake and his wife were in the living room. John Savage, his wife, and two young kids were running around. All I could think of was, *Manson is locked up, right?*

The day progresses and I forget about the murders, however, I did keep looking for where "helter skelter" was written in blood on the walls. As darkness approached, Rudy started the barbecue and people gathered around the piano to sing. Sally Kellerman sang, Valerie Harper sang, it was like $50,000 worth of entertainment for free! I couldn't help but wonder if this is what it was like the night of the murders, just a group of friends sitting around having fun until a pack of lunatics crash the party and kill the host. Robert Blake was very much to himself during the fun part of the evening, and the talk was about how strange he was around his wife.

We stayed late into the night, and I must tell you it was one of the most magnificent parties I have ever been to. Why? It was stars being people, not stars. They didn't have their "image" on, they were just Valerie and Sally and John. Here's the strange thing, talk about six degrees of separation, one of my very close friends is Stephen M. Schwartz, the songwriter. Stephen married Wendy Shaal, the actress. Wendy's father was Dick Shaal, the actor, and he married Valerie Harper. Years after the party, Valerie became like family to me (for a short time period), and what we had in common was that night in the hills at Rudy Altabelli's house in the shadow of Sharon Tate's murder.

All Night Talk

I HAVE LIVED IN CALIFORNIA since 1972. In that time, my mother has made it out to visit me maybe four times. Maybe. On one of those momentous occasions, when she's put her civic duty aside and decided to play mother, we had a confrontation that almost put me in the hospital. It took three months of therapy to recover when she left, and it was this trip that made me decide that perhaps four visits since 1972 was just enough.

She decided to come to California for some reason. I don't know why, maybe she had a coupon. I remember that my shrink had put me on medication because my anger towards her was so deep, I was unable to control it. I was on something to slow down my reaction time and give me time to think before I exploded.

She's in the house about two days and so far, it's going okay. She's saying hurtful things and I'm letting it roll off my back. I knew the medication was working when she said to me, "You're using too large a light bulb in the bedroom lamp."

"Which lamp?"

She walks me into the bedroom and turns on the bedside lamp, "You see, you're burning the shade right here," and she points to a place on the shade where there's nothing; no burn.

"I don't see anything."

She points again, "See, it's right here."

I'm thinking, *she's out of her mind,* but to her I say, "I'll change the light bulb." How else do you deal with a lunatic? *I'm* taking medication! We should be giving it to *her*.

About a day or so later, I get a call from The Ice House, could I do a show for them? I was thrilled. Finally, my mother was going to see me work. I agreed to do the show, and that night we drove out to Pasadena. For those of you who don't know the Ice House, it's one of the oldest clubs in LA. It opened in the heyday of the folk era and people like Lily Tomlin, The Smothers Brothers, and Pat Paulson got their start there. In the early 1980s, Bob Fisher bought the club and turned it from a dying white elephant to a dynamic Comedy Club, one in which the finest comedians in the country were getting their start. I shared the stage with David Letterman, Jay Leno, Tom Dreesen, George Miller, Gallagher, and on and on and on.

I was excited that my mother was in town when I was able to headline this club. I make a few phone calls telling people I'm working tonight, and like always, Fred and Mary Willard make the long drive out to Pasadena to see material they have seen at least a hundred times; the sign of true friends. To be honest with you, I don't remember who else was in the audience that night, but there were at least three other celebrities.

I do the show and it's gangbusters. I blew the roof off the place that night. The laughs were long and hard; they were continuous and loud. They were what comedians hope for every show. I got off stage and was a million miles high. I grab my mother from the audience and bring her back to the green room where I will greet people after the show. Within three minutes, the room fills with well-wishers. Fred and Mary were the most enthusiastic and they led the cheers. Everyone lingered for about half an hour, and as the room thinned out, I see my mother sitting in the corner, her knees tightly closed together, her arms crossed on her lap, holding her purse. Her face is forcing a smile.

We get into the car and head home. It's about a forty-minute trip. She's not said a word. It's killing me. I want something from her, some kind of recognition, anything. I get nothing. I can no longer take it.

"So, what did you think of the show?"

Like she was talking to a stranger, and with all the sincerity of a car salesman, she flips off, "It was nice."

"Nice?? Nice is all you can say? It was nice. Did you see those people? Did you hear the audience? That show was a lot of things, but nice wasn't one of them."

She looks at me and says angrily, "What do you want me to say? It wasn't my cup of tea."

I've got to tell you; I exploded, medication and all. I couldn't believe she could be so uncaring. I've seen her be nicer to hairdressers who just screwed up her hair. I look at her and say, "You know, at my age, I don't need a mother, I need a friend. And if you can't be my friend I don't want you in my life."

I guess this shook her, because she started opening up and we began talking about our relationship.

We talked the entire way home. I spilled my guts to her. I cried. I got angry. She cried. She got angry. We got home and I got undressed, and we were still talking. She made herself a cup of tea, and we were still talking. I told her things that I swore I would never tell her. I opened up. I bore my soul. I told her how hurt I was that she hadn't come out after the divorce and my nervous breakdown.

She replied, "I spoke to my sister and we decided it would be better for you to go through that alone."

This set us on another round of conversations. We talked and talked all night. Soon it was 4 a.m. and we were still going strong. It was a deep, intense talk that should cleanse the soul. It was the kind of communication you can only hope to have with a parent, and I was feeling the weight of the years of distrust and anger being lifted from my shoulders. It was a magical time. I looked at the clock and it was 5:45 a.m., we had talked the entire night. I finally said, "Mom, we've got to stop. I need to get some rest."

"I agree," she said. We stood, and she came over and put her arms around me. She gave me a real "mother" hug. "I'm so glad we had this talk, Stevie. It was important to get this all out in the open so you could see how wrong you've been." Then she glided into the bedroom like the Enola Gay after dropping the atomic bomb on Japan.

I stood there with my mouth open and my heart breaking. She had done it to me again. She let me in only to shut me out. It was at that moment I realized how much I hated her and loved her in the same emotion. I think they call that inner turmoil. She was the most frustrating woman on the face of the earth. She's not a bad person; she's a good person, just a horrific mother. It's taken me thousands of dollars in therapy to realize that. I could have saved that money if I had just listened to a woman I met in a doctor's office. She said, "When a mother says there's something wrong with the child, there's something wrong with the mother." That sentence hit me like a ton of bricks. She went on, "Because my son could murder someone and I would say, 'He must have had a good reason.'" I just looked at her in amazement. How lucky her son was! How unlucky I was. It would be so much easier if you could just pick your parents.

An Anxiety Attack

THE FEELING OF COMPLETE USELESSNESS, of worthlessness, of failure, is so strong in me I can't sit in my own skin. I sit here wondering what I can do with my life and all I hear is an audible hum in my head. It's like the hope switch turns off when it comes to me. I can help my friends; I can help strangers and lost dogs. I can't help myself, and no matter how much soul searching I do, I wonder if I'll ever rid myself of these feelings.

I'm told over and over again that I have to move on and forget the past. I have to forgive my parents and love them. I simply can't. I have such resentment towards both of them. They screwed up my life and then went on their merry way. They both remarried and told me how happy they were. They never asked if I was. They checked in with me when it was convenient for them. If you asked them, they felt they were the best parents they could be. If they were so wonderful, why am I such a mess?

I think the thing that upsets me the most is my plan didn't work. I had my life all planned out. I was going to be a star. I remember in the early days hanging out at the Comedy Store, Craig T. Nelson's wife came up to me and introduced herself. She said, "Everyone says you're the one to watch. You're the star." I never forgot that moment; I thought it was so strange, I didn't feel like a star at all. I felt lucky to be there, lucky that those people would accept me. Life is filled with irony, isn't it? Craig turned out to be the star. She was living with the star and she didn't know it. Craig, who was a writer at the time, has become a well-respected actor, and I became the nobody.

Here's a little-known fact: Barry Levinson, Craig Nelson, and Rudy DeLuca were a comedy writing team. They wrote for *Carol Burnett* and *The Tim Conway Show* for the longest time. Barry always wanted to do films and he left the group to direct his first film, *Diner*. It was Barry's film

And Justice for All that gave Craig his big acting break. Rudy went on to write with Mel Brooks. Rudy is the hit man in *High Anxiety*; see how incestuous the business is?

There's a reason I'm a nobody. I can remember the day I shut down. I had just come out of the hospital after my divorce and I went back to The Comedy Store to start working again. Mitzi Shore, who was my biggest supporter, had posted a sign in the hallway where the comedians hang out, "Steve Bluestein is in the hospital. Visiting hours are.... If you have the time, please go see him." Beneath that notice, comedians had handwritten jokes.

"I'd go visit him but I'm busy sleeping with his wife."

"I would go, but who's going to babysit *our* baby?"

It went on and on until all I could do is rip it down. I remember seeing those handwritten jokes supposedly written by my friends and feeling something die inside me. I had just been through the worst episode of my life, I found out the child I thought was mine was not. It was an episode that made my childhood look like a piece of cake, and all these heartless jerks could do was make jokes about my situation. I walked out of the Comedy Store and never returned.

I hate feeling this way, but I think it's important to put it out there. There is no "art" unless you are naked, and folks, this is about as naked as I can get. All I ever wanted was someone to hold me and tell me it's going to be all right. Isn't that insane? A grown man wanting to be held and feel protected. I think maybe that's why I take care of so many people, I don't want them to feel the way I do. I think if I take care of others, then maybe I'll protect them from feeling the pain I've felt all my life.

I know as Monica Johnson read this book, she shook her head, "Stop doing the 'self-pity', Steve." I wish I could, Monica. I wish I could just release it and be free of the anxiety, but I can't, it's embedded in my soul. It's what made Van Gogh cut off his ear; it's what made Levant chain-smoke and Joplin overdose. It's the pain of an artist, and I find that very ironic, since I don't feel like an artist. I feel like an unloved child. I suppose there are medications I could take to alter these feelings, but the friends I have seen on this medication are worse after they take it than before. I have to do this on my own, drug free, so I type my life away, pouring out my soul for the world to see. I'm either the bravest man on the face of the earth or the biggest fool who ever walked it. I guess time will tell.

Only I Can Change Me

I HAD AN EYE-OPENING EXPERIENCE TODAY. A couple of days ago, I sent out 702 emails from my computer address book telling everyone that I had changed my email address. I asked them to return the email so I would know they got it. Twenty-seven people responded. Talk about feeling insignificant.

It got me thinking: I need to be validated even for a change of address. I need to have the book readers email me what they think of my writing. I need to know my friends like their Christmas gifts. Let me put it in other words. I need *you* to make *me* feel better. Seriously, does it matter if 675 people didn't respond? Will my life be any better or worse knowing they got my change of address?

I was talking to a dear friend about this, and she said to me, "It's like you're a child." It hit me like a ton of bricks. She's absolutely correct. How you are and what you do has nothing to do with my wellbeing. My wellbeing should come from within me, but it doesn't or it hasn't. Why? Here's an example: I am forcing my friends to have a surprise birthday party for me. One of them said to me, "I just don't understand your need for a party. I don't need that, I got it all when I was a child." Like a bolt out of the blue, it hit me. I did not. Just like I have saved those scrapbooks because no one would, I plan my own party because no one will. It all comes back to that hole that was left in my soul. I am seventy. I think how can a man feel like a child? The answer is, the child never grew up. The child was never allowed to be a child. The child never had a childhood, and so the adult keeps trying to capture something that is long gone. I was never told I was enough, so I needed all of you to tell me, but 702 of you, 7002 of you, 70,002 of you can never make me whole because I never felt whole as a child. Question: how do you feel whole?

My friend Sandy, who had a similar upbringing to myself, sent me this long, wonderful email about self. One of the things she said was, "Does anyone in your family have twenty pages devoted to them on Google? Do any of them have your accomplishments?" I started to Google my cousins to see. Some have no page, some have two or three pages, but not one of them has twenty pages. Here's what I did with that information, *oh, my pages aren't as important as theirs.* Then I stopped myself. Yes, my pages are as important as theirs.

This past year I have had to let go of so many "comfort zones", zones that may be destructive to me, but have been a part of my personality. Giving up these pieces of my identity has been difficult, trying not to compare myself to David Letterman or Jay Leno or Gandhi or even Hitler, but trying to be Steve, the only person I've been all my life. I've got about twenty years left on this earth. Those twenty years will fly by faster than the last twenty. When am I going to give myself a break? When will I allow myself to feel good? I think the answer is, starting today.

I am filled with anxiety about this entry. This is the deepest I've gone. The hardest I've had to pull to change; the most open I've ever been. It feels strange, like I'm doing something wrong, and that tells me I'm doing something right. After my breakdown and my divorce, as I lay in the hospital, I said to myself, *everything you have done in your life has brought you to this point. If you get out of this bed and do it exactly the same way, you're an idiot.* When I got out of the hospital, I tried life differently. If that didn't work, I tried something else, and if that didn't work, and so on and so on. I've reached that point again in my life. Everything I've done in my life so far has brought me to the point where I still feel useless, unloved, and like a failure. If I continue to go on this way, I'm an idiot. I'm going to try something different. I'm going to try not to care about what the world thinks of me, try not to compare myself to others, try not to be who I was in the past. It's not going to be easy—I'm comfortable in my discomfort—but if I don't at least try, I'm an idiot.

Singing Waiter

THE DEPRESSION IS BACK, and it's back with a vengeance. I was supposed to go out to dinner with friends; I couldn't go. I was supposed to take a shower; I couldn't take it. I was supposed to go to a cocktail party; I just couldn't. Instead, I sat on the sofa in a coma. Knowing that I have to fight this, I went into my office to clean up my desk. Organization always makes me feel better, gives me a center. I have some control. I took my brand-new Dramatist Guild card and put it into a file where I keep that kind of stuff. The file slipped out of my hand and dropped to the floor. The papers scattered everywhere, and I let out a scream of frustration. As I gathered up the papers a Canadian two-dollar bill rose to the top of the pile. I looked at it with curious interest. I had no idea why it was in there and then, like a bolt out of the blue, it hit me. Two wonderful, elderly couples gave this two-dollar bill to me in 1968. It was a tip. I was their singing waiter on Cape Cod, and this two-dollar bill was their love note to me.

Oh yes, just when you thought you knew everything about me, there is yet another chapter to open, another can of worms to go through, another river to cross. In my youth, I had been known to carry a tune. Remember Susan from Van Johnson, the B'hai, Seals and Crofts? Remember her? She and I had gotten a job in college as singing waiters in a shithole of a restaurant. It paid the bills and provided me with a meager income as I struck out on my own.

After graduation, I heard about a place in East Dennis, Mass. on Cape Cod that was hiring singing waiters. It was called the Golden Anchor. I contacted them and was hired. It was my very first job in show business and my very first time on Cape Cod, despite the fact that I had been raised in Massachusetts.

We did twenty-one shows a week. Three shows a night, seven nights a week for two months straight with no nights off. Not only did we have to do the shows, but we also had to serve the meals and bus the tables. If I tried to do that today, they would have to take me home on a stretcher, but I was young and making really good money. Money that was going to take me to New York and help me find my first apartment.

There aren't a lot of details I remember about that place. I remember that we did a lot of drinking there and a lot of the group was smoking pot. I was very much against pot at the time. There was one more peculiar memory. I remember one of the girls kept a wish list of things she wanted to buy. I thought it was the most insane thing I had ever heard of, and then like twenty years later, it suddenly came to me that I should write a wish list of things I wanted. As I got each item, I would check them off, and suddenly I understood what a good thing a wish list is. For me, it puts down on paper my needs, and as long as my subconscious thinks my needs are being addressed, all is good. That's all I remember about that summer.

Oh wait, I do remember something else. As the used pats of butter came back from the tables, the owner would melt them down and use them as dipping sauce for the lobster dinners. To this day, I will not eat melted butter in a restaurant. Oh yes, and I remember one of my customers asking to take his steak dinner home for his dog. I brought it back to the kitchen and had to run out to do a musical number. When I returned, one of the other waiters had eaten the steak. I went through the trash, got a steak, and gave it to my customer (I haven't thought about that in thirty-eight years. Lord, I hope that guy really had a dog).

Suffice it to say, it was a very hard job, long hours, and very little rewards, but it was great experience, and it was at the Golden Anchor that I did my very first stand-up routine. It was there that I learned I could make a room full of people laugh. I had always been the funny one in high school and college, but that was only for small groups in private. At the Golden Anchor, I got to make a hundred people laugh at once. I remember the feeling, *I can do this,* and the germ of a career was planted.

We had regular customers that came in nightly to see the shows—or maybe it was the food. My ego wants to believe it was the shows that brought them back, not the lobsters. We were sort of local celebrities. I even had this older woman who wanted to get me into bed so badly that she would take me for long rides and park her car by the ocean. There were just a few things wrong: 1) She was married, 2) she had two kids, and 3) her husband was in the Mafia. No matter how badly I wanted to get laid, there was no way I was going to die for it.

The summer went on with its usual customers, twenty-one shows a week, and waiting tables. Then one night, two couples came in. They sat at my table and I began to take their order. They were really nice people; warm, sweet, sincere, caring. They were Canadians. I took their order, and just being myself, I made them laugh. They left me a very nice tip and came back night after night, always asking to be sat at my station. In a couple of weeks, we were friends. I knew them as Phyllis and Maurice, Gert and Hank. They knew me as the funny waiter, Steve.

One night after the show, we sat having drinks, and Phyllis asked me what I wanted to do after the summer was over. I told her I had dreams of working nightclubs and that someday, I wanted to work the Copa. The two couples came in a few more times, and then they came in to say goodbye, they were going back to Canada. I had grown very fond of these four people and was sad to see them go. I grow attached to people very easily. There's that need again.

I did my show and when I got off the stage they were gone. On the tip tray was a two-dollar Canadian bill. On the bill, they had written their names and addresses and phone numbers, and across the top in large letters, "SEE YOU AT THE COPA." I knew when I saw it that it was special. It was an expression of love that I had never seen before, and I folded it up carefully and put it in a safe place. I carried that two-dollar bill from Massachusetts to New York and from New York to Los Angeles. It's been many years and I still have it, in the same condition it was on the night it was given to me.

The way I hold onto things is indicative of how I crave love. Back then, I thought that note was a sweet thing to do, but years later I can truly see what a powerful gift it was. They had faith in me. They knew I could make it. I didn't know I could make it. I still don't, but they did. They did something that no one else had ever done: they told me.

Sometime in the 1970s when I was getting really hot, I called them in Canada. Maurice had died but the rest were still alive. I suspect they are all gone now, but not from my heart. It's not about their death, it's about their lives and how they affected me, and how some way, somehow, things are meant to be. You see, I had no idea what to write about. I had a note saying "singing waiter", but there were no memories there. That is, not until I dropped the file and their two-dollar bill fell out from where it's been for maybe thirty-odd years. Suddenly memories came flooding back and I remembered them and their sincere love of my talent. It reminded me that I had people in my life that cared; I just couldn't feel their love. It reminded me that the ones who have passed over are watching over me as well, protecting me from mudslides, inspiring me to write books, and pushing dollar bills out of folders. We are not alone, people. Our loved ones are all around us.

NYC Drugs

WHEN I SAT DOWN TO WRITE another NY story the word "drugs" came popping up time and time again. I didn't want to write about that period. I've been sober for thirty-five years, but I did do a lot of drugs in New York. It was my first time living on my own, away from the mother from hell, and I went out of my ever-loving mind with freedom. Since I'm telling all, I might as well tell you guys about my drug years. These stories aren't an endorsement of drugs; it's a recollection of a very confused period in my life.

It all began with Walter K. Walter was a friend from high school. To me, Walter was always one of the hip ones. He was in the right crowd, he joined the right club, he had the right friends. He just had it all. I always felt I didn't fit in with him and his crowd, but I peddled as fast as I could to appear to be one of his gang. When I heard Walter lived in New York, I contacted him. One night he came over to my one room apartment; we were going to a club or something. He starts the evening with a little announcement, "I brought a little something." He produces a joint. I was twenty-two years old and had never smoked grass before. I was petrified, but I was impressed. Walter K. smokes grass. Now you have to remember, I went through college and never smoked. I was in the theater department at Emerson College and never smoked. I worked as a singing waiter on Cape Cod and never smoked. Now my high school role model was standing in my very own apartment offering me the evil weed. Walter asks, "Do you want some?"

I *did* want some. I wanted some badly. I wanted to be a bad boy, but I was scared, "I don't know, Walter, what if I get addicted?"

He laughed and took out his lighter.

"No!" I wouldn't let him smoke in my apartment, "What if the neighbor's smell it?" I insisted we go outside. Walter was living in Queens or Brooklyn, I think, and still had his car.

He said, "I'll take you somewhere where we can smoke. No one will know. I'll protect you." Protect me? No one had ever offered to do that. We drove to lower Manhattan to the meatpacking district.

Visualize this scene. Cobblestone streets, old brick buildings with filthy loading docks, each dock with a metal roof covering huge wooden doors that had seen decades of wear. Through the doors was an opening allowing a track with hooks to pass through (this is where sides of beef would be hung). Rats ran Helter Skelter, and it was raining. I remember thinking, *I'm a junkie.*

Walter takes out the joint and lights up. He's doing some idle chat, but I don't hear a word of it. I'm keeping an eye out for the FBI. He hands me the joint. My life is over; I'm a drug addict. I can hear every bad thing I've ever been told about drugs being flushed from my mind, and yet I could feel my independence from that insane, overbearing bitch I called Mom. I take the joint and have my first hit as the rain intensifies. The sound of it pinging on the roof remains with me to this day. We pass the joint back and forth a few times.

"Feel anything?" Walter queries.

"No?" I sputter, because I didn't. I felt nothing.

Walter shrugs and starts the car. We're going to a club in Harlem. We're driving uptown and I happen to open the glove box. It's a mess. I pull everything out and start rearranging the papers. "What are you doing?" Walter asks.

"Cleaning your glove box."

He starts screaming, "Ha! You're stoned."

"No, I'm not. I'm starving. Have you got anything to eat?"

"Ha-ha! You're stoned!!" He screams again.

I find a half-eaten candy bar on the floor and devour it. Me, Mister won't eat unwashed fruit, I'm eating a six-month-old Snickers bar.

That was the first time I got stoned. It wasn't the last, however. I found a freedom in smoking grass that I had never felt before. I was funnier, I was brighter, I could talk to people, I thought I looked better. In retrospect, I was a mess, but it was the 60s and everyone was smoking grass, so I didn't feel *that* fucked up, just guilty.

Walter had introduced me to a world I had only read about, but I was a fast learner. I got the bong, I got the rolling papers, and I had the roach clip. I never bought grass, however. I was always too broke. I had been fired from United Artists and was now working at Alexander's Department store waiting for my big break in show business. There was this guy from Atlanta I worked with at Alexander's; can't remember his name. Must be the drugs. He was my main source for grass. I was living a block from the store, so he would come over at lunch break and light up. I never did. I had rules: 1) Not during working hours, 2) Not when you had to drive, 3) Not when your family was coming over, 4) Always wipe the joint off before passing it.

I was the most uptight pothead of the 60s. If I had gone to Woodstock, I would have insisted on having a reservation. One night after work, my Atlanta connection came over with a bag of grass. We smoked some and were planning on doing some more when the doorbell rang.

"Who is it?"

"Police!"

It's thirty years later, and I can still feel my heart sinking into my shoes. I turned to my friend. "It's the Police!!" I ran to turn on the air conditioning. It would clean the air; however, it was January and probably would look suspicious. I sprayed Lysol, because that doesn't look suspicious at all. We tossed the roach clips and bong out the window. In our final attempt to stay out of jail, we flushed $60 worth of grass down the toilet. Back then, $60 was like flushing the Hope Diamond.

I pulled myself together and buzzed the Police in. I lived on the third floor and it took them a few minutes to get to my front door. Tap-tap. I open it. Standing there is Stanley from Men's Shoes.

"You guys got any weed?"

It was like Reefer madness. We wanted to kill Stanley, and almost did. He made it up to us with a nice baggie of something he got for his birthday. The world was good again.

It doesn't take too long for me to start smoking on a regular basis. I guess all the pent-up, repressed feelings of being controlled by an insane mother came flooding out. I was finally on my own, doing what I wanted to do, and what I wanted to do was smoke grass whenever I wasn't being responsible. I was a weekend and evening smoker.

One weekend, I'm at Larry S's apartment in the Village. Larry had just gotten married to Francine, who would later divorce him and marry Corky, the drummer from Mountain. Remember them? I thought it was very strange, since I had been seated next to Corky at Larry's wedding and felt a very strange vibe from him when he looked at Francine. For now,

Larry and Francine were happy and married and living in a converted power station on Jane Street.

I was invited over for dinner, and I remember Larry having the best shit I had ever smoked. Francine is going to broil a steak, and she is in no better condition than I. She pops the steak in the oven, and within five minutes there are flames shooting out everywhere. The three of us are standing in front of the flaming oven.

"I always wanted a fireplace," Larry says. Larry and Francine are laughing.

I'm thinking, *this is how Chicago burned.* I take a pitcher of water and throw it at the steak. The flame shoots up around six feet. Larry kicks the tray off the stove with his foot and stomps it out.

Francine says, "You want mashed potatoes, or fries?"

We ate it off the floor.

I'm in Susan's apartment on the sixteenth floor for New Years. I remember it being a clear, crisp winter night in New York. Susan's place had a balcony, and at about 11:55 p.m. I snuck out there to welcome in the New Year. From this vantage point I could overlook the entire city. I was leaning on the railing smoking a joint, but I could hear the party inside, "Ten, nine, eight, seven, six, five, four, three, two, one," and then the appropriate, "Happy New Year!" I looked out onto the city and was so stoned I could actually "see" New Year's coming in. I could almost touch it on that balcony, and it's a moment in my life that I will never forget. I remember feeling good, for the first time in my life. I had an apartment, I had a job, I had lots of friends, and I was away from Boston and the insanity of my childhood.

Those were the feelings back then. In reality, I was a freight train heading for a brick wall. I had no idea how much damage those drugs were doing and how it was to affect me later in my life. This was only the beginning. It got much worse when I moved to LA. By then I was suffering from massive insecurity and inferiority feelings, and the worse I felt, the more I medicated. Only now I found a wife, and she was to become more of the problem than the solution. Everything in my life up until now, everything that I had considered horrific, was a piece of cake. The house of cards came tumbling down around me. It was a complete breakdown.

The Famous Manager

WHEN THE COMEDY STORE FIRST OPENED, the comedy scene was not like it is today. Today, comedy clubs are part of the American society much like movie theaters and drive-ins. Back then, they were a new entity. No one knew what they would become or how many careers they would give birth to. It was an adventure, an exciting adventure, and I was there from almost day one. In the very beginning, a comedian would just go to the club with hopes of getting on stage. Sometimes you'd wait around for hours and not get your chance, but there'd always be the promise of "tomorrow". You'd come back tomorrow and some big star would come in, and another night passed with you not getting on stage, but there was always the next night. Eventually you would get on, and that's how it went, night after night, month after month, year after year. It wasn't until Mitzi Shore took over The Comedy Store that scheduled shows were established. She had a line-up of comedians so a customer would know who would be on at 9 p.m. and who wouldn't. Comedians had to call into the club for time slots and then call back later to be told when their slots were or if they even got a slot. It was a hell way to get a career started, but hopefuls, like myself, would flock to The Comedy Store like moths to the flame. It was the only game in town.

There weren't many comedians back then, when I started. I would say maybe there were sixty. Today, I'm sure there are upwards of six thousand comedians working at any given night across the country. Today, if you have a suit and can string two words together, you can be a comedian. Back when I started, it was a club of exclusive entertainers, mostly men, mostly white, and surprisingly enough, being Jewish was not an advantage. They'd seen that. They were looking for the next big ethnic group to become popular. We had an Indian Comedian, Charlie Hill; one from Russia, Yakov Smirnoff; one from Bangladesh, and so on and so on. Back then, you felt special being a comedian. It was an exclusive club you belonged to, one that not everyone was invited to be a member of. Today, everyone is a comedian. Case in point, I was having a colonoscopy. I'm on the table and the doctor says to me, "So what do you do?"

"I'm a comedian."

"Really? So is my nurse."

"No, I'm a professional comedian. That's all I do. I don't spend my days helping you look up people's asses."

In any case, those sixty comedians were a tight-knit group in the beginning. We hung out together, we played together, we fought, we loved, we were a family. The only people who did not get along were Budd Friedman, owner of the Improv, and Mitzi Shore, owner of The Comedy Store, and here's why. There was always this feud between them as to who opened the first comedy club. Budd says he did, and so did Mitzi, but I will set the record straight right here and now: they both did.

Budd Friedman had the first club. There is no doubt about it. I went to the Improv in 1969 to see The Ace Trucking Company with Fred Willard. It was a small club with an outer bar where the acts hung out, and then a small show room right next to it. The building was a typical New York building, and as many of those buildings did in those days, it had an exposed brick wall where the stage was. That is why today, in most comedy clubs, a brick wall is used as the background to the stage. Budd had the first club, but here's where it gets sticky. Budd not only had comedians, he also had singers, piano players, and entertainers. His club was in the theater district, and so when the shows broke, many of the kids from the shows would come to perform at The Improv. Yes, Budd had the first club, but it wasn't an exclusive comedy club. It was a club that did have comedians though.

In 1971 or 1972, Sammy Shore decided to open a club on the Sunset Strip for only comedians. There was a popular club at the time called The Candy Store, so Sammy named his club The Comedy Store. The difference between Sammy's club and Budd's club was Sammy's was exclusively comedy. Why? Sammy was a comedian, and he needed a place where he could showcase his act. The irony being that The Comedy Store must have started at least a hundred careers to stardom, and not one was Sammy's. Just a footnote, in the very beginning, maybe once in a great while, a singer would get on stage, but ninety-eight percent of the time it was all comedy, and that was the difference between Sammy's club and Budd's. The purpose of Sammy's club was comedy, the purpose of Budd's was entertainment until the comedy thing took off, and there was so much money to be made, *then* The Improv became exclusively comedy.

When Sammy and Mitzi Shore (parents of Pauly Shore) were getting a divorce, The Comedy Store was dying. Sammy was not a great businessman, and the club had been run into the ground. There were no audiences anymore, and interest from the show-business crowd was waning. Mitzi got the club as part of the divorce settlement. She wanted it; Sammy did not. Mitzi has a reputation for being a little eccentric, which she might be, but she is a marketing genius. She took that dying club and gave it a look. The first thing she did was paint the club black. Then she created those turn-of-the-century signs that are so famous today. She had matches made with The Comedy Store logo on them so people would take them and talk about their night out. She changed the ways the shows were produced, too. She scheduled them so they had a beginning, middle, and end. She nurtured the comedians and created what is an industry today: The Comedy Club. Oh, by the way, she did it by not paying the comedians. She considered her club a school where people were learning to be comedians. That all changed with the comedian strike, which I was the PR person for.

Now you know the history of the comedy club scene in the 1970s. It was a very exciting time back then. Every night another star would walk in, every night a new guy would get on stage and there would be a buzz about him, every night it was something new and different. One of those new guys was Franklin Ajaye. From the moment he got on stage, he was special. He was intellectual, fresh, smart, good. He stuck out from the pack. He was immediately signed by a manager, an African American man named... well, I'll tell you later. I remember this manager well. He was slight of build, always had a smile on his face, and was a smart businessman. I had trouble talking to many of the managers, they scared me. They still do. I never had trouble talking with this guy. Why? He never looked down on anyone; he always was open and encouraging.

One night after the club closes, Franklin says to me, "Come with us. We're going to my manager's house. He's baking cookies." I thought it was very strange invitation, but the story was, the manager liked to bake cookies, and he wanted us to try a batch he had just baked. We all piled into our cars and met at the manager's house, which was a bungalow near Paramount Studio. I remember it because it had very high-pitched ceilings and I remarked at how I would love to live in a place like this, but you must know it was a very humble place, not a palace.

When everyone got there, the manager started to bring out cookie sheet after cookie sheet of the most fabulous chocolate chip cookies I had ever eaten. Being a starving artist, I pigged out and took some cookies home, much to the delight of the manager. I never gave it another thought, but whenever I would see the manager I would ask if had any of those fabulous cookies he baked.

It must have been about two years later, I'm driving down Sunset Blvd about two blocks from Hollywood High School, when I see a "coming soon" banner on an old House of Pies building. House of Pies had a distinctive roofline with a sharp peak; no matter what you would do to those buildings, they still looked like a House of Pies. In any case, I drive by and I see the manager standing out in front. I stop and he says, "It's my cookie store."

A store just for chocolate chip cookies.... You must be insane, I thought.

A few weeks later, the store opened with much fanfare. The manager had many show business connections, and they all showed up. It was a media event, and soon the buzz around town was these cookies were special and important people were giving them as gifts. It was the beginning of the gourmet cookie industry, and a comedian's manager started it. The rest is history, and I'm sure you've guessed it by now. The manager was Wally Amos, and the cookies were Famous Amos Cookies. Wally was and is just one hell of a nice guy. He took his passion for cooking, his smarts for business, and his knowledge of marketing and made himself a multimillionaire. It's been thirty years and I still am in awe of what that man did. Once again, I, Forrest Gump, was there when it all began. I guess life is like a box of chocolate… chip cookies, only in this case you know what you're gonna get. Inspiration.

Getting Into Emerson

I HAD GONE TO THE UNIVERSITY OF MIAMI my freshman year. It was the first time I had been on my own. I let my hair grow and had my first drink. I also had the first of many nervous breakdowns. With me, you fart and I have a nervous breakdown, but this was my first. I didn't keep a scrapbook about it, I just remember standing on my bed and slamming my pillow against the wall about a thousand times while screaming, "I can't take it anymore!" I remember the expression on Mark Hurwitz's face when he walked into my room, *Uh-oh. Looney tunes.*

You'd be slamming pillows against the wall too if you were going through what I was going through. I felt everyone was talking about me, and I heard voices as I walked through the quad. It was so bad I actually went into the dorm facing the quad—maybe I knew someone there and they were yelling out at me. I remember sitting in a diner and hearing laughter in the background and thinking they were laughing at me. I was not well-hinged.

I made it two semesters and could not take it another moment. I decided to transfer to some school in Boston, some place close to home and close to the friends I loved. I had heard about Emerson. It sounded like the kind of school I would like to go to. It offered Theater and Speech, and its student body was known to be bohemian. I sent away for the application and headed home for summer break. Here's the kind of support I got from my mother's family: "We're so proud of you. You actually lasted two semesters. We never thought you'd last that long." You have to understand, they were sincere. To them, that was a compliment. It's like saying, "Your baby is so ugly. She looks just like you."

I got the Emerson application, filled it out, and sent it in. My mother was not happy. She did not want me going to any school that offered theatrical training. There were two things going on here: 1) I wanted to be in an artistic school, and 2) I didn't feel I would be accepted academically in any other school. Emerson was my only hope.

The day of the interview came and I was a nervous wreck. I remember it like it was yesterday. It so amazes me the things I remember and can see in my mind like a photograph. I was ushered into the Dean's office and we began talking. He asked me what I wanted to do at Emerson and I told him I wanted to be an actor or a writer. We discussed movies that were out, we discussed actresses and actors, we discussed plays I had seen, and before I knew it the interview was over. He shook my hand and I was ushered out.

I thought the meeting went well. I felt we had a rapport. I was feeling good about the whole experience and I told my mother that. She was as cold as ice. She could care less. A few days later, we were fighting over what I was going to do next semester and I said, "I'm getting into Emerson so there's no need to worry."

"No, you're not. I spoke to them and you did not do well in the interview," she said.

I'm telling you it was like the rug was pulled out from under me. Where was I going to go? What was I going to do?

About ten days later, the envelope arrived. I put it on the kitchen table and just stared at it. I couldn't open it. Finally, I did. It started, "The President and Dean of Students are happy to inform you..." I had been accepted. I just sat there staring at the letter. Why had they let me in if I had done so badly at the interview? I guess they felt sorry for me. Later, my mother came home and I told her of my acceptance.

"Oh good," she half-heartedly cheered, and it was left at that. I was going to Emerson.

The following two-and-a-half years were lack luster for me. I spent my days walking around that school knowing that I had been let in because they felt sorry for me. I never felt good enough around the other students, despite the fact that I had a full social life. When it came down to the "who will be successful in life" daydreams, it was never me. I was defeated before I began, and I gave up. I never tried out for plays because there would always be someone better than me. I never joined any clubs because I knew they wouldn't have me. I simply walked the halls and barely made it through my classes.

Testing was a nightmare for me. I would get physically ill. I remember one class in which I excelled on all the oral participation and got a

D on the final. I was so distraught that I went to the professor to ask if I could take the final again.

"What happened, Steve? Why did you do so poorly?" I opened up to this man and explained about my testing anxiety. He was a real educator and he listened as I told him my story. He asked if I wanted to take an oral exam. I jumped at the chance. I got an "A" on the oral.

The years passed and I made it as a senior. It was then I met Jon Stierwalt and Bob Fisher, got an apartment in town, and was truly on my own. My mother was weaning me from being financially dependent on her and insisted I do the work-study program. I protested because, "What could I do that they'd want?" but I applied and was accepted. I was to work in the admitting office.

I fell into the groove of it right away. They allowed me to show prospective students and their families around the campus. I had it down to a science with interesting facts and funny stories. Word got back to the Dean that I was good on the tours and he commended me. It got me to thinking, if I was doing so well and they liked me, why had they told my mother I wasn't a good candidate for Emerson? It was then I got the idea to look up my file. It was easy, after all, I was in the admitting office. One day when no one was around, I slipped into the Dean's office and went to the student files. Quickly I pulled the "B's" and scanned for my name. There it is. I opened the file and my eyes welled up. Written in large letters in the margin it said, "Candidate is bright, witty, and well spoken. An excellent candidate for admittance." I just sat there staring at the file. Then, I heard someone in the outer office and quickly slid my folder back into its spot in the drawer.

I walked around trying to figure out what had happened. The answer came up the same every time. My mother, in an attempt to discourage me from wanting to go to Emerson, had told me I had not done well on my interview. For three years, I walked around that campus feeling like I didn't belong, like I wasn't as good as the rest of the students, like I should be lucky for being there, and all because of my mother's inability to accept my decision to be in the theatre.

When people say things like, "If you haven't gotten over it by now, you'll never get over it," they're absolutely right. I probably will never get over what was done to me. What I do is try, on a daily basis, to make it one day at a time. When I watch the Emmys or the Oscars and a winner thanks their mother for all the love and support, for taking them to acting classes, for always being there, I know that I will never make that speech... even if I never win.

Even More Sightings

WHEN I WAS WORKING in The Tomorrow Shop at Alexander's, we would get all sorts of high-profile people in to see what was hot for men's fashion. They never bought there; they just looked, and then went next door to Bloomingdales and bought there. Even in the 1960s, people were snobs. One day, I'm crossing the floor and I see this ashen looking man standing in front of me. He had the palest skin I've ever seen and thick white hair. I was transfixed on the hair because it didn't look real, and then realized it wasn't real, nor was the man. It was Andy Worhol. All I could think of was, *what is Andy Worhol doing in Alexander's?* Andy asked if I worked in the department, to which I answered "yes", and he stared at me for an instant, you know the look, like you're about to buy something, but you want to make sure it's what you need. He reached into his pocket and handed me a slip of paper, "You should come," and walked away. I looked at what he had handed me. It was an invitation to a party at The Factory. I didn't know The Factory; I was a kid from a small town. Factories, to me, were places where mattresses were made.

Now you have to understand why I didn't go. I felt worthless. I never felt I was good-looking, nor do I now. I could not understand why Andy Worhol would want to invite me anywhere, so I didn't go. Don't think I haven't contemplated what would have happened to me if I did go. I could have become a Worhol star, I would have met Jackie Kennedy, I would have.... Bullshit. Who knows what would have happened. I certainly will never know. I didn't go to the party; I stayed home and folded socks. I still fold socks. Come to my house tomorrow, it's sock-folding day.

Talk about the bizarre aspects of working for Alexander's. Must have been about six days after Andy was in the shop, and who should waltz in but Henny Youngman. Talk about being from another planet. He was the yin to Worhol's yang. He was old-school, but I recognized him immediately. He never stopped joking as he looked through the $89 suits. The man was on 24/7. He was a real comedian of the old guard, and I swear to you, I saw Youngman on *The Ed Sullivan* show in one of Alexander's $89 suits.

Some of the best sightings come from being backstage. It's where I met Shirley MacLaine and saw Robert De Niro. Backstage at *The Merv Griffin Show* was fun. They had a green room where all the guests waited to go on. I was a nervous wreck when I went on TV. Can you imagine me, fear of being judged, me, facing ten million people? This one time I'm in the green room and Norman Fell from *Three's Company* is there. He was seated next to the bar; I was across the room. The bartender asked me if he could get me something. I got up and crossed the room saying, "Yes, I'll have a…" and at that very moment the bartender sneezed. Without taking a beat I said, "Nothing," and turned back to my seat. Norman Fell laughed so hard, he almost fell off his chair. That's why they called him Norman *Fell*. Schmelman! Oh Dean!

Oh! This is a good one. I'm on a plane flying to Canada to do a TV show. I'm seated in first class, and who is seated next to me but Yvonne DeCarlo. She's working with a yellow legal pad and is furiously writing page after page after page. She never looked up, nor did she ever say a word to me. I was dying with curiosity trying to see what she was writing, so in my best I'm-not-looking-at-you head tilt, I peer out of the corner of my eye as I see her write in bold letters at the top of the page "DAVID" and she underlines it nineteen times. I guess she didn't like David. Then I realize she is writing her memoirs, on a plane, going to Canada.

Next day we shoot the TV show. The limo pulls up and she is standing next to me. She gets in and I follow.

She looks at me and says, "This is my limo."

The driver says, "I'm sorry Miss DeCarlo, there is only one car to the studio. He will have to join us."

I get in feeling like a leper. I spend the whole fifteen-minute trip staring out the window. We get to the studio and she gets out and never looks back or says a word.

We're in the green room, and I do not exist. She doesn't say a word to me. Mind you, we've flown up from LA together, driven in a car together, and are waiting to do a TV show. I'm not there. She's on first and does her spot. I do mine, and we share the sofa next to the host, who I think was Alan Hamel. She couldn't have been nicer. Complimentary. Laughing. Charming. The show ends, the camera shut off, and like a light switch clicks in her head, she turns to stone. I am no longer there.

Anyone who thinks show business is this huge family where we all sit around and sing "White Christmas" seriously needs to get shock treatments.

A Mary Willard Christmas

THE CHRISTMAS PARTIES started for just a few close friends in Fred and Mary's two-bedroom apartment in Brentwood. It was a small two-bedroom, but it was a home, Mary made sure of that. Their daughter was the centerpiece of that home. Come Christmas time, Mary dressed up that little place like it was Buckingham Palace. No matter what kind of money was coming in back then, Hope, their daughter, was always provided for at Christmas. Mary made sure of that, and it wasn't easy on a starving actor's salary.

The parties were always fun; we'd laugh and carry on. I think it was at one of these parties that Hope sat on my lap and said, "Uncle Steve, you have a big nose way out to here." Everyone laughed, and Fred, covering for what could be an embarrassing moment, said, "Oh pay no mind to the child. She's only mimicking what everyone is saying." I had my nose fixed four months later and have not let Hope forget it to this day.

Fred was always a gifted and talented actor. He was smart. His comedy was smart. There was always something special about him, but being special in this town can be a detriment, "What do we do with him?" The roles came little by little. There were lean years. He made a living, but he wasn't a star. Then he got *Fernwood 2 Night*. This changed everything. There was finally some money, and Mary made the best of it. She bought their first home in Brentwood. It was a wonderful ranch house with lots of room for parties.

That year the Christmas Party grew a bit; there were more celebrities because Fred had crossed over into the mainstream of show business. I would say there were about forty to fifty people there, and Mary, bless her soul, cooked for days.

She made this apple thing that I loved, I don't even know how to explain it. There was always a ham or a turkey, lots of side dishes, and wonderful desserts, but it was always about the people. This was a group of people that only met once a year at Fred and Mary's on Christmas. They were our connection, they still are.

We had some wonderful parties at the Brentwood house. One year, Mary made Christmas cookies in the shape of stars. I put one on my lapel and screamed, "She's making all the Jews wear these!" Fred happened to have the camera rolling, and it has become a good laugh for us when we watch the tape. The years roll on, and the party gets bigger and bigger as Fred worked more and more. One year, I arrive at the party and I get a parking spot right out in front. This is so rare. I knock on the door, gifts in hand, and there is no answer. I look in the window and the house is dark. I know I have the date right, but it appears that no one is there. Fred got a film and they flew to London and forgot to tell me the party was off. I got a lot of guilt dinners out of that one.

The parties continued as the years marched on, and then Fred and Mary moved from that house to their present location, which will remain a secret. Suffice to say, it's grand: huge backyard, tennis court, Olympic swimming pool, and the most perfect party house on the face of the earth. Mary took this New York Renaissance house and turned it into a New England charmer with all the warmth of a real home, a lived-in home that holds books and places to snuggle up to and read. It has a guesthouse on the property larger than their old two-bedroom apartment.

At this home, the parties really matured. They became not so much a party as an annual event. People looked forward to them with great anticipation, and they were getting huge. The more Fred worked, the larger the party got. Mary was still cooking all the food. One year she called me and said, "That's it, that's the last party. I can't do it anymore." I almost cried. She couldn't cut off my happiest day of the year! It was becoming too much for her. Then came the caterer and Maria! Finally, Mary could relax with the guests and enjoy the party with the rest of us, and that's when it took its present form.

Let's start with the house. I don't even know how to describe it. It's Christmas, but it's not obtrusive. You know how you go into someone's house and they've got Santa's Village—real size—in the living room, and it has all the warmth of a Macy's linen department? That's not what Mary's house is like, yet it takes her two months to decorate the place. She replaces pictures on the wall with Christmas scenes, she takes books off the shelf and puts Christmas books there, her lampshades are exchanged for red plaid, and her throw pillows are red and green. It's Christmas as you see it in those 1940s movies: warm and inviting, not brass and commercial.

The party remains exactly the same year after year, and this is how it goes: it starts around 7 p.m. and the dining room is set up with food. In the old days, if you got there late, there would only be turkey carcass. I usually got there late, and there would be that bird picked clean and string beans. I said to Mary, "I don't think there's ever food. I just think you put out that carcass every year and say, "Look how much they ate." The buffet lasts until about 8-8:30 p.m., and then the show starts. It's always the same. It starts with a play Mary writes. Mary's an award-winning playwright, and she writes this wonderful play about Christmas for the children at the party. It's always about the children for Mary.

That reminds me—I have seen women come to the party pregnant and over the years watched their children grow. Tonight, I asked one child how old he was. "Nine" was the answer, and all I could think of was, *where does the time go?*

Back to the play. It's acted by some of Hollywood's funniest comedy actors, people who appear on *The Simpsons* or in movies with Fred. It is adorable and the kids love it.

Then we start the Christmas Carols. Fred, who either tells a story or has written some original material, always interrupts these songs. Just when you think the singing is over, Joanne Worley knocks on the window from outside and Fred says to the crowd, "Oh my God, look who's here, Joanne Worley!" She's been at the party for an hour, which makes it hysterical. Joanne comes in with her piano player and says she just happened to be in the neighborhood and heard the singing. Fred asks her to sing a song and Joanne does an original material song every year. It's a joy!

Next comes the piano player, Bill Larkin. Unless you have heard this guy do his comedy songs, it is impossible to explain them to you. Just trust me when I say he's been doing the exact same songs for at least ten years, and each year I laugh harder and harder at them, and so does the rest of the crowd. He is a brilliantly gifted musician, and if there is a God, you will know his name someday.

Next comes the Jerry Lewis Choir, nine guys (myself included) who sing "Silent Night" a la Jerry Lewis. It's complete pandemonium.

Mary gets up and makes a speech, and I am always throwing insults at her. She is the perfect straight woman and we get huge laughs. Then we sing "The Twelve Nights of Christmas." Mary splits everyone up into groups and a special person does "FIVE GOLDEN RINGS." When I say special, I mean it's an honor. For the last couple years Bob Perlow has done it, and he's very funny. Bob was the warm up guy at *The Tonight Show*. Each time he would say "FIVE GOLDEN RINGS" he would find a funny way to do it. For instance, one year he had me call him on his cell phone right as he was supposed to sing. It got screams. It's the highlight of the song, and everyone waits for his part.

Paul Willson from *Cheers* plays "Silent Night" on his violin, and there isn't a dry eye in the house. It's like that year after year, decade after decade. It's my Christmas constant. It's the thing I look forward to more than Christmas itself. To me, it is Christmas.

This year, the crowd included Catherine O'Hara, Harry Shearer, Patrick Wayne, Mary Gross, writers from *The Tonight Show* and *Saturday Night Live*, Dan Castellaneta (the voice of Homer Simpson), comedians, actors, directors, writers; but for one night, they are not stars or show-business people. For one night, they are just people having a wonderful time at a wonderful party thrown by wonderful people.

Rosie O'Donnell

BECOMING A STAR in the business of show takes many complicated steps. It's a mix of luck and talent, with the emphasis on luck. I have had every bad break one could imagine in trying to make a career. I open for Donna Summer; she gets pregnant and is off the road. I open for Seals and Crofts; they break up. I get a contract with The MGM Grand, and it burns to the ground. I get a series with Tina Turner; she decides not to do it. The only thing that I have not done is ride in the car with Kennedy.

In 1985, I was riding high. I had just come back from Australia where I had starred in a show for three months. In a career, it's always important for the next step, and my next step was doing more TV. David Letterman and I had been friends from the early Comedy Store days, but David had gone to New York, and not-worthy me wasn't comfortable—unlike all my comedy friends—in calling him and asking to get on the show. Instead, I had my agents set up an audition in New York. I was going to be a gentleman about it rather than bother Dave. In order to do this, I had to be booked in New York. The only booking I could get for the week Letterman wanted to see me was opening act for Rosie O'Donnell at Caroline's. Rosie wasn't a TV star then, she was a club act with a good reputation, just like I was. In fact, the show would be two headliners. I thought it was a good idea and I accepted the gig.

The Letterman Show is contacted and they are coming opening night. Rosie is the draw—or not the draw as the case would be. The club is three-quarters empty. In a club that seats 250, maybe there were twenty-five people. Of those twenty-five people, thirteen were leather-wearing, tool-loving, tattoo-wearing lesbians with an attitude. Not my crowd.

I get on stage opening night, with the booker from *The Letterman Show* in this empty room, and I do my act to no one but lesbians. Silence. End of story for the *Letterman* audition. It gets back to me through Tom Dreesen that the booker told David, "He wasn't funny." This is how my career has gone from day one. One night at The Comedy Store, the *Tonight Show* came in to see me. Right in the middle of my act, a guy stands up and screams, "You suck!" and was so drunk they had to throw him and his entire party out.

I resign myself to the fact that *The Letterman Show* would not be on my agenda, and move on. The rest of the week, the crowds get bigger. We have a "commercial" crowd—or normal people—in the audience and my shows are great. *The Letterman Show* did not see any of those shows. Naturally. The whole point of the story is this, Rosie and I get to know each other that week. I found her to be a very warm and kind person. She's funny as hell and very complimentary to me about my show. She's very open about being gay and tells me about her lover at the time and how hard it was for her to keep a relationship because she was just about to take a job on VH1 as a VJ, but her lover wanted to stay in LA. My entire experience with her was very positive. I felt close to her as a friend even though I wasn't.

Rosie gets the job as a VJ and parlays it into her own comedy show on VH1. I think it was called *Stand-Up Spotlight*. The show consists of Rosie doing stand-up followed by three guest comedians. It was a very popular show. The second year into the show, I get a call from Rosie, would I do her show? I couldn't say yes fast enough, and I do it. I do the show, and again, Rosie couldn't be nicer. I watch her set and it's hysterical. I tell her how funny she is and she's self-deprecating and humble. I do my set and it goes very well. Rosie asks me back for a second and then third time. Each time, she could not have been nicer, kinder, funnier. Rosie is one of the smartest women in comedy. She has taken her talent and used it to go from one step to the next.

You have to be hard in this business. If you're not hard and hold on to your dream, you are pulled in sixteen directions by people who want to tell you what they think your career should be all about. Basically, it's all based on money and how what you are doing is affecting their pocket. Rosie never let those people bother her. She had an eye on a goal, and she headed for it. Nothing was going to stop her. I, on the other hand, would let anyone tell me anything and would listen to them. It's all about self-esteem and self-worth. When you don't have any, it's easy to be swayed. Unfortunately, if you are a woman and know what you want, you are labeled a "bitch." A man is difficult or crazy; a woman is a bitch. Nice, huh? The more successful Rosie got, the tougher she got; the tougher she got, the more flack she took; the more flack she took, the harder her skin got, and so on and so on until she became the person she is today. Basically, under all that tough exterior is a kind, warm, wonderful person.

A Thought

I CANNOT TELL YOU why this happened, but I can tell you that I remember it in such detail that to relive it here tonight is a piece of cake. I was about nine years old. My father was home this night. My father being there was peculiar, because usually he came home from work, ate dinner, changed his clothes, and was out the door. The atmosphere in my home was one of distrust and alienation. They fought nonstop. They could not be in the same room for five minutes without her screaming at him or him blasting her with a barrage of insults. My father's way of dealing was to get dressed and leave. In any case, that night he was home.

My mother walked into the room dressed to go out. I hadn't heard anything about her going out and so it seemed strange to me.

"I'm going out. Daddy will stay with you."

Folks, it's been years and I can still feel the feeling I felt when I heard those words sheer panic. I got hysterical. Instantly. "No, you can't leave. I don't want you to leave!"

For everything that ever happened in my life, I can give you a reason. I can tell you the motivations of this and the understanding of that, but this night I had not a single reason for this sudden and complete panic. It was instantaneous terror. I began to scream. I remember running to her and clutching her thighs.

"No, you can't go. Don't leave me. Don't leave me!"

She pulled my arms from around her legs and said, "Stop it."

The more she pushed me away, the more I screamed. I was hysterical, the kind of crying you get with that machine gun gasping for air on the intake. She would have none of it and was out the door. I ran to the window.

Screaming at the top of my lungs. I flung myself against the huge living room picture window. The trails of my nine-year old hands made a path through the condensation that accumulated on the warm interior panes as I slid down to the floor. The water collected in icy puddles on the sill as she got into her car and drove off. I collapsed into a ball of screaming terror. My father was on the sofa, four feet from me, motionless. Through all the hysterics, he had not said a word. Not a single word. He was watching it like the whole thing was on TV. He had no words of calm for me, no nurturing understanding. He just watched me like I was a science project.

As I watched, her car turned the corner at the end of the street and disappeared into the cold winter's night. I turned to him to see what he was doing. Nothing. He had a transfixed gaze on his face. I had quieted down now, just the repeating gasp of the machine gun air intake. There was nothing I could do. She was gone. I picked myself up off the floor and went into my bedroom where I closed the door and remained for the rest of the night. I thought the horror was over but it was not.

The next morning, my mother was furious, "What is wrong with you? How could you act that way? Do you want the neighbors to talk?" The neighbors. That's what she was worried about, what the neighbors thought.

"I am not having them think I raised a little animal. Today you are going to every single neighbor and apologize for the scene you made last night."

I could feel the fear in my feet. I was going to have to go out and knock on doors and apologize to everyone for being a scared child. I remember going to that first door looking down at my feet and mumbling something like, "I'm sorry I made noise last night." I cannot tell you how they responded. I simply don't remember. I do remember going to at least five doors and repeating the embarrassment over and over. Even at that age I was ashamed. I have wondered over the years if that was fitting punishment. Should a child be made to pay the price for a screaming fit? Should they have to apologize to every person on the plane or in the supermarket aisle? I don't know. Should they?

I don't know why this memory came to me. It just did. It happened so long ago and the pain of that night still remains with me. Some people can move on and get over it. I have not learned that skill yet. I can't tell you why, I just haven't. Somewhere in me, I think maybe it's because I never got closure. I never got to understand the why this happened or why that happened.

As most of the world sleeps, I relive a childhood trauma, or the death of a friend, or a painful experience; a loss, a pain. It's my life and I've learned to deal with it. How, you ask? By getting out of bed and putting it into written form. By getting it out of my mind and down on paper. That's how I deal. I am a writer. I write. If I were a songwriter, I'd put it to music, but I'm not a songwriter. I'm a word-writer, and so I put it into words. To stop me from writing is to negate my very existence. I have grown enough in the last couple of years to know that I will not feel guilty about writing or expressing myself. What I have learned is that when I do put it down on paper, someone else who is unable to sleep reads it and says, "I'm not alone." To me, that is what this whole thing has become. Me helping you, through my pain.

Epilogue

I WILL CONTINUE TO WRITE. Maybe there is another book in me, I don't know. I sit down as often as I can to document the insanity of my life. When I write now, I am not encumbered by the fears that I'm not good enough or that I don't know what I'm doing. I know what I'm doing. I know how to do it. I can communicate with the written word. I can bring a smile to a face or a tear to an eye. I am a writer. Yet there is always that voice in my head telling me I'm not enough. Telling me the next time, they'll figure out I'm a fraud. I try to ignore that voice, try to tell it to go away, but it stays with me like my dog that lies at my feet. Maybe it's what drives me? Maybe that voice is where my creative juices originate? Who knows? Accept and move on, Steve, accept and move on.

This has been my story. I've shared it with all of you for better or worse, in sickness and in health. We've marched down the aisle of my life hand-in-hand, and I've said, "I do," or, "I will," or whatever they're saying these days. I've let you in like I've never let anyone in before, and it feels right. I can't say it feels good, but it does feel right. I hope I have been able to do the same for you. Let's plan to remain friends, okay? I'm only an email away. Remember that when the dog howls or the ghost of some distant trauma floats down the hallways of your psyche. If I can make it through my life, then you can make it through yours.

Thanks for letting me share.